ZAKROS

The Discovery of a Lost Palace

of Ancient Crete

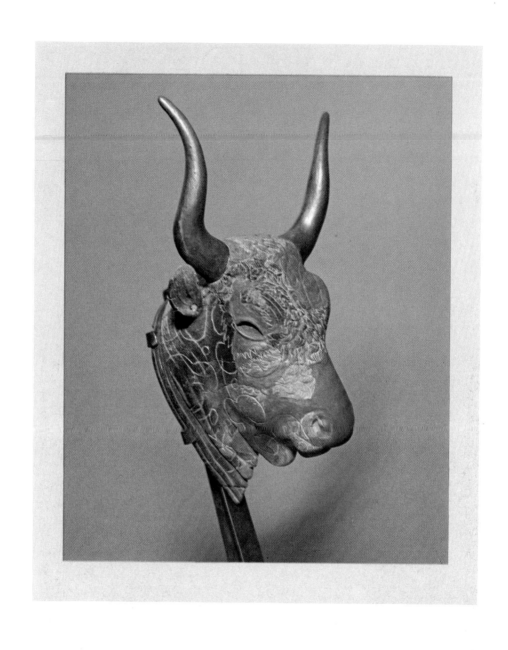

PUBLISHED BY

CHARLES SCRIBNER'S SONS · NEW YORK

ZAKROS

The Discovery of a Lost Palace
of Ancient Crete

NICHOLAS PLATON

Acknowledgments

Both in connection with the excavations at Zakros and in the preparation of this book, I wish to express my warmest thanks to a number of individuals and organizations. The excavations were made under the auspices of and with financial assistance from the Archaeological Society of Athens. Without the generous financial support of Leon and Harriet Pomerance of New York, the work could not have begun or been continued; they have provided not only financial aid but moral support as well. My wife, Anastasia Platonos, an experienced archaeologist, has collaborated in the work at Zakros from its beginning and has had a part in many important discoveries in the Sitia area, as well as providing valuable help in the preparation of the book. All the members of the Zakros expedition—archaeologists, architects, technicians, photographers, and supervisors—made important contributions to the work; special mention is due to archaeologists Helen Zaganiari-Frantzi and John and Effi Sakellaraki; architects Joseph Shaw, Maria Lygidaki, John Demetriades, Kyriaki Manola, and John Knithakis; and photographer George Xylouris. Dr. Stylianos Alexiou, director of the Heraklion Museum, and his colleagues provided understanding and help during the excavations and were responsible for the restoration of the finds and their exhibition in the Museum. As regards the book, Joseph and Maria Shaw and Helen Wace collaborated in the translation under my direction; Kenneth Heuer and Alice Roberts of Scribners and Walter A. Fairservis, Jr., of the American Museum of Natural History provided valuable editorial assistance. Most of the photographs were taken by Anastasia Platonos, Emil Serafis, and George Xylouris; specific credits for all illustrations are given on page 337.

Four-lobed sacred-communion chalice of veined marble,
from the Treasury of the Shrine

6

The palace from the north

Contents

7

Contents

Contents

IV: DESTRUCTION AND MEMORIES

Mace heads of veined marble, from the Treasury of the Shrine

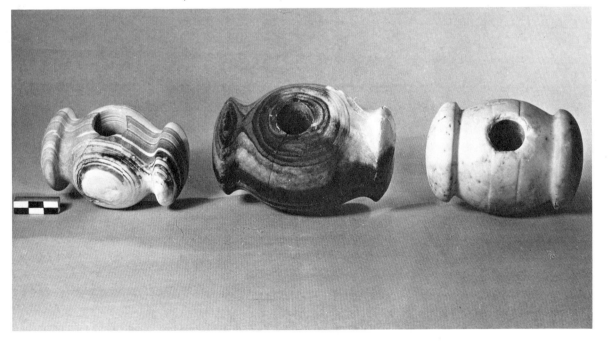

*Veined-marble amphora with curved handles,
from the Treasury of the Shrine*

The golden diadem showing the Mistress of Wild Goats

Illustrations

Illustrations

Illustrations

Conical rhyton of veined marble, from the Treasury of the Shrine

14

ZAKROS

The Discovery of a Lost Palace
of Ancient Crete

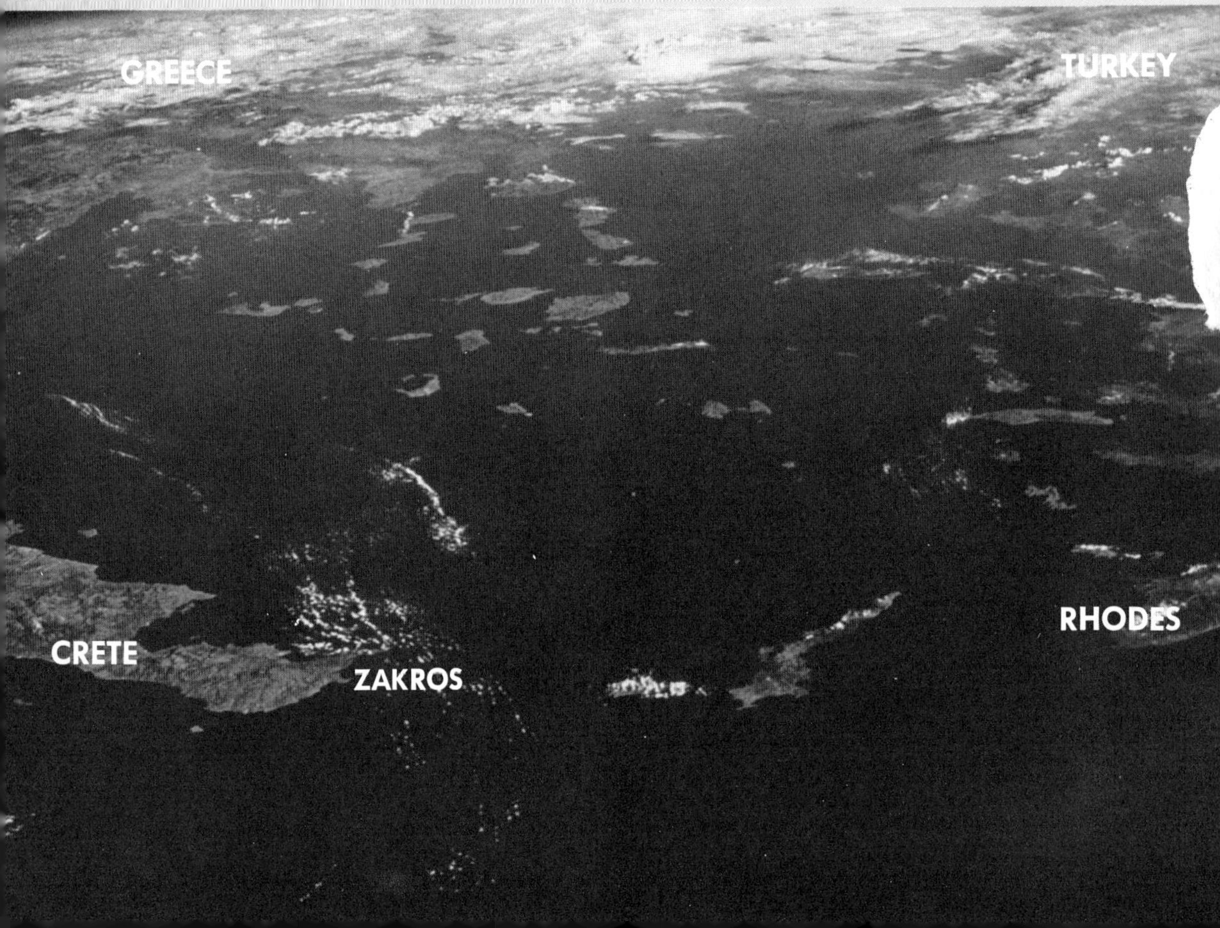

The eastern Mediterranean as seen from Gemini 5

GREECE

TURKEY

RHODES

CRETE

ZAKROS

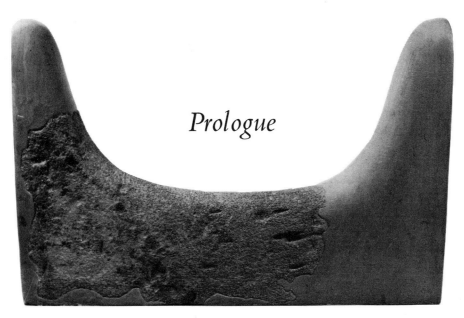

Prologue

Stone horns of consecration

To speak of Cretan civilization is to evoke illusory pictures of a colorful and dramatic period during the second millennium B.C. when for the first time in history a European culture played a forceful and dynamic role on the international scene. Civilizations until that time had originated and developed along fertile river valleys where crops could flourish and their abundance furnish the subsistence basis for cities and states. Tightly geared to the cycles of the seasons, Sumerians and Egyptians viewed the world as the realm of immortal forces which all men must acknowledge, whether one was a humble farmer or a royal craftsman. This acknowledgment most frequently took the form of ritualized subjection to the cycles of the natural world, as if one were literally a stalk of wheat or a fish in the river.

Sir Arthur Evans's archaeological revelation in the early part of the twentieth century of the Minoan city of Knossos in Crete put historical substance where legend had prevailed. Evans's discoveries, along with those of others, described a civilization whose basis was commerce—a commerce motivated by Crete's geographical position between the sources of raw material in Europe and the markets of the ancient Near East. The sea was not a barrier but a natural highway needing only maritime skill and individual acumen to provide the motivation for its use. As early as two thousands years before Christ Cretan objects appeared as far up the Nile as Thebes, and Egyptian artifact styles were increasingly found in Crete itself. An international awareness marks the Cretans. Though their world too had its animism and there were needs to acknowledge the supernatural, the ancient Cretans seemed to be masters of their own fate—much more so, at least, than the civilized men of the ancient Orient with whom they had to deal. In ancient Crete, then, lies the genesis of European civilization.

For all the archaeological evidence that has accumulated since Evans's day, for all the study devoted scholars have made, there still remains much to be learned about this all too shadowed civilization. The earth of the island of Crete still conceals many secrets, secrets whose revelation will help not only in evidencing more of the ancient Cretan world but also to cast stronger light on the very character of civilization itself.

The following pages contain the step-by-step account of how modern archaeology works in its constant search for these ancient secrets. The detective story recounted describes the clues whose interpretation led to the discovery of a lost palace at Zakros in eastern Crete. This palace in turn was a lodestone which opened graphic vistas wherein the Crete of the Minoan kings stands forth as never before. The reader who moves with the methodical pace of the author can sense the way archaeologists work and the reasons their work is crowned with success upon success. For here, by the careful compounding of archaeological evidence, literary sources, geographical knowledge, and learned conjecture, the ancient world is revealed not as a thing of exotica, though it is exotic, but rather in its realistic actuality a proof of a major step in the history of man's civilization.

The Search for the Palace

Modern archaeological technique is methodical, painstaking, and frustrating to the amateur. The search for and the discovery of the Zakros palace complex was a slow and careful process in which all possible clues were appraised and decisions based on those clues made with caution. Here lies the amateur's frustration, for what may seem obvious is often not so. However, as this account makes clear, certain clues lead surely to the goal.

1 Why does an archaeologist choose a given place for his work of investigation? Clues out of the immediate past direct his attention to that area. Here in the recovery of gold objects by an old Cretan peasant was the first clue.

A Treasure of Gold Objects

Not long before the outbreak of the Second World War, Dr. Stylianos Giamalakis, a surgeon and art collector of Heraklion, acquired a unique treasure consisting of three most remarkable gold objects. At the time, the doctor told how the objects came into his possession. Some years earlier, he had operated on and cured an old peasant from the village of Epano (Upper) Zakros, who was suffering from a ruptured hernia. Knowing that his patient came from an area where archaeological discoveries had been made, Dr. Giamalakis did not ask for payment for his services, hoping that later the peasant would give him some antiquities or indicate a place where such things were to be found. This the man, when he was leaving for his home, actually promised to do. The doctor had almost forgotten the incident, when he unexpectedly received a message from his former patient, asking him to come to the village to receive certain valuable objects for his collection. In those years travel between Sitia and Epano Zakros was difficult, and the doctor had to travel on muleback. By the time he arrived at the peasant's house it was late at night, and he found the old man seriously ill. In a private conversation the peasant told the doctor that he had long had in his possession some gold objects of great archaeological value which had been found at Kato (Lower) Zakros; now, feeling his death near, he wished to give them to the doctor who had once saved his life. He then told how, during the 1890s (consequently before the major excavations at Knossos and Phaistos had begun), the treasure, consisting of five gold objects, plainly of great value, had been accidentally found during the cultivation of a field; he did not mention the exact location. Two of the five objects were flattened cylinder seals with engraved representations of human figures and animals; these he had sold to an employee of the "Eastern" Telegraph Office at Heraklion, then operated by the English, but he had refused to part with the others, recognizing their value and never having been under serious financial strain. Now, in a gesture of gratitude, he wished to contribute these objects to the doctor's famous collection, but having obligations toward his own family he felt he should receive something in return; he would accept whatever the doctor was willing to give him. Then he produced the objects, which were a diadem, a small shallow bowl, and a necklace pendant in the form of a bull's head. The doctor gave him in exchange a gold watch, a few English sovereigns, and a small amount of Greek money.

Naturally, it is not possible to decide whether this narrative is accurate in all details, though it gives the impression of being true. Later, at Zakros, I tried to obtain more information about the treasure. Many tales were told there about the discovery of gold objects within burial caves or during the cultivation of the fields years before. Among these was one about the discovery of a bull and a vessel, both in gold, but I was not certain that any of the accounts corresponded to Dr. Giamalakis's story. In the meantime, however, certain scholars, some of them specialists, had questioned the authenticity of the treasures, pointing out unusual features both of techniques and of decoration. The Heraklion Museum, of which I was then director, had meanwhile purchased the entire Giamalakis collection, and after careful examination of the objects, I became convinced of their authenticity, which was later confirmed.

The quality of the objects themselves suggests a royal derivation, and two of them seemed to be closely connected with Minoan religion. If they came from a tomb, it must have been that of a king or prince or of a high official, probably one who held a religious post. All three articles are of pure gold, and their workmanship is most extraordinary. The diadem SEE PAGE 11 is adorned by a central medallion with a representation of a woman taming wild goats, which she holds upside down, one in each hand. This is the familiar Minoan type of *Potnia Theron*, "Mistress of the Animals," here represented as a goddess of wild goats. The fact that this aspect of the goddess was proved to have been the one most often worshiped at Zakros lends further support to the authenticity of the treasure. On either side of the central medallion there is an octopus in a slanting position—a favorite theme during the flowering of the palace culture. The other decorative motifs are double whorls and spirals, designs very frequently used in Minoan decoration to express movement; these are closely related to motifs on gold diadems from the royal tombs at Mycenae and on a sword found in a royal tomb on the island of Peparethos (modern Skopelos), which may be that of the settler Staphylos from Knossos, since his name survived as a place-name in that location.

The pendant in the form of the head of a young bull is indeed admirable, not only as a naturalistic rendering of the vigorous animal, with the hair, the folds of the skin, the eyes, and the relatively short horns splendidly executed, but also for the decorative effect of the spiral rosette in filigree technique on the forehead and the very fine granulation applied on the contour of the plaque at the back. The pendant was suspended by means of a small cylinder at the upper part of the nape.

The bowl, the sides of which incline outward in an elegant shape known from other examples, also has a whorl of embossed spirals in repoussé technique forming a rosette, so similar to that on the bull's forehead as to suggest that both were works of the same craftsman.

All three objects were undoubtedly the products of a royal workshop and probably the possessions of a person of high status in Minoan society, perhaps even a member of the royal family. The fact that they had been found at Kato Zakros was a significant indication that a palace had existed in the region.

2   Somewhere in the region of Zakros there was perhaps an ancient palace. But where? Were there other hints as to its possible location in the work of past explorers?

Early Investigations at Zakros

The valley of Kato Zakros was identified as an archaeological site by the English explorer and cartographer Captain (later Admiral) Thomas A. B. Spratt as early as 1852. At the close of the nineteenth century the area was visited by three famous pioneers in Cretan archaeology, the Italian explorer Lucio Mariani, the Italian archaeologist Federigo Halbherr, and the English archaeologist Arthur John Evans who obtained and made known the first archaeological information about it. However, the first systematic excavations were made by the English archaeologist David George Hogarth, as part of a program of the British School of Archaeology in Athens for a more general study of the region of Praisos and the discovery of buildings of a prehistoric settlement.

Hogarth's work was accomplished with great success in the spring and summer of 1901. Excavation was ultimately interrupted in August by torrential rains, which with the resulting floodwaters swept away 4,000 trees, flooded the greater part of the cultivated areas, and carried down great masses of earth and boulders, threatening the lives of the workmen and making further excavation impossible. The rivulet changed its bed and at present flows in a more easterly direction, forming a small delta at its outlet to the sea.

The investigation by Hogarth revealed a dozen buildings, almost all on the slopes of the northeast hill, remains of some others on the southwest hill of Hagios Antonios, and two shrine deposits next to the little church there. The results were important; these scattered structures constituted

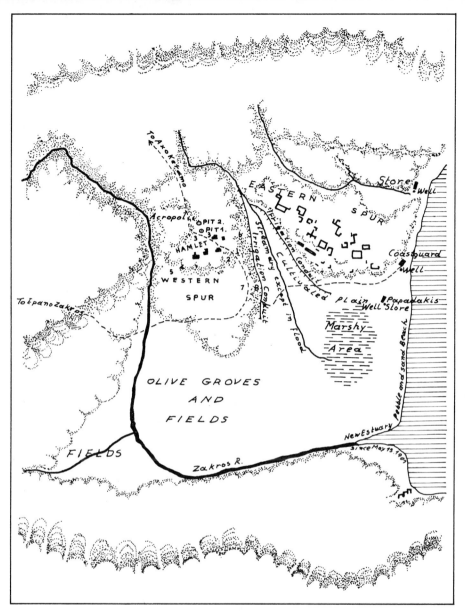

The Zakros valley, showing the area excavated by Hogarth in 1901

the first discovery of a Minoan harbor town. Moreover, they were well
built and contained quantities of household furniture and implements
belonging to the mature phase of the civilization first made known through
the great excavations of Knossos and Phaistos. Unfortunately, many of
the buildings at the top of the hill had lost the protective layer of earth
overlying them and had suffered severe damage. Of two or three houses

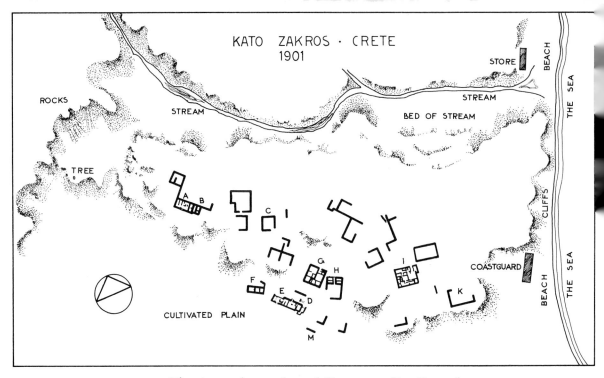

The site on the northeast hill excavated by Hogarth

Plan of houses A-B and D-E excavated by Hogarth

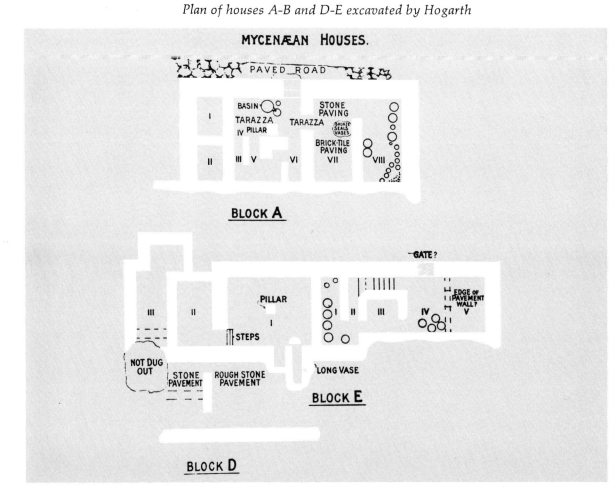

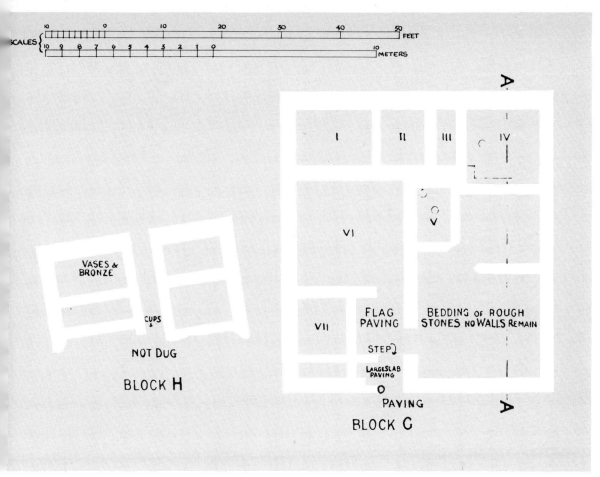

Plan of houses H and G excavated by Hogarth

the exterior walls had been preserved to some height, but in only a few cases was the organization of the interior still clearly discernible. The investigations were focused on spots where walls could be clearly seen projecting above the surface of the cultivated fields. By this method, however, while sporadic houses could be located, no continuous section of the Minoan town was exposed.

Hogarth designated all the houses excavated by the letters A to M, although in some cases he only traced their contours without digging into their interiors. Most important among the excavated buildings in regard to state of preservation, plans, and the objects found in them were the complexes A–B, D–E, and J. House A, which Mariani had identified as a "temple" because of its cyclopean masonry, had eight rooms on the ground floor, some reached from above through trapdoors and some, partially

27

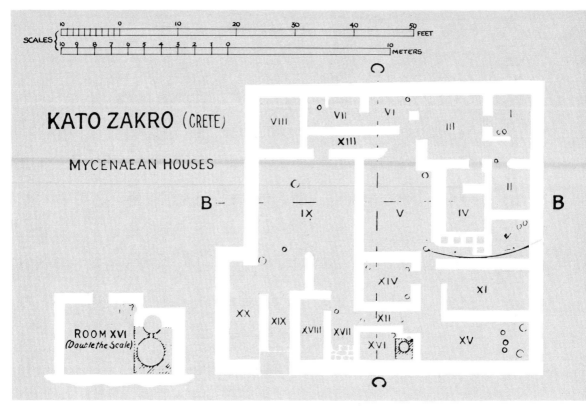

KATO ZAKRO (CRETE)

MYCENAEAN HOUSES

B –

VIII   VII   VI   III   I
      XIII
            IX   V   IV
                 XIV   XI
XX   XIX   XVIII   XVII   XII
                   XVI   XV

ROOM XVI
(Double the Scale)

B

Plan of house J excavated by Hogarth

separated from one another by mud-brick partition walls, reached directly through the outside door. The floors were in some places covered with baked mud bricks. Some of the rooms contained installations of an agricultural character—a winepress, for example—while others served as religious shrines. In one of the latter was found an important deposit of clay sealings, undoubtedly belonging to archives which, the excavator believed, must have been kept originally in the upper floor of the building. A clay tablet with incised signs in the script later designated Linear A confirmed the hypothesis. The impressions suggested seals of various forms, a great number of them three-sided, some bearing representations of cult scenes, while others bore curious creatures of monstrous, daemonic form, creations of a tormented imagination. Some of the representations were undoubtedly from the engraved bezels of gold rings. The total group of sealings is exceptionally important both as examples of glyptic carving in miniature and as clues to Minoan religion—of equal significance with other groups found in the royal villa of Hagia Triada in the region of Phaistos and in the Palace of Knossos itself. The presence of the sealings indicated that

House A had been used for the safekeeping of archives of a palatial character, and consequently that it was an annex of a main center of political and religious control. In any case, it was an important building, for in addition to the rooms of the ground floors and a contiguous complex of storerooms, designated by the excavator as House B, there were other compartments, unfortunately poorly preserved, on the flat ground above to the north, and other corresponding rooms on the upper floor from which bronze tools had fallen onto the ground floor. Comparable tools, mostly used for woodworking, were found on the ground floor of another house, unfortunately stripped completely; among these were five saw blades with straight and curved dentation.

In a less important house (G), the southwestern exterior wall was preserved to a height of 5 meters, due to the fact that it had served as a main retaining wall for the terrace on which the house was built, but the interior walls were preserved to a low height only. Beyond the lobby and the vestibule of the entrance, the rooms surrounded two sides of an interior square court. In House J the interior organization of the rooms was much easier to distinguish, but again the walls were quite low. At the entrance there was a massive monolithic threshold, and here also the angular arrangement of two series of rooms framing a court was repeated. This house contained more than twenty apartments, in many of which floors of concrete were preserved, as well as the stucco coatings of the walls. Here too were recognizable installations connected with the production of artifacts or with agricultural processes, such as a winepress connected with a vat for the collection of the liquid, and another installation with successive little basins in a row, provided with a drain conduit, perhaps used for dyeing, as well as a storeroom containing small widemouthed jars (*stamnoi*), pitchers, wine amphoras, and other vessels. Further testimony of home industry was provided by numerous loom weights fallen from an upper floor, and by an unusual utensil apparently used for blowing the fire to raise the temperature to the melting point. Two rooms that may have been used for worship were one with a square pillar and an adjacent lustral basin and another with a deposit.

The complex designated D–E deserves special mention, for it is located on an area of the hill which subsequent discoveries have shown

SEE PAGE 27

SEE PAGE 26

Terracotta winepress, from a house on the slope of the northwest hill

to be significant. Hogarth interpreted the complex as two contiguous houses, one with a spacious entrance hall, paved with concrete, leading through a door at the back to a storeroom full of pithoi; the other with a main room containing a square pillar in the center, and subsidiary spaces used for storage, as well as a small staircase on the north side, leading to an upper level where the rooms had been destroyed.

Clay and stone utensils, bronze tools, and small artifacts were found, but these were rather few in number. There were enough, however, to prove the existence at Zakros of notable workshops, especially for the manufacture of pottery in the Floral and Marine styles—that is, the styles chiefly characteristic of the Neo-palatial period during which the town must have been at its acme.

Of the buildings on the slope of the other hill, only a small part was explored, for the excavator, noticing that the bedrock was exposed at many spots, decided that this section of the town had been completely destroyed. However, as later investigations proved, the richest quarters of the Minoan town were in this precise area, and considerable remains have survived.

The two deposits—called "pits" by Hogarth—in the vicinity of the church of Hagios Antonios, which probably belonged to a sanctuary at the top of the hill, were found to be full of fragments of clay and stone vessels which had been discarded after having been used in the sanctuary ritual. These vessels varied in shape, and many bore interesting decorations, painted in a light color on a dark background, and mainly using motifs from nature, such as vine tendrils. There were also fragmentary pots with black decoration on a most brilliant light surface, enlivened by the addition of very fine patterns in white. This ceramic style was subsequently dated to the transitional phase between the Middle Minoan and Late Minoan periods—that is, around 1600 B.C. In the same deposits were found numerous loom weights, as well as single-nozzled clay lamps; the latter were perhaps used to provide light during nocturnal ceremonies at the sanctuary, which unfortunately could not be located. At a short distance from these deposits there is a small rock peak on which survive some stone walls in cyclopean masonry; it seems probable that the sanctuary was constructed on this height.

Hogarth also looked for the cemeteries of the settlement and explored various small caves and crevices on the slopes of the northern heights. Most of the burials, however, he discovered in the caves of a ravine, which during the investigations in the 1960s was named the Gorge of the Dead, because of the multiplicity of burials found there. On the basis of the accompanying pottery he attributed these burials to older Minoan times, the period which Evans defined as Early Minoan. Some of the pots had a lustrous black surface, some a gray one, with incised decoration, usually consisting of rectilinear and occasionally curvilinear motifs, which on

Part of the Gorge of the Dead, between Epano Zakros and Kato Zakros;
burials date mainly from the Proto-palatial period

other pots was rendered in a dark, shiny color on a light ground. These
finds showed that habitation at the bay of Zakros had begun in Early
Minoan times, around the middle of the third millennium B.C., although
no clear remains of the early settlement were found during Hogarth's
investigations.

The results of Hogarth's excavations in the region of Zakros were
important enough to encourage further research over a larger area, and it
is rather curious that investigation was not renewed for sixty years. Access
to this isolated region of easternmost Crete was of course difficult because
of the lack of roads, but even when a relatively usable road artery up to
the village of Epano Zakros put an end to complete isolation, nobody

thought of conducting investigations in this crucial spot. The British School, which had carried out the initial excavations, was occupied with other enterprises, especially as it had inherited the weighty task of continuing Evans's excavations at Knossos. Perhaps there was a fear that further investigations would reveal only isolated houses, mostly stripped of their original contents. However, evidence gathered during a broader survey of Sitia in the intervening period showed the necessity for a more careful look at Kato Zakros.

3   Ancient man no less than modern man was concerned about the place where he lived and carried on his daily tasks. In modern geography then are the clues to those optimum places where men can reside in harmony with the demands of their daily activities. In the geography lies the next clue to Minoan Zakros.

Eastern Crete as a Palace Site

From the very beginning of the search for the main centers of Minoan civilization, it was evident that eastern Crete must have played an important role in the formation and further development of the culture. This section, which today constitutes the region of Sitia, occupied a particularly advantageous position in relation to the East and to Egypt. The basic, vital area of central Crete, controlled by the major palaces, was encircled by two large mountain ranges, that of Ida (today Psiloritis) and that of Dikte (today the Lasithi Mountains), and extended north to the coastline. Directly to the east of the latter range, at the narrowest part of Crete, deeply penetrated on the north by Mirabello Bay, is the narrow low isthmus of Hierapetra. The total width of the island here is no more than 12 kilometers, and the passage from sea to sea is quite easy. According to the "law of isthmuses" formulated by the French classical scholar Victor Bérard (1864–1931), in any age when circumnavigation was perilous, transporting goods overland across a short distance and reloading them on ships provided an adequate solution. This explains the prosperity of the Minoan town of Gournia, which controlled the isthmus of Hierapetra, as well as that of other sites situated at the wider region of the isthmus, from as early as the Pre-palatial period. Sites such as that of the small peninsula of Mochlos, a little to the east of Gournia (today an islet close to the shore), and the small island of Pseira, on the eastern side of

Mirabello Bay, contributed considerably to trade, through their double, or, as Homer characterized them in the *Odyssey*, "twin" harbors.

Beyond this isthmus the imposing range of the Sitia mountains rises abruptly, essentially isolating the extreme end of eastern Crete. That area, though lacking in broad fertile plains, had the advantage of safe harbors, an important factor in the frequent trading operations between Crete and the East and Egypt at that time. The relative isolation imposed by the mountain ranges, on the other hand, could provide security to people fleeing to the farther valleys in times of invasion. Even today, the one road artery that leads to the eastern end of Crete climbs the steep slopes with great difficulty, suspended, as it were, over the northern coast, and winds around in a way particularly awesome to people traveling in buses. The mountains are bare and desolate, and in only one place along this high passage the scantily running water of a spring feeds a small fountain next to a plane tree at the very edge of the precipice. Farther on, however, small green valleys open up between the mountains, today occupied by the picturesque main villages of the Sitia region. Almost in the very locations of the modern villages were the Minoan settlements, recognizable by a few remains and by the chance discovery of occasional tombs, not yet systematically investigated. Still farther to the east, where there are vaster, vital areas with an outlet to the bay of the town of Sitia, were the centers of the Eteo-Cretans at Praisos. These people—the name means "true Cretans"—seem to have been the descendants of those Minoans who at the time of the Dorian invasion (at the end of the twelfth century B.C.) had fled to eastern Crete to pursue life according to their old traditions. Even in classical Greek times, they continued to speak their old language and to write it, though in a Greek alphabetic script, as a few fragments of inscriptions show. Toward the bay of Sitia certain rivers, which today have become simple torrents, formed with their deposits a fertile valley, about which rose important Minoan centers.

Still farther east rises the last mountain range of Sitia. This range seems to have been given the name Dikte, which was formerly applied to the central range, when the Eteo-Cretans came as refugees to eastern Crete. The foothills descend rather abruptly toward the east coast, where there are little bays more or less protected from the winds, with small alluvial plains around them. The main Minoan settlements had already been founded on these bays in early Minoan times, but they flourished mainly when trade relations with the East and Egypt became more intensive during the Neo-palatial period. These sites, together with those located in the area of Praisos, possessed a culture equal to that developed in central Crete around the great palaces at Knossos, Phaistos, and Mallia. Such a comparable culture in eastern Crete could be explained only by assuming that there too a large and rich palace had existed. Such a palace should be in one of the two main areas, the central area at Praisos or the region along the coast where the harbor settlements were situated. Since Crete had depended for its growth and prosperity on close trade relations with the outside world, the second alternative seemed more plausible. Moreover, most of the pottery of the renowned Marine style derived from this area, suggesting the presence of palace workshops. The precedence of eastern Crete in the formation of this style had been recognized by many scholars.

The Zakros Area

Where the range of Dikte descends toward the sea, the torrents flowing down from the mountains carried silt which accumulated to create small valleys between the foothills. In areas where water was withheld by impermeable strata, springs gushed up, and luxuriant and varied vegetation developed. One of these favored areas is Epano Zakros, today one of the richest and largest villages in the district of Sitia. The spring gushes up in a rocky landscape, next to a small ravine in which plane trees and walnut trees abound. Just before reaching the area of the village, the streams form small waterfalls which in the past were used to power flour mills. Nowadays the propelling force of the water is not needed, but the distribution of the water throughout the settlement is useful for everyday needs and, moreover, contributes to the picturesqueness of the village. Farther on, the spring water has been channeled off into conduits for irrigation, and these have recently been extended down to the region of Kato Zakros.

However, the surrounding mountains are bare, and, as a result of their geological make-up, which is predominantly schist, they assume an unusual violet hue, which in places turns into brown or light green, depending on the texture of the layers of sedimentary schist. The single main road follows, with many bends, the lower parts of these schist foothills, until it reaches the green valley of Zakros. Recently a rough, steep side road toward the overhanging mountain region has been built but it is not usable during the winter. This connects with the plateaus of Karydi and Ziros, where rather poor villages subsist on limited cultivation and farming. On these plateaus the British School of Archaeology, in 1902–1903, discovered remains of Neolithic settlements, as well as later small settlements of Pre-palatial Minoan times. In the well-irrigated valley of Epano Zakros, however, the existence of much more sophisticated settlements during the Proto-palatial and Neo-palatial periods could be deduced from the remains found from time to time and especially from the discovery of a significant mansion near the village, which controlled the road leading down to Kato Zakros.

Farther away, toward the northwest, a peak sanctuary from the Pre-palatial and Proto-palatial periods was found at Traostalos and excavated by C. Davaras in 1963. It proved similar to all the other such sanctuaries that had been found at various points in central and eastern Crete, always near large settled sites. A comparable sanctuary at Palaikastro, on the height of Petsofa, was excavated in 1901 by the English archaeologist Sir John Linton Myres and yielded masses of offerings, especially terracotta figurines of male and female worshipers.

The foothills framing the valley of Epano Zakros descend in steps toward the still smaller valley of Kato Zakros, which lies at the inmost point of the small bay of the same name. Between two of these hills a rapid torrent carved a deep, narrow ravine with steep sides, splitting the limestone rock for a distance of about 8 kilometers. This torrent fed the small river which still waters the valley and which is constantly changing its bed as a result of flooding after prolonged periods of rain. Toward the south end of the bay, the water forms a kind of shoal, full of reeds which add color to the landscape. The ravine opens out in some places and elsewhere narrows considerably, becoming quite rugged. At its widest point SEE PAGE 32

Entrance to the Gorge of the Dead

there is a flat area of some expanse, on one side of which rises a small rocky peak. The top is so small and so difficult of access that the habitations of which remains were found must have belonged to refugees driven by the invasion of the Dorians into such impassable and well-concealed areas. During this same period—approximately the eleventh and tenth centuries B.C.—cavelike crevices and little caves opening out onto the steep sides of the ravine, which here reach a height of 150–200 meters, were used as burial places, succeeding other earlier burials of the Pre-palatial and Proto-palatial periods. Today only scattered fragments of pithoi and of offerings to the dead are to be found at the entrances and within the narrow interior spaces, the result of pillaging at various periods but especially during modern times. This ravine is the one investigated by Hogarth and later named by our expedition the Gorge of the Dead. Walking through the ravine, one follows a winding path, which sometimes climbs the slopes in order to avoid the frequent obstacles at the bottom and elsewhere descends toward the bed of the stream, where occasionally vegetation grows thickly, and miniature waterfalls leap over the rocks. The ravine changes from time to time from a wild and threatening chasm with overhanging rocks to a calm and picturesque landscape with abundant, babbling, and often playful streams of water. During the heavy rainfalls in the winter the water rushes down through the ravine carrying with it anything it finds in its way, flooding great expanses of land, and leaving large deposits of gravel and boulders, which render uncultivable the once productive fields. Luckily, such destructive floods rarely occur on a large scale, but the one already mentioned, which terminated the first excavations of Kato Zakros in August 1901, in a single day utterly changed the appearance of the area. The repercussions of this catastrophe were felt for many years, and the people of the area had to work very hard to make their fields productive again.

The recently constructed side road follows the south brink of the ravine for some distance and subsequently winds down gradually to the lower foothills until it reaches the valley of Kato Zakros, where it turns toward the shore. On the slopes of the foothills burial enclosures belonging to the Pre-palatial and Proto-palatial periods have been found, and some of these have been excavated by our expedition. From this point one can see the little bay in all its expanse, defined by its two promontories. At the point where the bay penetrates most deeply into the land, there are broad beaches with thick sand, perfectly suited for sunbathing and swimming by natives and visitors alike. Between two large beaches projects a cliff, on top of which a combination coffeehouse and restaurant has recently been built to replace the hastily erected shed which was previously the only refreshment stand of the area. The single road follows the shoreline and along it in recent years an increasing number of small buildings have arisen, not yet forming a hamlet but serving the inhabitants of Epano Zakros as temporary quarters when they are engaged in farming and fishing during the summer.

The valley of Kato Zakros is not broad, and the cultivable area is even more restricted by two rocky hills, one on the northeast and the other on the southwest, on both of which the Minoan settlement once stretched. The decay of the ancient buildings left heaps of stones which increase the difficulties of cultivating these barely productive hills. The natives have tried to confine the stones to spots where they serve the purpose of retaining successive terraces on which small plots of cultivable land have been created. In the area of the stone heaps a few sickly little trees provided shade for the cultivators during the heat of summer. A narrow strip of cultivable land was formed between the two hills, which widens as it approaches the sea. By digging a few wells and utilizing the scanty streams this area was made into an extensive orchard of various kinds of fruit trees, and in some sections bananas were grown. Among these enough space was found to plant small groves of olive trees, which proved more productive than other crops on the heights and in the broader zone of the valley. Recently, cultivation has expanded over the entire valley, since water has been channeled down from the springs of Epano Zakros through cement conduits. Farm machinery for cultivation has also been introduced, though its use is restricted by the Archaeological Service, in order to prevent ancient buildings from being damaged or destroyed. At many places groups of cypress trees flanked the pathways or marked the limits of neighboring fields.

Outside this narrow valley between the two hills there is less cultivation. Certain areas are marshy or covered by gravel carried there by the torrent. Elsewhere the bedrock comes to the very surface, rising steeply near the two promontories and considerably eroded in many places. Toward the south end, the rocky heights rise gradually to form terraces, on one of which were found the fossilized remains of a hippopotamus. At some points the sea penetrates deeply, forming small fiords. On the side of one of these is a very deep, cavelike cleft called the Black Ditch (Mavro Avlaki), which was used for burials in Pre-palatial times. Burials have also been found in rock cavities—the largest of which is called Spiliara—on the steep slopes of the heights which enclose the valley of Zakros on the northern side.

SEE PAGE 3 The bay of Zakros is one of the safest of eastern Crete, providing a secure refuge for small vessels, especially sailing and engine-powered boats used for fishing and sponge-diving, which put in at Zakros mainly in the summer season. The fishermen spread their nets on the sand to repair and rearrange them. Loads of fish are transported to Epano Zakros and thence to Sitia and Hierapetra. The sponge-diving boats, in small fleets, usually from the islands of the Dodecanese and especially from Kalymnos, put in at the bay for two or three days before starting for the regions of Dernah and Benghazi on the coast of Libya, at the beginning of the sponge-collecting season. The waters of the inner bay stay relatively calm, even when strong and violent winds blow from the northwest, descending with great force from the steep cliffs and down through the deep ravine, literally sweeping the land. During the winter, residence in the area of the bay with its inadequate accommodations is difficult, even painful, and as a result very few inhabitants stay there throughout the year. Only recently have the operation of excavations and the systematic irrigation of the valley put an end to Kato Zakros' almost complete isolation.

4 It is eastern Crete then, and particularly the region of Sitia, that must be thoroughly explored. The author now begins his own investigation.

Explorations in Sitia

Both archaeological evidence and geographical conditions thus combined to cause me to undertake a systematic archaeological investigation in eastern Crete. I planned a program of work in the two main regions, which was expected to extend for ten years. On the basis of both older and more recent finds, I decided to explore first certain parts of the valley of Sitia and of the adjacent narrower valley of Praisos, since these were the major vital areas which would have been under the control of a king and of district governors. Easy access to the sea at Sitia Bay provided an outlet for trade into the southern Aegean Sea and consequently secured direct communication with Egypt and the East. Since the Praisos–Sitia region was fairly accessible to the eastern coastline where the harbor sites of Palaikastro and Zakros were, a major palace, if one existed, could have administered the coastal zone and used its natural harbors.

Exploration under my direction started in 1952 and was continued for ten years, at the end of which time the region of the bay of Zakros was reached. Investigations were carried out every year, but only for a limited time, usually not exceeding a month, because of parallel administrative and archaeological work undertaken by the Archaeological Service proper, and the limited financial and technical means available. The excavations were conducted under the auspices of the Archaeological Society in Athens, with professional and technical personnel supplied by the Greek Archaeological Service. Preliminary annual reports were published in *Praktika*, the Proceedings of the Archaeological Society.

The results fully justified my expectations. Four large Minoan mansions were found and excavated, as well as two peak sanctuaries, and cemeteries and burial caves of the Minoan and early Greek periods. Many other significant Minoan buildings and cemeteries were traced but were not investigated for lack of time.

From 1920 onward, small elegant heads of female figurines from Piskokephalo in Sitia began to be brought into the Heraklion Museum. Also known from the same area were curious female figures with pleated dresses that must undoubtedly be Minoan, although the graceful heads with high hairdos and tied-up chignons resembled the heads of Hellenistic figurines. When, in 1930, more fragments of figures were brought in, along with terracotta beetles having the characteristic curving horn of the species *Rhinoceros oryctes,* it became extremely probable that all these items derived from a Minoan peak sanctuary, but the opportunity to look for the specific source did not occur until I began my investigations in the 1950s.

The location of the deposit of the figurines was found on the slopes of a height near the village of Piskokephalo, and within a few days of digging a great number of various types, mostly male and female worshipers in various postures, were brought to light. The men were shown in the customary Minoan short loincloths, while the women appeared in pretty dresses almost modern in fashion, with open bodices. Their date was determined by the accompanying pottery as being in the first phase of the Neo-palatial period—that is, the seventeenth century B.C.

The curious likenesses of the beetle *Rhinoceros oryctes* were collected by the dozen. That these insects were dedicated to the deity is unquestionable, since they were shown climbing upon two of the worshipers and were also depicted in the interior of clay models of shrines, which could easily be identified by the sacred double horns which crowned them. It is interesting that even today representatives of this species of beetles continue to live in the same place; specimens have been exhibited in the Heraklion Museum along with their clay imitations. One of the latter shows a beetle carrying its little one on its back.

Naturally, such dedications have been found in many other peak sanctuaries where the deity was apparently worshiped as a goddess of the heavenly world, but the idols of Piskokephalo, being the latest of a series, were more highly developed and indeed more refined.

The discovery of the sanctuary of Piskokephalo made it most likely that there was a contemporary settlement in the surrounding region. The governor should have had his dwelling in a place guaranteeing his control of the area and at the same time enabling him to use the harbors near the present-day city of Sitia. The ruins of a house and farm building were actually found, by my wife, between Piskokephalo and Sitia, near the former bed of a small river, now dried up, and only 2 kilometers from the shore. Most likely the river was navigable for small ships at least to the point where the house stood. This fact would explain its unusual layout and form: the rooms were distributed in three successive terraces on a hill sloping toward the river; two long staircases flanked these and led down to the river, where there was a small wharf. Today a thick layer of sand lies in front of the wharf. Unfortunately the buildings were partly destroyed by the modern highway, which cut through the center, and by mechanical cultivation which extended over the terraces, but one can recognize the doorkeeper's lodge at the bottom of the main staircase, some basement rooms, and on the façade facing the river some larger rooms, surely the remnants of the principal apartments. Other small staircases provided communication between rooms at various levels.

The house had been plundered either during or after its destruction, but the scanty remains found can be dated within the early phases of the Neo-palatial era, not later than the end of the sixteenth century B.C.

The modern city of Sitia, lying on the western side of the bay of the same name, is supplied with excellent drinking water from a spring on one of the hills which enclose the previously mentioned valley on the northeastern side. The place is called Zou. The spring gushes up in a thickly planted area, watering a narrow valley, toward which the hill slopes down abruptly. During construction of the highway which runs over the hill, the ruins of another Minoan mansion were discovered.

On excavation, the mansion proved to be quite extensive. It consisted of several groups of rooms distributed among successive levels connected with one another by either staircases or ramps. Certain of the more spacious rooms behind the façade were evidently used as living quarters

44

because of the beautiful view from them toward the green valley. Fortunately, the entrance system of an ascending corridor terminating in a small sitting room has been preserved. The room has a corner bench and a wide, low window looking onto the picturesque area of the spring. From this other rooms were accessible, whose character as workshops could be deduced from their interior arrangement and the utensils and tools found in them. One group had been used for the manufacture of pottery: this included small rooms for baking the vessels, a workshop with a basin for kneading the clay, an adjacent area for drying the molded articles, a horseshoe-shaped kiln, and areas outside for storing the finished pots. Other wide spaces surrounded by low walls were apparently intended to be used as stables and pens for domestic animals. In many rooms were found small built-in cupboards for storing vessels. In one of the façades the windows of ground-floor apartments were preserved.

Some graves consisting of small hollows were found on the steep slope below the mansion, but only a few of these were excavated.

Not far away, on a great height dominating a wide valley near Praisos at a place called Sphakia, a peak sanctuary was discovered with part of its few original rooms preserved. The sacred nature of the building was determined both by its location and by the ritual vessels and the fragmentary clay animals found in dedication deposits in it. Its date was determined on the basis of these finds as the Proto-palatial period, to which most of these sanctuaries belong.

The third Minoan mansion which the expedition found and excavated is in the area of Achladia, 12 kilometers from Sitia. Its exterior walls of cyclopean masonry were visible through the thick vegetation that covered it, and I had actually discovered it before the Second World War. During the explorations in Sitia, the entire structure was uncovered and proved to be, not a simple unit in the form of a mansion, but several buildings spaced close together. This series of establishments, chiefly of an agricultural character, resembles the group of three large villas at Tylissos in central Crete, 21 kilometers northwest of Knossos, which was excavated between 1919 and 1924 by Dr. Joseph Hazzidakis, head of the Cretan Archaeological Service.

At Achladia, only one of the buildings was excavated, the one which had first been noticed and which was apparently the best preserved. This had two entrances, a main one with a ramp leading up to it and with an enclosure nearby, used as a stable or sheepfold, and a postern entrance apparently for servants. From the anteroom beyond the entrance one entered on the left into the main living quarters which were furnished with benches along the walls. Here also was a room perhaps used for religious ceremonies, since there were twin depositories just outside it, full of vessels which were most probably used in ritual. To the right and to the rear were storerooms containing pithoi for the storage of agricultural products. Twelve rooms are preserved, but originally there must have been at least twice as many, as a second floor can be deduced from the base of a staircase and from material fallen from above.

The numerous clay and stone vessels and the few tools found in the villa at Achladia date it to the same period as the villas of Piskokephalo and Zou. However, remains of another settlement, which may belong to the Neo-palatial and early Post-palatial periods, were found about a half-hour's walk to the east. Our attention was attracted to this area because an important tholos tomb, now known as the tomb of Rhiza, had been discovered at Achladia before the Second World War. This monument was fully preserved, even to the keystone of its spacious beehive chamber. Though it had been largely plundered, in it were preserved a clay coffin, within which the dead had been laid, and many clay and stone vessels placed there as offerings. The chamber had a diameter of approximately 4 meters and was constructed in the corbel system of cyclopean masonry. Though the influence of Mycenaean tholoi was obvious, the monument presented certain Cretan peculiarities, such as a blind door for the communication of the dead with the upper world and a long, tunnel-like passage (dromos) covered with slabs, leading to the burial chamber. The door had strong piers and a heavy lintel. The tomb was constructed in the middle years of the Post-palatial period, perhaps a little after 1300 B.C.

Not far from the tholos tomb was a pottery kiln of a characteristic shape, interesting because it is one of the few kilns known from the Creto-Mycenaean world. The lower compartment in which the fire was built, the bench supporting the grid on which the clay articles were placed, and a portion of the walls of the curving main chamber had survived.

The largest Minoan villa found by the expedition was on the height of Prophetes Elias, not far from the village of Tourtouloi. It occupied the entire top terrace of a peak that dominates the access roads to the main area of Praisos. Unfortunately this villa, which the expedition investigated only partially, had suffered great damage from the removal of cut limestone blocks for the construction of modern roads and bridges. Today one can distinguish more than forty rooms, on successive terraces of the hill, communicating with one another by means of stairs and corridors reaching to the top. On the steep side of the hill, the building was supported by a strong, high retaining wall; on the other side one can walk up the gently ascending slope.

Despite the very extensive damage, one can recognize many living rooms, storerooms, workshops, winepresses or kitchens. Many utensils had remained in their original places and this made possible the identification of the different sorts of workshops. Thus, there were terracotta winepresses with their characteristic outlets, and others joined permanently with the buckets for collecting the must still in place. There was no evidence for a second story, and the establishment may have been limited to the ground floor, perhaps to avoid the effects of destructive earthquakes to which the place was susceptible. The date, based on the household supplies, is the same as that of the other three villas discussed—the first Neo-palatial period.

Praisos, the cradle of the Eteo-Cretans, would be a logical site for an extensive palace, the seat of power not of a simple governor or feudal lord, but of a king, controlling the larger, central area of the present-day district of Sitia. Such a hypothesis is still plausible, although the kings of Praisos would probably have been of an inferior status, subject to the more extended authority of the rulers at Zakros. Early excavations conducted in this area by the British School of Archaeology exposed the remains of a substantial building at Hagios Constantinos which could have been a small palace, but investigation did not advance far enough to clarify its nature. It should now be investigated more thoroughly. Both early and recent excavations have revealed a whole series of tholos tombs, small but well constructed. Some of these belong to the Neo-palatial period but most of them to the Post-palatial period, which suggests continued growth in this area after decline had begun in central Crete. Even in the latest period, when the arrival of new Greek settlers was being heralded by the introduction of new customs and habits, the area of Praisos produced notable artifacts of gold, bronze, and ivory, samples of which were found by my expedition in a luckily unplundered small tholos tomb.

The explorations in Sitia were occasionally guided by fortuitous discoveries of objects and ruins. In these instances research was limited to that absolutely necessary for the salvage of antiquities. However, the results often made significant contributions toward clarifying problems connected with the evolution of Minoan culture. One of the most important of such investigations was conducted within a small natural cave at Maronia, in which were found burials of the second Pre-palatial period —that is, dating to 2400–2100 B.C. The funerary offerings included vessels of the so-called Vasiliki style, with its characteristic mottled decoration produced by oxidation while firing, as well as ivory seals.

At many sites unplundered rock-cut chamber tombs belonging to Post-palatial years were also found, containing interesting objects used as offerings, especially diverse ceramic articles. A very large cemetery was excavated near the village of Myrsini. In this and neighboring areas remains of settlements were traced. A tholos tomb in the area of Myrsini proved to belong to the Pre-palatial period and was of the familiar type of the tombs of the Mesara Plain. The dead were placed in clay coffins and in pithoi and were accompanied by many clay and stone vessels.

Interesting from the point of view of further cultural development at Sitia is the discovery and investigation of cemeteries of the Early Greek Period (1100–700 B.C.) in which the old forms of tholoi or chamber tombs were inherited, along with many Minoan burial customs such as the use of terracotta coffins and pithoi. Small natural caves, enlarged by rock-cutting, also continued in use as burial places. In many of these graves were found objects dating from the Minoan period, especially seal-stones and golden rings.

The systematic exploration of Sitia was discontinued when discoveries at Zakros demanded complete concentration of effort there.

5 The search narrows down to the bays of the region. Here previous excavations had proved the existence of Minoan settlements but not of a significant sort. The evidence suggested something more dramatic and important.

Palaikastro

To reach the small bays of easternmost Crete by land, one has two choices. Either one must climb over the high mountains which isolate the coastal zone as they slope down rather abruptly toward the sea, or, taking the longer route, one must skirt the mountain range along the north, following the north coast and then crossing the low pass which separates the area of Itanos and the promontory of Samonion. Even in Minoan times it was much easier to follow the latter route, in spite of its length, than to climb up the steep mountain path, and either land route was preferable to circumnavigating Samonion, even today called the Accursed Cape, which presented serious dangers with a rough sea. The pass over the narrow isthmus is not far from the Monastery of Toplou, which was built in post-Byzantine times and was provided with a high circuit wall. Since the Turkish name Toplou refers to a place equipped with cannon, the monastery apparently also had such a weapon for defense against pirates. From this point it is a short and quite easy descent to the open valley in which lie the modern village of Palaikastro (meaning "old castle") and, close by it, the Minoan settlement.

From the early years of Cretan excavations, the area of Palaikastro inevitably attracted the attention of archaeologists. It seemed a suitable location for a Minoan settlement, which could have taken advantage of a good natural harbor, protected by an islet (Grandes), and also of a fertile valley capable of producing many kinds of crops. Indeed, investigations conducted by the British School of Archaeology over the years 1902–1906 revealed extensive remains of an entire city. In contrast to Gournia, a town of a completely rural-manufacturing character excavated almost simultaneously on the Isthmus of Hierapetra by the American archaeologist Harriet Boyd Hawes, the city at Palaikastro was an important mercantile center. A whole series of house blocks, each consisting of many buildings and forming by their close interconnection a unified complex, extended over a practically flat area. The blocks were connected by a network of roads, and the central artery was entirely paved with slabs and supplied with gutters and drains and occasionally with causeways. The houses had many rooms and normally possessed a second story, where the rooms were allocated according to their function. Small open-air interior courts with four-columned porticoes were used in the more substantial houses to provide light and air to the subsidiary rooms and afford comfortable resting places for the inhabitants. At many points were found small cult shrines with accompanying depositories of ritual vessels. Workshops and industrial establishments were identified in certain other spots.

In a site with such an advantageous position and of such high cultural standards, the possibility of discovering a small palace, used either by a district governor or a king, was not to be excluded. But no such building was found in the entire settlement. On the other hand, the discovery of the Dictaean sanctuary of Greek times, with an inscribed stone containing a hymn to Crete-born Zeus, led to the hypothesis that, exactly in the part of the Minoan settlement where these remains were found, there must have been an important shrine during Minoan times.

The city at Palaikastro, of which the Minoan name is not known, was not far from the coast, but because of the subsidence of the eastern coast of Crete, any possible harbor installations must have sunk into the sea. Their traces could probably be found only by underwater exploration.

In recent years the British School of Archaeology began new research in a small section of the city, particularly in order to clarify, through stratigraphic study, the question of the succession of cultural periods and phases. New houses were then found with interesting installations and with impressive façades, well built with dressed ashlar masonry, facing the central paved road of the city. These investigations afforded an opportunity to study other aspects relating to the evolution of culture in eastern Crete. Simultaneously an effort was made to repair the damage caused by the Second World War in the area excavated earlier. Today only a small part of the entire investigated settlement is visible, for the early excavators covered over most of the exposed remains, leaving uncovered only the principal parts, especially the houses on either side of the main street and part of the shrine area.

The numerous finds from Palaikastro, both of the Minoan and the Greek periods, are today in the Heraklion Museum. Among the Greek ones are part of the sculptural decoration of the Temple of Dictaean Zeus and the inscribed stone with the hymn to the god. In this hymn an invocation is addressed to the young god, asking him to return every year in the company of the Kouretes, to bring fertility to the earth and fecundity and general well-being in works on earth and in the sea. The ritual dance of the Kouretes, led by the young god, achieved through magic the result requested in the hymn. In this ritual one recognizes the survival of very ancient concepts of Minoan religion.

The ancient palace should be a substantial structure. Somewhere in the known ruins of the past of Kato Zakros should be traces of that building. But where? Detailed investigation must be undertaken.

New Evidence at Zakros

During my extensive investigations in eastern Crete I became convinced that the area of Kato Zakros had played an important role in the island's relations with Egypt and the East and that therefore the natural bays of the easternmost coast, and especially the safest of them at Zakros, must have been utilized for harbor towns. The highly developed culture, demonstrated by artifacts of royal character such as the treasure of gold objects and the splendid pottery, and the presence of an archive, attested by numerous sealings and by a tablet inscribed in Linear A script, strengthened the hypothesis.

A detailed survey of the area, undertaken to collect other more definite indications, achieved results in 1961, exactly sixty years after the first exploration by Hogarth. I visited first the excavated remains of houses on the northeast hill. The exterior walls of the main complexes were still clear, but the interior arrangement had been obscured by the fill accumulated above and the heaps of stones formed in the meantime. The remains of Hogarth's complex A–B could be distinguished clearly, but the form of the building remained confused.

Large stone heaps, some several meters long, had accumulated on the slopes of the two hills or divided the narrow, closely planted valley. The peasants had pushed the stones aside in order to cultivate the intermediate area. The main stone heaps had been piled on top of ancient walls, which the peasants, to avoid excessive effort, had decided not to demolish. Even after being cleared, the fields still contained so many stones and weeds, and the bedrock came so close to the surface, that the soil was barely productive. The peasants had noticed that the legumes that grew there were easily cooked and had a good flavor, apparently as a result of the enrichment of the soil with fatty substances, which usually happens in long-inhabited areas. The Cretans today describe such areas as "Lenika" (*Hellenika*—Greek lands).

During the planting of the vineyards, especially in the strip between the hills, the peasants encountered sturdy walls, parts of which they had to demolish. In some places they found walls constructed of large, carefully dressed blocks of poros stone. They extracted many of these blocks and placed them at the edges of their lots. When they needed building materials, especially for the corners of houses and for doorjambs, they dismantled parts of visible walls. Luckily, only a small number of buildings were constructed in that almost deserted region, and the use of cultivating machines had barely started at the time of the investigation. On some of the poros blocks which had been extracted, incised signs could be distinguished.

From the very beginning, the presence of dressed poros blocks was taken as a substantial indication of the possible presence of a palace in the narrow valley where most of the squared blocks were found. There is no local supply of poros stone in the immediate vicinity of Zakros, but mainly limestone and schist. The poros, then, must have been brought from somewhere else, perhaps from far away.

I asked the natives where this stone could have come from. They informed me that extensive beds of poros existed along the coast, especially at Pelekita, a place a few miles to the north, that quarrying had plainly been done at some time, and that the stone had been transported by sea to the bay of Zakros. Fishermen confirmed that marks of quarrying the material into squared blocks were clear; the final dressing of the blocks seemed to have been done after they were transported to the construction site. Later I visited the quarry myself, to check the information and take photographs. SEE PAGE 54

This evidence added one more important indication of the existence of a palace and of its possible position. Quarrying on a large scale and

Minoan quarry of poros stone at Pelekita

transportation by boat presupposed organized, painstaking, expensive labor; this would hardly have been undertaken by simple citizens for their own homes, especially when hard limestone was abundant at the site. The fact that poros blocks were most numerous in the narrow valley suggested the most likely location of the conjectured palace. The great expanse over which this material was distributed showed that the building complex must have been of considerable size. A wall of poros blocks was also found at the bottom of a well excavated in the same area, not far from the road that led to the shore.

Other indications accumulated, supporting the hypothesis of a palace and helping to define its location. In one of the wells nearby, intended to supply water for the irrigation of the fields, workmen found a long bronze sword of a familiar Minoan shape, with a blade strengthened by a projecting midrib; unfortunately, during the clumsy process of extracting the sword, the edges were damaged. One fragment was handed over by the workmen immediately, and the rest when the trial excavation started. On the fringe of the flat area of the valley not far to the south, a large, tall column base of dark stone was found on one of the lower terraces. Judging from its size, it undoubtedly came from a vast structure, probably of palatial character, for large column bases were not found in any of the Minoan houses. Not far from this base appeared the sturdy corner of a building which at first seemed likely to be the structure to which the base belonged. However, subsequent excavation exposed only houses of the Minoan town, disproving the hypothesis.

The provisional survey had already made it clear that in all probability there was a palace at Zakros. I decided to conduct the first trial excavations at the end of the same year, 1961, since the necessary conditions for a more extended systematic investigation were not yet settled.

7 For archaeologists there is only one way to confirm what is hinted by surface evidence: that is to excavate—to probe the earth in search of the materials, artifacts, ruined walls, which confirm the presence of what is sought.

The Trial Excavations

For the trial excavations points were chosen at which there were definite indications that important structures might be found; two on the slope of the southwestern hill facing toward the narrow valley, where one could distinguish two solid corners of buildings of large, dressed stones; the third on the flat area, not far from the location of most of the cut poros blocks and at a spot where the owner of the land had found the opening of the mouth of a pithos, which he had not removed. The latter could possibly be related to the palace, if the guess about its location within the narrow valley was correct. The three sectors were termed A, B, and C.

Results from the first were most encouraging, for excavation revealed critical parts of Minoan buildings. Naturally there was a possibility that at least part of the palace might extend onto the terraces of the southwestern hill, with its main section occupying part of the level area of the valley between the hills. As excavation proceeded, however, it became clear that the building complexes found on the slopes were large houses belonging to the town, while the small section of successive storerooms on the level area, with their rich wares, seemed more palatial in character.

Of course the significance of the results could not be fully estimated at the end of the preliminary excavation, though the theoretical basis on which the excavations proceeded made it most likely that the location of the palace had been identified, along with an important section of the Minoan town near it. In the latter area (sectors A and B) brief and limited excavation had brought to light parts of two houses which seemed to be sturdily built and quite large. Parts of façades made of large blocks appeared, and the first interior apartments were investigated, although neither the plan of the houses, their full extent, their relation to one another, nor the stages of their development could then be defined.

In sector C, a complex of storerooms, of which two small rooms opened into a corridor, seemed quite similar to the Corridor of the Bays in the East Wing of the Palace of Knossos. All of the pithoi and masses of other terracotta wares in the storerooms were *in situ*—that is, in the positions where they had been when the buildings were destroyed. Many of the smaller vessels had apparently fallen from a higher floor, along with a few loom weights for weaving, several mud bricks, and a few stucco fragments painted with continuous rosettes. Not a few of the pots were beautifully and unusually decorated.

These findings were not enough in themselves to prove that this was the location of the hypothetical palace, but combined with other indications they aroused considerable optimism. My first report, published subsequently in *Praktika* of 1961, contained some discussion about a possible palace and expressed a hopeful outlook for future excavations. However, the extensive and systematic investigation warranted by the results of the trial digging required larger scientific, technical, and economic means than the Archaeological Society could immediately provide, since it was then involved in an extensive program of excavation over all of Greece.

By a most fortunate coincidence, shortly before the main investigations started in Kato Zakros, unexpected help made possible the organization of a carefully planned, systematic excavation. In a letter addressed to me as director of the Heraklion Museum, Leon Pomerance of New York, a friend of arts and antiquities, and his wife, Harriet, expressed their willingness to help finance an excavation in the area of Knossos. The couple had recently visited the Museum and had admired its treasures. The statement in the introduction to the Museum Guide that the soil of Crete contained an inexhaustible supply of such works of art, which could be easily recovered if the means were available, had given them the idea of offering financial aid for an excavation. An initial offer of $3,000 was made to begin the work.

Naturally, this donation was gratefully accepted, after the necessary permission was obtained from the appropriate Greek ministry, with the express agreement that the excavation would be conducted throughout by the Greek Archaeological Society under the direction of the Ephor (general supervisor) of Antiquities. The site of Zakros in Sitia was proposed, as it had yielded positive signs promising the discovery of important Minoan buildings. The donors would be allowed to be present at the excavation but were not permitted to intervene, and the provisions of the Greek Archaeological Law were to be observed in regard to both the conduct of the excavation and the treatment of the finds. The benefactors were also warned of the difficult living conditions at Zakros and the lack of most basic facilities there. They agreed to all these provisions, and preparations were begun for the commencement of work in September 1962.

The palace from the southeast

8   What preliminary trial excavation suggests can only be substantiated by full-fledged and systematic clearance of the remains. Large-scale excavation is a demanding matter. While financial help, skilled assistants, and governmental support are the necessary tangibles, even more pressing is the need to plan a strategy so that maximum results can be obtained in the all too short run of a yearly excavation period.

These problems solved, the excavations begin, and the climax of a long search is the proof that the palace of Zakros is found.

The Discovery of the Palace

The investigations met with unique success in the very first season. Not only were important houses of the Minoan town discovered very early, but the excavations soon revealed part of an extensive building which all evidence indicated could indeed be a palace. Work was concentrated in the three areas fixed through the trial excavation—namely, sectors A and B on the southwestern hill, where the houses were revealed, and sector C in the flat area between the two hills, which seemed to be the SEE PAGE 84 site of the palace. In all these sectors, but especially in the building considered to be a palace, rich discoveries were made, especially of many and varied types of ceramic and bronze objects. The houses proved to be quite large and to have suffered only minor disturbances as a result of reoccupation during the Post-palatial period. Of the palace itself a considerable section of the storerooms and of adjacent spaces on the ground floor was revealed. The storerooms were full of pithoi and other vessels, while both large and small pots had fallen from an upper story. From a treasury in

The contents of one of the West Wing storerooms, as found

the upper story came bronze ingots and ivory tusks that had been intended
for use as raw material by craftsmen.

Excavations started at the "Corridor of the Bays," first located during
the trial excavation, and at a massive corner of large cut stones which was
faintly discernible in the midst of a long and high pile of loose stones. At
the beginning both the donors and the assistant archaeologists were skeptical about the likelihood of finding a palace in such a location, but by
the end of the season, there were few doubts left. The exceptionally high
quality of the pottery found, the series of storerooms with great numbers
of pithoi, the stores of imported raw materials, the careful construction of
the building, all provided essential evidence.

Even thus early in the investigation, numerous indications pointed
to the destruction of the palace in a sudden catastrophe followed by a
widespread conflagration. The house pottery helped fix the date of this
destruction to the end of the third phase of the Neo-palatial period, around

Bronze ingots and elephant tusks, as found in a room
of the West Wing, fallen from the story above

1450 B.C.—that is, the same time as the destruction of the other Minoan palace centers. Along with the pottery were found stone and bronze utensils, tools and weapons, a gold and silver vessel, and various miniature objects which seemed to have remained exactly where they had been on the day of the catastrophe.

An impressive façade extended toward an open space to the west, apparently the West Court. In order to expose that section it had been necessary to remove big heaps of stones and considerable amounts of earth fill, which, by shielding the building, were responsible for its relatively good state of preservation.

The discovery of many cut poros blocks, some incised with masons' marks, made it clear that the similar material which had been removed by the owners of the land was derived from the building. Two swords with gold studs on their handles, found in one of the rooms, were of the same type as the one found in the nearby well before the excavation began. Most significant was the realization that the building had not been disturbed after its destruction and apparently had not been plundered, a

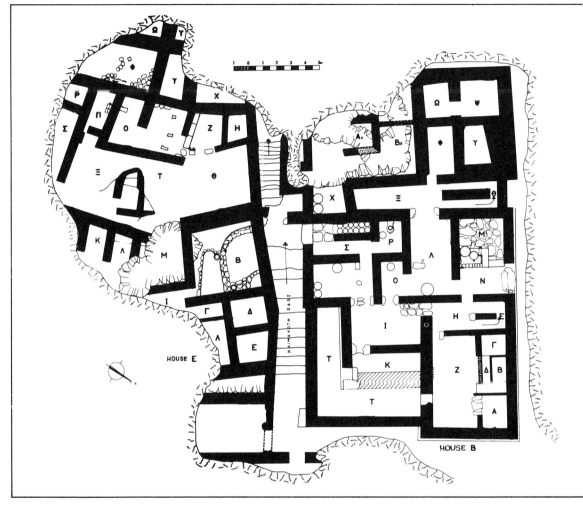

Plan of houses A, Γ, Δ, Z, on the slopes of the southwest hill

circumstance that promised important discoveries. No previously excavated palace, Minoan or Mycenaean, had escaped plundering.

In the other two sectors excavation was conducted with the help of young assistant archaeologists. The exposed sections of the houses proved exceptionally interesting. These buildings undoubtedly had at least two floors with many rooms and a good interior arrangement. The rooms included storerooms, industrial establishments, workrooms, main living quarters, and cult rooms. The household equipment, though simpler than

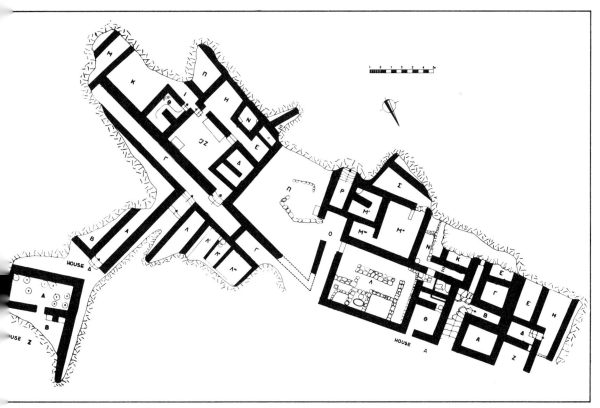

Plan of houses B and E on the slopes of the southwest hill

that of the palace, consisted of numerous terracotta vessels and a few of stone and bronze. In some parts of the houses alterations and adaptations for different use could be identified as having been made during the Postpalatial period, thus explaining the presence of pottery of this phase.

Furthermore, research was extended to areas where graves might be or had been found, for instance in the Gorge of the Dead, previously mentioned, and the Black Ditch and the slopes of the Spiliara. Although the small caves had been robbed, several burial offerings, mostly of Pre-palatial and Proto-palatial Minoan periods, were recovered.

All these discoveries delighted Mr. and Mrs. Pomerance, and they promised to continue their support during the following excavation seasons. The excavation was thus assured a sound economic basis, especially since the Archaeological Society increased its annual contribution to match the sum offered by the benefactors. A total of $60,000 had been allotted for the work through 1970; more than half of this was contributed by the Pomerances. Meanwhile, the Greek Government started taking the necessary measures for the expropriation of land and the subsequent payment to compensate the landowners. It also took essential steps to consolidate and protect ancient remains at the site. Unfortunately, because of the bureaucratic formalities involved, and other difficulties, expropriation and compensation have so far been accomplished only on a limited scale.

Excavation started with great optimism in the fall of the following year, 1963. Results indeed surpassed our highest expectations. At the end of the season practically all archaeologists who had expressed reservations about the identification of this vast building as a palace withdrew them or at least withheld them awaiting the discovery of additional evidence. It was by now clear that the exposed section was only part of one wing of a new palace laid out in a labyrinthine manner comparable to the plan of the Minoan palaces discovered much earlier.

Various rooms of the palace sanctuary were now revealed next to the groups of storerooms and compartments into which storage jars, bronze ingots, and ivory tusks had fallen from above. These included a small cult room, a lustral basin, repositories, an archive room, and the shrine's treasury. To the sanctuary also apparently belonged a pantry, a small workshop, and a storeroom full of pithoi. All these spaces had remained untouched since the time of the catastrophe, and all the articles of cult and house equipment were still in their original positions. Once again a shrine's treasury had been found with all the ritual vessels stored in it—the first known example being the Temple Repositories of the Palace of Knossos, where the faïence snake goddesses and many other cult objects had been found. The vessels and symbols within the treasury at Zakros had evidently been used in ritual ceremonies, and most of these, especially rhytons and chalices for sacred communion, were admirably carved in a variety of choice stone.

Next we started uncovering a vast hall, perhaps used in palace ceremonies. Here, apparently fallen from a corresponding hall above, were found two stone ritual vessels that were unique in form and artistic treatment—a rhyton in the shape of a bull's head and another bearing a repre-

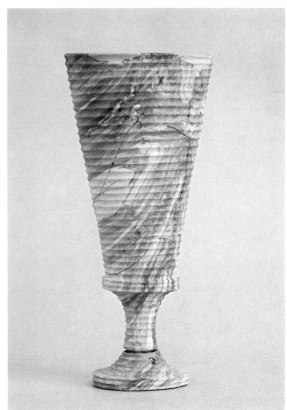

From the Treasury of the Shrine: (left) *ovoid porphyry rhyton;*
(right) *sacred-communion chalice with horizontal grooves*

Rhytons and chalices, as found in the Treasury of the Shrine

sentation of a peak sanctuary in relief. This hall was provided with a light-well surrounded by columns.

Then excavation revealed an annex, probably used for industrial purposes, at the west side of the building, as well as part of a spacious hall adjacent to the complex of storerooms. Everywhere great quantities of pots and other objects were found.

In the other two sectors within the Minoan town on the southeast slope of the hill excavation also continued. Two rather extensive, apparently two-storied buildings with twenty and twenty-four rooms respectively on the ground floor, had already been fully disclosed. In them were found more industrial establishments, storerooms, and small unroofed spaces with simple hearths. Remains of five or six other houses also began to emerge. A slab-paved lane with smaller passages branching off from it was exposed, leading up the hill between two houses. Each house had its own character. The storerooms were found full of vessels, pithoi, large amphoras, squat storage jars, jugs, pitchers, and other smaller pots. Two winepresses, with the vessels used for the extraction and collection of the juice, were found *in situ*. A third press was built in and provided with a tublike collecting container. In one of the houses was found a small stone capital. This is the first example of a stone capital from either Minoan or Mycenaean areas, and its discovery proves that Evans was correct in his restoration of wooden columns in the palace of Knossos. Further indications of reoccupation of certain houses during the Post-palatial period gradually emerged.

SEE PAGE 30

In the same season, important results were obtained during investigations in the small burial caves in the Gorge of the Dead. Although most of these had been pillaged, considerable material rejected or overlooked by the robbers was collected and research proved generally interesting. One object was similar to the utensil previously mentioned as being found by Hogarth and had apparently had a similar purpose—that of kindling a fire by blowing, in order to raise the temperature to the melting point. Since the one here had been placed in a tomb as a funeral offering, the person buried had probably been a metalworker, and this unusual article one of the tools used in his craft. In a small narrow cave with side passages and a double exit, located at the end of the ravine toward the valley,

Stepped lane in the town on the southwest hill

Stone capital, from a house on the southwest hill

were found undisturbed burials furnished with pottery of the Vasiliki style, having a mottled decoration produced by oxidation firing, and other pots of a gray color decorated with incised triangles and half circles, clearly pointing to Cycladic influence. Among the offerings was an exceptionally important round pyxis (cosmetic box) of schist, decorated with closely set, incised geometric motifs. The lid of this box had a handle carved in the shape of a reclining dog, identical with the famous one found in 1905

Schist comestic box with a handle in the shape of a dog,
from a tomb in the Gorge of the Dead

by the American archaeologist Richard B. Seager in a grave on the islet of
Mochlos. Both boxes were apparently made by the same craftsman, who
must have lived during the second phase of the Pre-palatial period, around
2300–2100 B.C. This beautiful box, on which the artist had so skillfully
combined the naturalistic and decorative elements, was found on September 13, 1963. By an extraordinary happy coincidence, on this same day
the contents of the shrine treasury of the Zakros palace were discovered,
as well as part of an important hoard of Oriental cylinder seals and
Mycenaean golden jewelry in the palace of Cadmus in Boeotian Thebes,
in an investigation which was also under my direction. The remainder of
the latter hoard I recovered, after my return from Zakros, with the help of
Mrs. Stasinopoulou-Touloupa. The treasure, which confirmed the old
tradition that Cadmus had come originally from Phoenicia, was shown
to date to about 1300 B.C.

During the following season, in 1964, investigations progressed to
the point that even the slightest remaining doubts as to the identification
of the complex as a palace had been removed. By the end of that season,
almost the entire West Wing was exposed, as well as a large section of the

Central Court with part of the interior façade of the East Wing just in view. The rapid pace at which the disclosure of the palace was proceeding obliged us to suspend excavation in the surrounding Minoan town and to limit additional research within the cemeteries to points which were threatened by further pillaging. However, to avoid further damage, excavation was begun on a rural Minoan mansion in the vicinity of Epano Zakros, already partly destroyed as a result of the construction of a road leading to Kato Zakros and the installation of a new water conduit. This proved to be a substantial building with numerous rooms, storerooms, and agricultural equipment, such as a double built-in winepress.

Excavations in the West Wing of the palace progressed to the total revelation of a vast hall with a series of columns supporting an upper floor, a pier-and-door partition, and a lightwell surrounded by columns. Next to it was found a brilliantly decorated spacious room, used perhaps for banquets, judging from its contents. Next were revealed both the official and the secondary entrances from the Central Court into this wing, and the connecting system of corridors. The communication from here to the various sections of the palace thus became clear. A large apartment reached through a small portico at the north side of the Central Court must have been used as a kitchen. The investigation moved from there into the East Wing, where we expected to find the royal apartments, and perhaps also the throne rooms, to judge from the pillared, stepped passage which appeared there. Finally, at the south corner of the Central Court, we came across a channeled fountain well, reached by means of a flight of steps, which must have supplied fresh drinking water. Once more housewares and other objects found in place in most of the rooms were so numerous as to confirm the conclusion that the palace had not been disturbed after its final destruction. In the following four seasons, from 1965 to 1968, excavation progressed relatively rapidly, considering that the digging season never exceeded twenty-five days and that we had to cope with many difficulties, such as the seepage of water through the soil at lower levels and the necessity of removing enormous heaps of stones where the palace building spread up onto the slope of the northeast hill.

The Minoan Villa of Epano Zakros, which we considered crucial to excavate in the years 1964–1965, proved to be one of the most notable

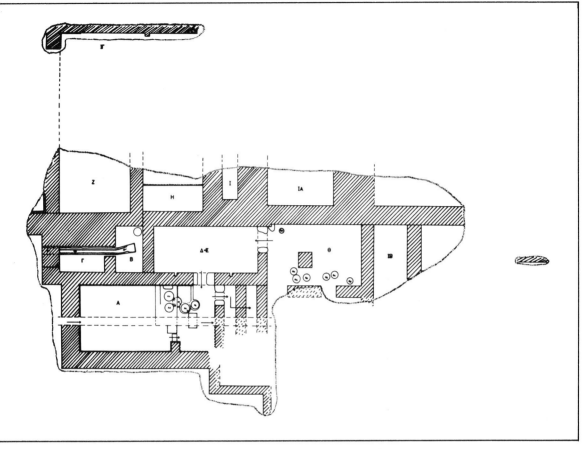

Plan of the Minoan Villa near Epano Zakros

buildings in the entire Sitia region. Aside from its great extent, with apartments built on successive terraces on a slope, it contained extraordinary installations for agricultural industries, and storerooms full of pithoi, one of which was inscribed with the longest inscription so far found on a pithos, containing twenty-six signs in Linear A script. The walls of the villa had been decorated with noteworthy paintings with floral and abstract motifs. Unfortunately the partial destruction of its halls, especially where the road to Epano Zakros passed through, made it impossible to form a complete picture of this attractive building.

In 1965 an essential section of the East Wing was exposed. There, as had been suspected from the beginning, the royal apartments were located. Unfortunately, cultivation had penetrated deep into the soil, and damage was considerable. Careful study of the scanty remains, however, made it possible to recognize with certainty the various apartments with their lightwells, as well as a bathroom. The royal bath, to judge from its sacred ornaments, had also served as a lustral basin for purification rites. A vast rectangular hall with a curious circular structure at the center, into which a well-preserved staircase descended, now began to be exposed. In the following year the whole complex was elucidated: it was an official hall with a colonnaded spring-cistern at the center, the source of abundant water coming from a spring which was located nearby to the south, at a spot where an underground spring chamber, also reached by means of a staircase, had been specially installed. Perhaps the grand complex was actually the throne room of the king.

In 1966 and 1967 part of the South Wing was explored, where workshop establishments used in the manufacture of luxurious artifacts of crystal, faïence, and ivory, as well as in the production of perfumes, were found. The housewares and other objects were neither so numerous nor so exceptionally well made as those from the area of the shrine in the West Wing, but they were most interesting for a better understanding of everyday life within the palace. The main passages from the east and south toward the Central Court began to appear in 1967. In the same year more of the East Wing was traced. A broad antechamber into the vast square hall and a slab-paved inner courtyard to the north of the hall, with an elaborate underground system of drains, were uncovered. The main SEE PAGE 90 entrance to the palace, first discovered at that time, was connected by a ramp with this courtyard. A slab-paved road, apparently starting at the harbor, led to the entrance. One could reach the inner court by walking down the slanting steps of the ramp and thence reach the rest of the rooms in the East Wing. Next, exploration was begun on the north side of the palace, which was constructed on successive terraces on the slope of the hill. Parts of these structures had apparently been used only in the older phase of the Neo-palatial period; subsequently these had been filled in. From an archaeological point of view it was important that certain buildings and pottery could be safely attributed to this phase—a result not attained in the case of the rest of the palaces.

The Discovery of the Palace

In 1968 and 1969 excavation continued along the northeast slope, and notable establishments built on successive terraces were found, communicating by means of ramps or small or large staircases. These buildings presented great interest, for they belonged to successive Minoan periods, starting in the Proto-palatial and ending with the last phase of the Neo-palatial. One of them was located to the north of the main palace entrance and of the royal road nearby. However, by the fall of 1968 it was not yet clear whether these structures belonged to the palace, were annexes, or were simply parts of the houses of high officials living in the immediate vicinity. Later research confirmed the suspicion that Hogarth's excavations had reached the boundaries of the palace. One of the complexes found had actually been partly excavated by Hogarth. At the end of 1969 the complexes on the North Slope had been proved definitely to be annexes of the palace, separated by small lanes branching from the main roads.

During the 1967 season, certain vessels found by chance led to the discovery and systematic investigation of two burial enclosures with about two hundred burials, furnished with interesting offerings, mainly clay and stone vessels and seals which date from the end of the Pre-palatial period. Some of the dead had been placed within pithoi and clay chest-like sarcophagi. In the course of the excavations, a great many objects were collected, some found by chance in the process of land cultivation and

Rock-crystal seal, from a burial enclosure at Kato Zakros

others discovered within the stone heaps which were removed in order to trace the palace and the houses of the town.

By the fall of 1969 an expanse of about 6,500 square meters of the palace area and the annexes had been exposed, and still the outer limits to the structure, at least to the east and south, had not been reached. The original prediction that the new palace would not be essentially smaller than the palaces of Phaistos and Mallia seemed now to be confirmed. However, the complete excavation of the building, with its surrounding courts and the roads leading to its entrance, will require at least three or four more seasons of digging. More work will be needed in order to explore the surrounding town, to trace the royal graves and the various cemeteries, to note possible harbor installations, and to clarify the development of the Minoan settlement at the site from the earliest Minoan periods down to the latest habitation. Part of the town quarters have already been investigated, but additional systematic research and study will undoubtedly require a long time and the participation of other scholars.

*Rhyton with octopus decoration, from installations
of the Post-palatial period in a house on the southwest hill*

The Palace of Zakros

Having made the great discovery, the culmination of a long search, the excavator is overwhelmed by the scale of his finds. Daily a multitude of precious evidence confronts him, demanding its due and accurate reporting. Not a piece can be moved without its position being noted, for the very character of a room may be revealed by the finds of humble objects within it.

What follows is the author's description, section by section, of the palace. The description could only have been made through attention to the countless details of recovered evidence. Here then is the Zakros palace resurrected by science, casting in one splendid stroke a strong light on the Cretan past.

*General view of the palace, looking toward the West Wing
and the northwest sector*

9   The location and physical character of a building give an insight into its purpose. Palaces reflect the climate of the time, for their location points to peace or war and their physical construction is a barometer of wealth.

Site and Design

The palaces of Knossos and Phaistos were built on strategically located hills dominating road arteries, which connected vital areas within each state. These hills, unlike the Mycenaean citadels, were not fortified. Such a position was at first considered a standard feature of Minoan palaces, but the later discovery of a third palace at Mallia showed that this was not necessarily the rule; its site was on a flat plain near the coast. The fourth palace, at Zakros, presented still another situation, in which the palace was built partly on flat land, partly on a hill. The main part of the palace extended over the flat, narrow zone between the two hills of the valley of Zakros, while what were probably supplementary sections were on terraces on the slope of the northeastern hill. This hill and the opposite one, at the southwest, were occupied by buildings of the Minoan town.

At first the location seemed curious, for the palace gave the impression of being in part dominated by the hill houses, while its main section was open to attack from the sea and from the surrounding hills. Gradually, however, the reasons for this unusual position became clear. The structures on the northeastern hill were either extensions or annexes of the palace, directly under its control. The main palace complex nestled within the narrow valley and was thus protected from the powerful prevailing winds from the northwest, which today still harass the region during most of the year. Moreover, the fertile land here made possible the cultivation of gardens, which must have added to the attractiveness of the premises

General plan of the palace

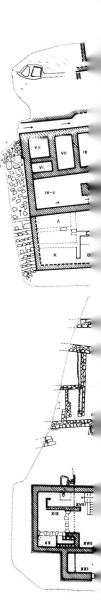

I–VIII	Storerooms of the West Wing
IX	Reception lobby, West Wing
X	Staircase of the Shrine
XI	Room with painted amphoras (see also XV)
XII	Room of the swords
XIII	Pantry of the Shrine
XIV	Corridor of the Shrine
XV	Room with painted amphoras (see also XI)
XVI	Archive Room of the Shrine
XVII–XXI	Workshops of the West Wing
XXII	Deposit room of the Shrine
XXIII	The Central Shrine
XXIV	The lustral basin
XXV	Treasury of the Shrine
XXVI	Workshop of the Shrine
XXVII	Storeroom of the Shrine
XXVIII	Hall of Ceremonies
XXIX	Banquet Hall
XXX	Entrance, antechamber, and staircase of the West Wing
XXXI	Service entrance and corridor
XXXII	Kitchen and dining quarters
XXXXIII	Kitchen storeroom
XXXIV	North portico
XXXV	Corridor to the bathroom
XXXXVI	The queen's apartment
XXXVII	The king's apartment
XXXVIII	Corridor to the Central Court
XXXIX–XLI	Unit of the built well
XLII–XLVIII	Workshop unit of the South Wing
XLIX	Southern approach to the Central Court
L–LI	Service rooms of the Kitchen
LII	Staircase leading up to the Banquet Hall
LIII–LIV	Storerooms of the North Wing
LV	Stepped ramp
LVI–LVII	Storerooms of the royal apartments
LVIII–LX	Bathroom, antechamber, and small corridor
LXI	Dressing room
LXII	Hall of the Cistern
LXIII–LXIV	Inner paved court
LXV	Terraced parterres
LXVI	Ascent to the harbor road
LXVII	Storeroom
LXVIII	Enclosure with service installations
LXIX	Northeast Entrance and passageway
LXX	Southeast court
LXXI	Spring Chamber
LXXII	Well of the Fountain
α–λ	North sector of apartments belonging to first palace phase
A–I	Northwest sector, first palace phase
D I–D III —E I–E V	Oblique Building, Protopalatial period, rebuilt in first palace phase
A–Z	Northeast annex of the palace

80

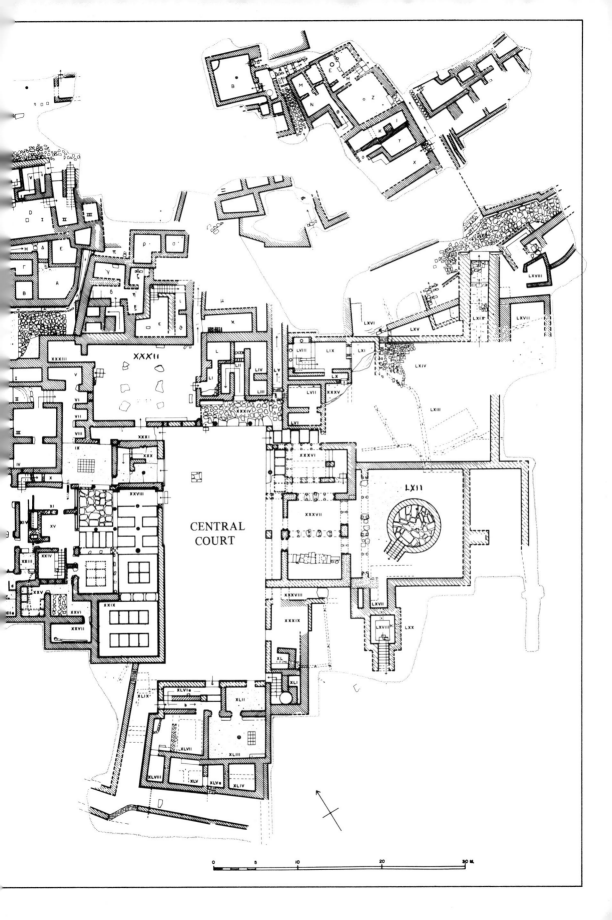

CENTRAL
COURT

and provided a pleasant resort for members of the royal family. The problem of water supply, both for drinking and for general use, was solved without difficulty, for the underground water was easily tapped by means of special installations. The advantage of direct access from the sea, by means of slab-paved roads, was important for a governmental center preoccupied with trading activity, which took place chiefly at the harbor.

The development of Zakros as a maritime base made it possible to fend off sudden invasion by means of ships moored in the harbor or patrolling the shore. Indeed, scholars believe that a strong navy was used instead of fortifications at Minoan sites. A comparable means of guaranteeing safety was used in the British Isles in modern times. The central location of the palace between the two sections of the town, moreover, had practical advantages.

Architecturally, the Zakros palace is closely related to the other Minoan palaces. Like the rest, it was organized around a central court, unifying the structure into four wings: two main ones, the west and east, and two secondary ones, the north and the south. A court, originally paved, extended in front of the west façade. Similar to the others also was the arrangement of the interior. The west wing contained chiefly rooms connected with the shrine and related cult rooms and storerooms which may also have belonged to the sanctuary. The east wing contained the main living quarters of the royal family, as well as a ceremonial hall which might have been the throne room. Other areas served as workshops; others, such as kitchens and service rooms, were for daily use. The layout was as labyrinthine here as that at the other palaces, and the whole structure was made even more complex by the addition of one or more stories above the ground floor. The presence of these upper stories is inferred from staircases, from collapsed building materials, and from the sturdy construction of walls on the ground floor. There was considerable use of timberwork to strengthen and give elasticity to the walls, and various openings were found which indicate the positions of windows and doors. The masonry of outer walls and of inner divisions was analogous to that of the other palaces. Wooden columns standing on stone bases were of the typical tapering shape, and the various series of lightwells, pier-and-door partitions, porches, colonnaded verandas, and benches were also char-

SEE PAGES 80-81

82

acteristic of palace architecture. The walls were adorned as usual with paintings, but at Zakros only decorative motifs seem to have been used; no representational scenes have as yet been found. There is a slight dissimilarity in orientation, for at Zakros the main axis of the palace deviates slightly from the precise north-to-south orientation found in the others. In describing the Palace of Zakros, however, the orientation is treated for convenience as though it too was exactly north to south.

Despite these customary characteristics, the Palace of Zakros had certain unique features, dictated by such factors as adaptation to the landscape and climate, the use of local building materials, the nature of its relation to other political centers, and conditions existing at the time of its construction and renovation. Since the part of the main building and the annexes already revealed occupies at least 6,000 square meters, and the palace areas at Phaistos and Mallia are not much over 9,000 square meters, the difference in scale between Zakros and those palaces is probably not significant. It cannot, of course, be compared to the peerless palace of Knossos, which is over three times as large. The Central Court at Zakros, considerably smaller than that of any of the other palaces, is about one-third the size of the one at Knossos. Nevertheless, though inferior in size, in charm this palace is certainly comparable if not superior to Knossos.

Building Materials

Even though architecture in the Neo-palatial period depended on old traditions and long previous experience, it became more ambitious in order to fulfill the aims of grandeur, grace, and comfort that characterized the new era. Naturally, results in each case were governed by the means available and by economic considerations. Local materials were used for most of the construction, while rarer or harder kinds of stone were restricted to more important areas. Limestone was abundant and was used for basement walls. Unbaked mud bricks made of local clay were used in upper floors and interior wall partitions. Extensive cypress forests provided a relatively convenient source of timber, and cypress

(Above) *The site of the palace; (below) view toward the West Wing,*
with the Hall of Ceremonies and the Banquet Hall in the background

beams were incorporated within walls in order to make them more elastic in the event of earthquakes, and were also used for columns, piers, door and window framing, ceilings, and roofs. All these materials were locally available at Zakros. In the vicinity of Knossos and Phaistos there were excellent quarries of crystalline gypsum, and this highly decorative material was used for lining walls, paving floors, and making columns, pier bases, and benches. At Mallia and Zakros no gypsum was locally available, and since this material is difficult to transport, less luxurious materials, such as slabs of hard black ironstone, poros stone, or local limestone, pavements of schist, and bases of hard stones, such as breccia, ironstone, and serpentine, were employed instead. Decorated stucco was applied on walls and limestone or concrete prepared with lime and small pebbles on floors. On some of the floors at Zakros tiles or burned bricks were combined to simulate carpets. Synthetic substances may have been used there on the floors of official halls; this possibility is discussed later.

Dressed poros stone was extensively used in the palaces of Knossos and Phaistos, particularly in the Neo-palatial period, chiefly for the construction of important façades, walls of lightwells, and living quarters. At Mallia, sandstone, which is less resistant and less attractive, was used instead, but at Zakros poros stone was again widely used in the construction of walls facing interior courts and for lightwells and entranceways. Since this stone did not occur naturally within a wide radius around the palace and its transportation over the mountain ranges from farther west seemed impossible, its presence at first presented a mystery. However, the discovery of poros quarries in the coastal area of Pelekita, 5 kilometers north of the bay of Zakros and immediately south of the small bay of ancient Karymai (present-day Karoumes), showed that the stone could have been transported by boat, and, as I mentioned earlier, the recognition of this fact was one of the chief indications that there was a palace near the bay of Zakros. As one approaches the coast of Pelekita today, one can distinguish from a distance the layer of poros stone sloping down toward the sea, overhung by masses of limestone. Rocks projecting into the sea made it possible to tie and unload small vessels. Although the shore must have been greatly transformed by subsidence since antiquity, the way the stone was quarried, transported, and loaded can still be discerned. The

SEE PAGE 54

main areas where stone was cut are recognizable. There is a very deep and wide cut in the poros layer, gaping toward the sea. On the steep side there are stepped platforms of various heights, showing where the blocks were extracted. Quarrying activity is most easily traced on the rock facing to the north. Two or three blocks still lie about, their surfaces badly eroded with the passage of time. Across from the big cut there is a smaller cliff of poros stone, which was quarried on all sides, so that it is now easy to climb. One can distinguish the grooves made for the wedges used to extract the blocks. On the opposite side of the ravine, to the northwest, huge poros masses had crumbled down.

Condition of the Palace

As excavation at Zakros progressed, a most important fact became clear: the palace had escaped plundering and was only slightly disturbed. Storerooms, various compartments, repositories, treasuries, with practically all their contents, remained as they had been on the day of the destruction. A great deal of household equipment which had fallen from the upper floors was lying where it fell. Most of the valuable objects were still in their original positions. Tools lay where they were being used on that day, and raw materials and unfinished artifacts were found in workshops. The finished products were still in the storerooms. In the kitchens and their annexes there were remnants of food, together with cooking utensils either in use at the time or in storage compartments. The only exception to the generally undisturbed condition was the East Wing, where cultivation had penetrated deeply into the soil and as a result very few objects and architectural elements survived.

There does not seem to have been any significant rehabilitation of the palace after its destruction in Minoan times. There were only scanty remains of unimportant structures in a limited area and in a higher stratum. The greatest damage was brought about by the repeated building of rubble retaining walls for the cultivated terraces of the hill, and by the installation of irrigation conduits, one of which penetrated down into the

Minoan layers in the East Wing, where the overlying layer of accumulated earth was very shallow.

All evidence pointed to a sudden and terrible catastrophe which caused the buildings to collapse and burn. Many traces of this violent conflagration could be seen throughout the palace. The people living in it apparently had barely enough time to collect their more valuable portable possessions and escape. They never came back to retrieve what was left of their riches or to reconstruct the building and reinhabit it. Only a few objects of precious metal were found—for example, a small silver jug decorated with gold inlays and a thick simple ring of gold. The fact that there is no indication of a reoccupation of the palace also seems curious, since there is evidence of resettlement in the town site on the south-

The small silver jug found in a storeroom of the West Wing; the view at right shows the gold decoration more clearly

western hill, where certain houses were partially rebuilt after 1380 B.C. One must assume that following the destruction the area of the palace was considered sacred and inviolable—under a kind of tabu—as was the case with other palaces, especially those of Phaistos and Mallia, where, apparently, only shrines were later raised. Even the situation at Knossos is perhaps comparable, for the structures attributed by Evans to the "reoccupation period" had a predominantly religious character. It is noteworthy in this connection that the area of the palace of Cadmus in Thebes was described in classical times as an *enelysion*—that is, a prohibited sacred precinct, which had been struck by the thunderbolt of Zeus and was not to be trespassed upon; only an enclosed shrine to Demeter, the walls of which were revealed by excavation, had been allowed to rise above these ruins.

As an unpillaged palace of its period, Zakros is unique. All the other great Minoan and Mycenaean palaces had been robbed and stripped of their treasures long before their discovery by archaeologists. Any precious objects found in them were only those left behind by robbers or buried under floors laid on top of the ruins by later inhabitants. Thus in the Palace of Knossos remnants of the contents of the treasuries were dumped into the temple repositories after the destruction which struck the palace around 1600 or 1500 B.C. Scraps from the central treasury were moreover covered over by floors built during the final reconstruction of this palace. In the palaces of Phaistos and Mallia no valuable objects dating later than the final catastrophe were found in their original locations. In the Palace of Mallia only a few precious weapons were preserved under later floors after the destruction of 1600 B.C. The palaces of Mycenae and Tiryns in mainland Greece had been so thoroughly plundered that practically no valuable object was obtained through excavation. In the palace at Pylos only masses of broken clay vessels and numerous clay tablets from the archives, resembling those of Knossos, remained in their original positions; all precious objects had been removed. Only the Palace of Zakros can provide an adequate picture of the equipment of a royal Aegean household of the second millennium B.C.

10 There is an ancient axiom that the entrance to a building sets the mood of the visitor. Feelings of awe, wonder, puzzlement, even terror can be motivated by the combination of approach, entrance, and façade.

Approaches

The need for direct communication with the harbor suggested that the main entrance to the palace should be sought at the eastern side, where a road beginning at the sea must have terminated. Excavation has not yet exposed the limits of the East Wing, and as a result the presence of a gate on the east remains hypothetical, though strongly suggested by an east-west passage running around the main rooms and ending at the Central Court.

A major gate has been located at the northeastern side of the East Wing, at which terminated a paved road with a northeast-to-southwest direction—that is, oblique to the façade of the gate. It has not yet been possible to trace the entire length of this road, which, with its central causeway of poros stone slabs, and its gutters next to the building flanking it, resembles roads connected with other palaces. Its general direction indicates that it could have started at the northeastern end of the bay, and presumably it went around the northern hill, upon one of its lower slopes. This road led to the main entrance, which was at a higher level in relation to the main part of the palace and the Central Court, and the passage leading from it was therefore constructed in stepped, slanting platforms. The visitor reached the palace proper by first entering an interior court from which the apartments of the East Wing were accessible. The unusual form of the northeast gateway resulted from the need for an entrance which could be completely controlled and which would

*The end of the paved road from the harbor,
at the Northeast Entrance*

connect the main road from the harbor, lying at a higher level, with the main part of the palace on the flat land at a lower level. The solution was indeed very efficient. Through the gateway on the side of the road one entered a roofed passage with four broad ramps leading down into the interior court. The flanking walls of the passage were beautifully lined with dressed poros stone in regular courses. The floor was covered with irregular slabs, except for a causeway running along the axis of the passage, which was paved with regular slabs in the manner familiar from

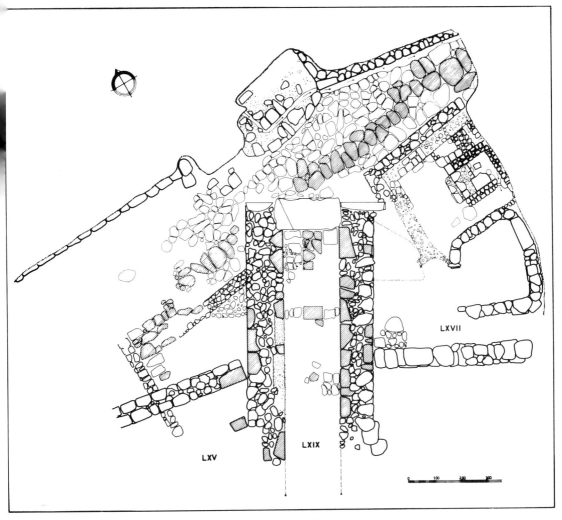

LXV *Terraced parterres*   LXVII *Storerooms*   LXIX *Northeast Entrance and Passageway*

Plan of the Northeast Entrance and the road

similar passages in other Minoan palaces. This median strip must have
given the impression of a carpet covering the central part of the ramp.
Much of the pavement is destroyed, but one can still visualize the original
effect. The threshold of the outer door was the largest found in the palace
and was made of dark limestone, 2.3 by 1.1 meters. However, there are
no visible dowel holes or cuts for holding what must have been a heavy,
two-leaved door, or for keeping such a door closed. The wooden doorjambs stood on limestone slabs which were narrower than the threshold;
hence, wood must have lined the ends of the two side walls of the gate-

way on its exterior and the leaves of the door attached and fastened to this by means of bolts.

This entranceway seems to have been constructed during the last phase of the palace, for there is evidence of changes in the original layout of the road and of the buildings flanking it. At first, the road apparently extended farther west and perhaps terminated at a ramp. There are only a few traces of the older arrangement left, including the possible use of the small door located at the northeast corner directly outside. Little is left of the ramp. The area of successive terraces, north of the interior court, was reorganized after the construction of the new gateway, and a wall was built which followed the direction of the road and the adjacent buildings. The purpose of these small terraces is not clear. Perhaps they were planted with flowers, providing an attractive decor for the little square at which the royal road terminated. Many fragments of stone vases were found in the area of the gate, but the most noteworthy find here was a sardonyx seal with a schematic representation of an ox's skull over an altar-like structure with branches growing out of it.

Another passage, apparently unroofed, led directly into the Central Court at its southwestern corner. This ran along one side of the South Wing and at its southwest corner three approaches converged to meet it. The floors of these passages were simply beaten earth, and apparently their level changed during the various periods. Excavation has not yet extended far enough to show where these passages began, but the fact that they follow three different directions would suggest that they connected with roads starting from the east, west, and south. They led directly to the Central Court, the starting point of communication among the various sections of the palace.

No direct approach was found from the west, where the façade seems to have been compact and uninterrupted. During the Neo-palatial period the palaces of Knossos and Mallia had no direct access from the west; the only passage to their central courts went around the south side of the west wings. The situation at Zakros was similar. An explanation for this may be that the shrines located within the west wing were to be kept completely safe and inviolable, and access to them controlled. In the Palace of Phaistos alone, an early system providing direct access

*Sardonyx seal with a representation of an ox's skull above an altar,
from the Northeast Entrance area*

to the interior from the west court was maintained. At Mallia in the later years of the Neo-palatial period a service entrance, undoubtedly patrolled by sentries, was opened through the west façade.

Investigation within the complexes of the North Wing at Zakros has not progressed enough to show whether there had been a passage leading from the top of the hill to an entrance. The existence of one is not unlikely, despite the presence of the northeastern gate, as passages on this side were found in all the other palaces. To be certain, however, the nature of the various architectural units within this section of the palace will have to be clarified.

11   Rooms around a court are characteristic of buildings in much of the Mediterranean area even today. How early this "Mediterranean style" developed is a matter of conjecture. Yet, as seen at Zakros, the court was important even in Minoan times.

The Courtyards

In all the Minoan palaces, the west court, stretching in front of a compact west façade, played an important part in the life of the palace. The townspeople often gathered there to attend formal festivities and sacred ceremonies. These slab-paved courts already existed during the Proto-palatial period and often remained in use in the later periods despite radical architectural changes brought about in the meantime.

At Zakros there is as yet little evidence of a palace earlier than the one we discovered. The West Court, however, at least in the exposed sections, bears signs of successive phases, all dating to the Neo-palatial period. At least two main phases have been recognized, one during which an inclined paved courtyard gently descended the slope of the hill, and a second in which the courtyard was rebuilt in successive stepped terraces with steps also following the slope of the hill. Parts of the early paved courtyard were preserved beneath the later terraces. The later court, small parts of which were preserved near the façade, was covered with a layer of concrete made of lime and large river or sea pebbles. Beneath the older pavement were found houses which must date to the period before the construction of the palace, a date also indicated by the pottery found in them. Staircases or ramps must have allowed communication between the terraces of the later court. These must have been located farther to the west in that section of the court which is not yet excavated. Probably the stepped road discovered in 1969 outside the northwest quarter of the buildings on the north slope was a continuation of such an access. At deeper levels appeared remains of much earlier buildings, only partially investigated, apparently going back to the beginning of the Proto-palatial period. An unusual drain, starting from two large upright slabs outside the façade of the West Court, apparently served to collect water from the roofs during the last phase of the palace, unless it was used during ceremonies which, according to the evidence from other palaces, took place in the courtyard in front of the west façade.

Excavation has not yet extended to the area directly beyond the south façade of the West Wing. The presence of an enclosure wall, delimiting the main passage leading to the Central Court from the south and provided with an opening giving entrance directly to the west, which was blocked later, makes it quite likely that there was another court at the south, probably used in daily life.

Most important for the life of the palace was, as usual, the Central Court, which at Zakros, as has been noted, was a good deal smaller than the central courts of the other palaces. (The measurements are 30 meters long by 12 wide, or, according to Professor J. Walter Graham's calculation, 100 by 40 Minoan feet.) Acting as the heart of the palace, this court controlled communication in all directions and served as the meeting place of courtiers and officials during celebrations. Ritual processions, dances, formal sacrifices, and feasts took place here during religious ceremonies. Aside from religious functions, the court served as a place for political, social, or even private meetings. It was not paved with slabs but was floored with tamped earth reinforced with lime. Around it rose the monumental façades of the wings, which with their diverse arrangements and their richly colored eaves, door frames, columns, and piers contributed to the striking appearance of this open central area. The greater part of these façades was made of ashlar masonry of poros stone, arranged in successive courses in a pseudo-isodomic system. Within these walls timberwork of vertical and horizontal beams was incorporated as in the other palaces. The timber was from tall cypress trees brought from woods which at that time must have covered the now denuded mountains of eastern Crete.

As can be deduced from various traces preserved and from the small

*The walls of the antechamber at the entrance to the West Wing
from the Central Court, showing incised double-axe symbols*

mortices for fastening tenons on the poros blocks, the façades of the West
and South wings facing the Central Court were pierced with a series of
double windows, similar to those typical at Knossos. These windows provided light to the large room behind the façade of the West Wing and to
the smaller compartments of the South Wing. Comparable windows must
have existed in the upper floor.

There were three main entrances leading from the Central Court
into the West Wing. The middle one, with a large monolithic threshold,
served as the main passage and was provided with an anteroom, which
originally had a central column, and flanked by a small angled corridor
that probably housed the staircase leading to the upper floor. The symbol
of the double axe was repeatedly carved upon the stone blocks of this
anteroom, signifying that the premises to be entered were sacred. Surely
it is not accidental that outside this area was found a quadrangular base
which appears to belong to the altar of the Central Court. This base was

Wall of ashlar masonry in poros stone
at the entrance to the West Wing from the Central Court,
with double-axe symbols incised in the stone

at first thought to be a small enclosure for a sacred tree, but the interior was found to contain compact clay, in which no tree could have grown.

Of the other two entrances, the one on the left led to the main Hall of Ceremonies, the one on the right to a corridor through which the store-rooms, kitchens, and service rooms could be reached. The existence of windows and other openings upstairs, corresponding to those on the ground floor, can safely be assumed.

A small portico with two columns occupied part of the north façade facing onto the Central Court and provided access to the rooms of the terraced North Wing, to the service rooms, and to the upper floor by means of a central staircase. Above this portico must have been a colonnaded veranda serving the adjoining rooms on the upper floor. The red columns of this veranda and the interior decoration showing through the balconies were among the architectural arrangements that enhanced the effect of the Central Court.

The small portico, of which both the column bases and the paved floor were preserved, served also as a waiting room or resting place, as indicated by a bench built alongside its north wall. This seat was framed by a wooden cornice and provided with upright slabs covering the wall behind it. This space afforded protection from heat and rain.

Despite considerable destruction due to cultivation, and partial disarrangement of the stylobate blocks caused by the installation of a later drainage system, there was enough evidence for a fairly certain reconstruction of the façade of the East Wing. This façade, fronting the royal living quarters and provided with an entrance leading directly to these, was more monumental than the others. Most of its northernmost section consisted of a rather narrow portico which belonged basically to the rooms behind and which was divided into two parts, marked by wide openings between square piers and columns. The visitor here had to walk up two steps on which rose two piers on either side of a slender column. Directly to the left was another, narrower entrance between piers leading directly into the interior court already described. The remainder of the portico had larger openings between piers, with a central pier set upon the stylobate running along the court. Similar though more elaborate porticoes existed in the other palaces, and it is not difficult to visualize a colonnaded veranda above the portico comparable to those attested in other palaces, especially at Knossos. There too the general effect must have been one of variety of form and color, which contributed to the charm of the building. The royal couple and their retinue must have appeared frequently on the portico and the balconies above during celebrations, when crowds of people gathered in the Central Court. At other times these same places would have served for entertainment and relaxation.

Directly to the south of this portico was the opening of a corridor, most likely one that would have passed outside the rooms of this wing and led to the conjectured east gate, if that existed. A pair of large stucco horns, a symbol of the sacredness of the palace, had fallen from above the cornice of this entrance upon the floor of the court and smashed into pieces. Fragments of similar ritual horns were found at Knossos, testifying also to the religious character of the place. Evans imagined whole series of such double horns crowning the building. The remainder of the façade of the East Wing at Zakros was marked by small doors leading into the complex which contained a fountain well.

Finally, the south façade within the court was carefully built of dressed poros stones arranged like those of the west façade. A central door with a large monolithic threshold led to the rooms in the southern quarter of the West Wing which were given over to manufacturing activities. The large opening between the West and South wings led to the passage already mentioned, at which several approaches converged.

The general effect of these façades, with their pseudo-isodomic masonry, their diverse elevations, their various entrances, their single or double windows, both on the ground floor and in higher stories, their porticoes and colonnaded verandas above, all enhanced by polychrome decoration, could not have been basically different from that of the other Minoan palaces, especially Knossos. The smaller size of the court and the relative simplification of certain architectural features may have detracted from the impressiveness of the building, but the greater concentration and the frequent variation of these features, which here assumed most graceful proportions, must have added to its charm.

Besides the West and Central courts, there were other smaller interior and exterior courtyards. At the north end of the West Wing, beyond the corner of the West Court, and directly below the structures defined as the northwestern complex, there was a small paved court surrounding the exterior angle of the northernmost storerooms. This could well be what is left of a higher paved terrace of the West Court from an earlier phase. As is explained later, during the first phase of the palace the northwestern section from this terrace could be reached by means of a staircase. When the West Court was rebuilt in stepped terraces, part of the higher one was isolated by means of a wall in ashlar masonry, turning at a right angle, and remained as a small court within an enclosure, perhaps after the original pavement was covered over. Under the new flooring and along the northern retaining wall ran a drain.

Another interior court, which was mentioned in connection with the main northeastern gate of the palace and is described later, was reached directly by way of the stepped approach starting at the gate. This court was spacious, 13.5 by 14 meters, and presumably entirely slab-paved. Only part of the pavement at the northwestern corner is preserved today, the rest having been destroyed by cultivation. The destruction of the pavement made it possible to study the drainage system running underneath, which is discussed in Chapter 23. The court was useful not only because of its direct link with the outer gate, which made possible easy access in all directions, but also in providing light and air to rooms of the East Wing and especially to the large square Hall of the Cistern, described in Chapter 18. Moreover, it provided the palace people a place to sit, as an alternative to the Central Court.

Incised double-axe symbol on a poros-stone wall

12   The west wing in the Minoan palaces had a special function related to religious ideas. Religion and rulership were closely connected in the ancient world, where leadership had a powerful mystique.

Character of the West Wing

The two functions already attributed to the Minoan palaces—cult center for the deity and seat of political power of a king—were strikingly confirmed by the new elements found at Zakros. The fact that here, as in other palaces, the main rooms of the sanctuary are concentrated in the West Wing is not a mere coincidence. There must have been a special reason for this location, one probably connected with the religious beliefs of the time. The special development of the West Court and its attested use for the cult ceremonies is probably not unrelated to the placement of the shrine in the West Wing. At Zakros, this court has not been entirely excavated, so that its religious functions cannot be confirmed. Certain dressed stones of the exterior west façade, however, bore the incised sign of the double axe, a symbol which, as previously mentioned, was repeated on the walls of the anteroom of the main entrance to the West Wing, as one enters from the Central Court. Apparently, as elsewhere, the shrine complex occupies the entire wing and contains the same categories of rooms related to religious activities.

The wing is bounded on the north by the small paved court and the rooms of the kitchen, and on the south by an unroofed area which supposedly contained another court with a passageway along its west side. Both the West and Central courts flanking this wing were directly connected with the shrine, a situation evident in other palaces as well. The conjectured altar in front of the main entrance shows the close link of

The Palace of Zakros

Plan of the West Wing

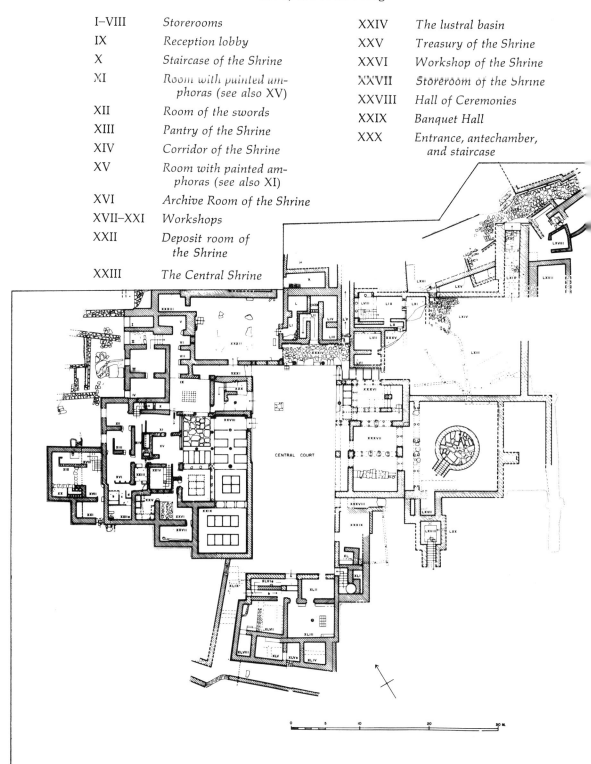

CENTRAL COURT

0   5   10   20   30 M.

the Central Court with the West Wing. In later times, an unusual annex was attached to the West Wing, taking over some of the area of the original West Court. This annex consisted of a small anteroom and a larger compartment, divided inside by a pier-and-door partition and other mudbrick walls into smaller rooms. The pier-and-door partition, here rudely constructed, made it possible, by opening or closing the doors, to use the interior space either as one or as two units. The small inner area to the south had a series of nine rectangular, rather shallow basins which did not communicate with one another; a similar arrangement was found in one of the houses excavated by Hogarth on the northeast hill. Perhaps this room was used for some industrial activity, possibly dyeing fabrics. It was served by an underground drain. Behind a partition which closed off the north side of a space under a small stucco-coated staircase leading upward, there was a latrine on a low dais with an opening toward a ditch. The septic pit extended outside, toward the West Court, and was apparently covered with clay tiles.

The layout of the shrine compartments was dictated roughly by the same principle adopted at the other palaces, especially Knossos—that of serving most effectively the needs of the cult, and of storing and administering the treasures and revenues of the sanctuary. The triple entrance from the Central Court, with a wide central gate which must have been higher than the others, recalls the arrangement of the tripartite façade of the central shrine at Knossos. The central threshold, 2.1 meters long, was second in size only to that of the exterior northeastern gate. One entered through a small anteroom, originally provided with a slender central column, into a spacious, nearly square room with a concrete pavement that had in the center a quadrangular covering of tiles, perhaps simulating a carpet. The square room must have been used as a lobby where people could wait and be checked before entering the shrine proper. Immediately to the north one entered two sets of storerooms belonging to the shrine; through a nearby corridor the North Wing and the Kitchen could be reached. Two areas to the south were accessible through two entrances. One area contained the principal rooms of the shrine proper and the rooms of the sacristy used for preparations connected with the cult; the other rooms were used for ceremonies and sacred banquets. An angled wooden staircase, accessible through the first ante-room of the complex of the shrine proper, led to the upper floor, which was apparently also connected with the shrine. The occupation of the entire West Wing at Zakros by rooms related to the shrine confirms an analogous assumption by Evans about the west wing of the Palace of Knossos and supports the theory that a theocratic government existed in Crete, especially during the Neo-palatial period.

Storeroom Units

In the west wings of the other three great palaces, an extensive row of storerooms lines one or both sides of an elongated corridor. At Zakros the storerooms are arranged in three groups, but in certain features they resemble those of the other palaces. Three recesses or bays, formed by parti-tion walls along the side of a corridor, contained altogether five pithoi and a great many other pots. (This storeroom group corresponds to what Evans called the Corridor of the Bays, in the east wing of the Palace of Knossos.) At the end of the corridor there was another room used for storing small pithoi and a variety of other pots, and from this one could reach another room behind the west façade, which received light through a large win-dow opening into the West Court. Six pithoi had been placed along the walls of this last room. Opposite the northernmost recess of the corridor a flight of five steps led down into another unit consisting of two spacious rooms lying partly below ground level. The staircase passage was lit by a small window and was used for the storage of medium-sized pots which stood on a dais. The low storerooms, which were full of pithoi and other storage vessels, were provided with light through windows opening high up, narrower than those mentioned previously. Their size is deduced from the bedding of the lintel, which could be traced in one case. The walls were preserved to a height of more than 3 meters, a height rarely encountered in prehistoric sites.

In these two large storerooms there were eleven and twelve pithoi respectively, placed along the walls, as well as numerous medium-sized pots. Many small pots, a number of them beautifully decorated, had

Pithos with two tiers of handles, from a storeroom in the West Wing

fallen from an upper floor, together with many stone vases and the elegant small silver jug inlaid with gold already mentioned. The number of pots found within these rooms alone was estimated at more than five hundred. Most of the pithoi must have contained oil, which would have fed the fire that reduced this section of the palace to ashes. Nevertheless, the accumulation of ash, which formed a thick layer coming up to the very tops of the pithoi, needs another explanation.

The pithoi had two sets of handles, one around the shoulders and one around the base. Their short round necks would have made it practical to tie fabric over their mouths; however, flat circular terracotta lids were found in the storerooms and other spaces nearby. Almost invariably the pithoi were decorated with relief imitations of ropes in zigzag and wavy lines. This decoration must derive from the practical habit of tying pithoi tightly with ropes to insure their safe transportation.

The ewer with nautilus decorations resembling the "Marseilles ewer,"
found in a storeroom in the West Wing;
another view is shown on the facing page

There was an amazing number of brilliantly decorated pots, especially of medium and small size. These were luxury equipment for use
within the palace. All styles of ceramic decoration typical of the period
between 1500 and 1450 B.C. (in Evans's terms, Late Minoan I B) are here
represented. Pottery of the Floral style is decorated with such motifs as
reeds, palms, and lilies, as well as wreaths of flowers and leaves; that of
the Marine style with porphyry shells, nautiluses, seastars, corals, and
sponges. A most elegant ewer, with a delicate decoration of rhythmically
repeated floating nautiluses, is practically identical with the famous "Marseilles ewer" found in Egypt where it must have been sent filled with fine

107

Funnel-like vessel in precursory Palace style, from a West Wing storeroom

wine from Zakros; both were obviously made by the same artist. Other pots are decorated with designs arranged in friezes or connected spirals, networks, garlands, chains, and festoons. There was a variety of shapes—amphoras, jugs, pitchers, wide-mouthed jars, large hole-spouted vases with so-called bridge-spouts. Other vessels, probably all intended for ritual purposes, include rhytons, libation vases with an opening at the base to pour liquids, a tall elegant jug with decoration imitating a metal prototype, a brilliantly decorated fruit stand, a funnel-like vase with an attractive pattern of spirals above a line of arcs, and various braziers and strainers. There is a surprising number of patterned cups, some decorated in a ceramic style of an earlier time, that is, with white paint on a brown or reddish ground. The stone vases were more restricted in variety, and most of them either bore a simple engraved decoration or were plain and apparently intended for everyday use. Along with the pottery were a few bronze tools. Surprisingly, in the storeroom containing the eleven pithoi was found the gilded neck of a ritual rhyton with relief representations, other fragments of which were later found dispersed elsewhere. Apparently this had fallen from an upper floor, along with the other ritual clay vessels already mentioned and a bronze double axe, which was surely a religious symbol. Certain rooms upstairs would therefore seem to have been used

Clay jug designed to resemble a metal one,
from a storeroom in the West Wing

Ovoid rhyton in Marine style, from a storeroom in the West Wing

Jug in precursory Palace style, from a pantry of the Shrine

for storing vessels and other shrine property. Nearby there must have been a loom, since clay weights, used to hold the threads vertical, were found scattered in the storerooms of the ground floor and of the basement. The looms were of the vertical type—with the help of the description in the *Odyssey* one can picture noble ladies of the palace moving back and forth in front of them constantly as they wove.

The upper floor was reached by means of a small staircase, the well of which was south of the half-basement storerooms. It started at a nearby

Cup in Floral style, from a storeroom in the West Wing

room with three or four stuccoed steps and then made a right-angle turn, continuing with a flight of wooden steps supported by small partition walls. A small space under the staircase was used for storage. Within this space, which could be entered through the square lobby, were found two long-toothed saws, folded one within the other, a large stirrup jar, a three-

Jug in Floral style, from a storeroom in the West Wing

legged terracotta pot, and some other ordinary vessels. Thus the series of storerooms and the spaces above were immediately connected with the main rooms of the shrine which lay to the south. It is logical, therefore, to assume that these storerooms were used for objects connected with the shrine, a function comparable to corresponding spaces in the other palaces, where supporting evidence was also obtained.

Bridge-spouted wine pot in precursory Palace style,
from a storeroom in the West Wing

13   To ancient man the whole world was inhabited by spirits and by living beings. The line between was never clear. Shrines to aspects of the spirit world were commonplace features of the settled landscape. There, in rites of magic and supplication, sacrifices and offerings were made to insure the cooperation of the supernatural in the affairs of the day.

The Central Shrine

From the square lobby previously described one proceeded into the complex of the Central Shrine, which consisted of eleven rooms of various sizes and shapes. These were connected internally by means of small and narrow corridors, straight or turning in a labyrinthine arrangement analogous to but not identical with that of the other palaces.

The functions of the rooms are not always easy to define, although the equipment found in them helps. However, many of the objects found within the rooms had fallen from above, as can be inferred from their position and from the fact that their fragments were widely scattered. The upper floor was reached by means of the same staircase that led to the rooms above the storerooms. The first two rooms next to the entrance received abundant light through large, probably double windows of a type familiar from Knossos. The bedding of the windows and traces of carbonized material from their wooden framework were preserved. The light came from the colonnaded lightwell of the adjacent large hall. These two rooms were probably used by the priests, who controlled access to the shrine and managed its operations. There were two depositories behind these rooms: one a simple niche defined by clay partitions, the other a wider cist plastered on the interior. Oddly enough, no objects were found stored in these spaces. To the east side and partly beyond in the nearby lightwell, a group of at least twelve large four-handled amphoras had fallen from the floor above, together with great quantities of calcined material from the collapse of walls and partitions of the upper story. The amphoras were splendidly decorated with plant motifs in spiral or curving compositions, with interlinked spirals or with patterns simulating the surface of conglomerate or veined stones. They have broad, elegant bodies, base rings that project considerably, and cylindrical or curving round necks with flattened rims. While these amphoras retain decorative elements dating back to the Proto-palatial period, they anticipate to some extent the so-called Palace style prevalent at Knossos during the latest phase of that palace. The use of dark paint on a light ground is enlivened with fine details in white and with orange-colored bands that encircle the body of the pot.

With these large amphoras were also found many smaller pots, especially pitchers, amphoras, bridge-spouted vases, wide-mouthed storage jars, and various types of cups ornamented with beautiful floral motifs and spirals. Rather curious were certain vessels with large, coiled, figure-8-shaped handles and with a horizontal internal partition pierced with holes around a central opening. Similar pots, decorated with spiral polychrome pattern against which were depicted helmets and figure-8-shaped shields, were found in the Tomb of the Double Axes at Knossos, where they were undoubtedly used for ritual purposes, and are also shown in representations of religious ceremonies. Here, therefore, they formed part of the shrine equipment and performed analogous functions. Fragments of three plastered offering tables, each with three feet, as well as six cylindrical faïence pots, were found in the second room and may also belong to the shrine.

A very important group of objects, which had probably been kept in a small storeroom in the upper story, had fallen in a heap to the west of the first room, near the passage leading into the corridor near the clay partitions. There were six bronze ingots, quite similar to the ones found in the treasury of the Summer Palace at Hagia Triada near Phaistos, and three large elephant tusks, two well preserved, the third badly damaged. These were obviously raw materials imported from abroad, the ingots from

SEE PAGE 61

Four-handled amphora with painted decoration,
from the apartments of the Shrine

Bronze ingots found in the West Wing

The Palace of Zakros

Fruit stand with spiral decoration (left) *and decorated
stirrup jar* (right), *from the storerooms in the West Wing*

The West Wing viewed from the south

View from the Central Court toward the Hall of Ceremonies

The Well of the Fountain

Cyprus, the tusks from Syria. They provide concrete evidence for a commercial contact between the harbor of Zakros and the East. The ingots were roughly as heavy as those from Hagia Triada—that is, 29–30 kilograms each. No incised signs, such as appear on some of the latter, were discernible on these. The largest and best preserved of the tusks is 0.7 meter long and bears clear signs of having been burned by the fire that destroyed the palace. Traces of the same fire are also visible on some of the pots which fell into the east end of the room and the adjacent light-well. A large four-handled amphora, decorated with symbols of sacred double axes, was distorted by severe burning but has now been restored; another fairly large pot was so badly distorted that its shape could not be reconstructed.

A little farther in, at the passage next to the western room, were found at least two dozen curious pots, all similar in shape, which had probably fallen from the same storeroom as the ingots and the tusks. These pots are characterized by a cross-shaped partition in the interior, masking an aperture which opened into the hollow stand, and seem to have been either incense burners or fruit stands. As incense burners, they would have contained coals, and the openings would provide enough draft to maintain the fire. If they were fruit stands, the hole would have allowed the water with which the fruit was sprinkled to drain out. The large number of these pots suggests that they may also have been connected with a ritual, a supposition supported by the discovery of similar pots in the nearby deposits of the shrine which contained equipment serving the cult.

Two very long bronze swords with golden nails and a midrib, and one of the legs of a three-legged bronze caldron, the latter probably fallen from a floor above, do not help to identify the function of the room directly to the west, behind the exterior west façade, where they were found. The corner of this room projecting into the courtyard was preserved to a great height and was one of the two spots at which excavation started. At a rather high level and behind the second corner block was found the skull of a small child, the only instance of human remains in the palace. Obviously this could not be one of the victims of the catastrophe, and its presence here is still unexplained.

The room directly to the south was certainly a pantry for storing clay pots, mostly small ones. These must have been placed on shelves or in cupboards, carbonized remains of which were found along the walls. These pots filled the entire space along the west wall, reaching up almost to its preserved height. A partition, at the doorjamb of one of the two entrances at the south side of the room facilitated the installation of additional cases. The equipment consisted mostly of various types of cups, jugs, pitchers, and bridge-spouted vases, with two or three stirrup jars. Many were beautifully decorated in the Floral or the Marine style. Among the largest is a remarkable nine-handled pithamphora bearing a decoration of octopuses, one of the best-preserved examples of the Marine style. Bridge-spouted vases and also stirrup jars decorated with sea motifs can be compared to the best known examples—for instance, the famous stirrup vase with octopuses from the Minoan town of Gournia.

SEE PAGE 123

    This room, like the one just previously described, received light from the West Court through a window. On the floor above there was apparently a workshop for the manufacture of stone objects and perhaps also

Stirrup amphora with octopus decorations, from the pantry of the Shrine

Bridge-spouted jug in Marine style, from a storeroom in the West Wing

for metallurgy, as can be deduced from several pieces of steatite, sheets of bronze, the handle of a gigantic caldron, and a few bronze tools that had fallen to the ground-floor rooms and the nearby corridor. Perhaps the foot of a bronze tripod found close by in the other room came from the same workshop. The small corridor which bent at right angles and passed in front of the principal rooms of the shrine provided access to the various compartments in this area and connected the large ritual rooms of the West Wing with the small staircase leading to the floor above.

The space directly south of the pantry containing the small pots proved to be the archive room of the shrine, which is discussed later. Through it, by means of exits on two sides, one could reach immediately a small centrally located room, the shrine proper.

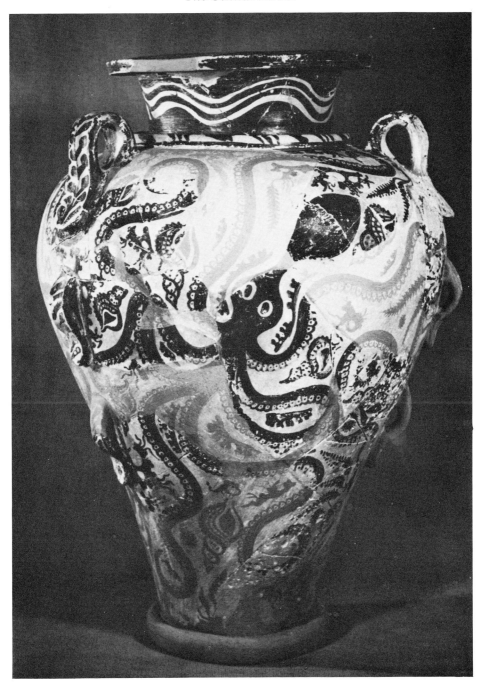

*Nine-handled pithamphora with octopus decorations,
from the pantry of the Shrine*

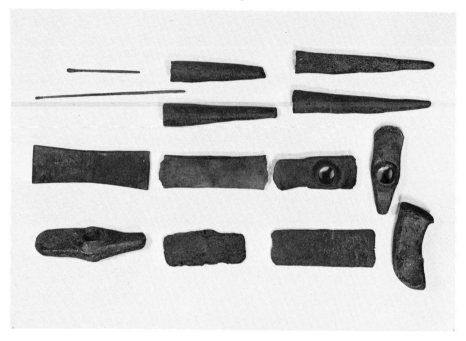

Bronze tools found in the West Wing

The Shrine

The shrine at Zakros corresponded to the standard type of small sanctuary chamber with a ledge, familiar from the other places. These shrines were intended for the worship of the images of the deity, with the mediation of the priesthood. Their small size indicates that they were made only for a small number of worshipers; they surely were not accessible to everybody in the palace. The most typical one is that at Knossos, known as the Shrine of the Double Axes, though this belonged to the period after the destruction of the palace—that is, after 1380 B.C. In it, images and symbols were found on a ledge at the back of the room just as they had been laid down, and in front of them on a lower dais lay ritual vessels. Quite similar and also built in the Post-palatial period is a small shrine in the area of the former bathroom and lustral basin in the Little Palace at Knossos. Images and symbols here were similarly placed on a high ledge in the rear. Sometimes no images were found on these ledges,

124

and only ritual vessels and small altars indicated the nature of the room. This was the case also with a Post-palatial shrine at Hagia Triada with a plaster floor beautifully painted with dolphins and octopuses, and with the shrine next to the throne room at Knossos, which dates from the latest phase of that palace (1450–1380 B.C.)

Zakros's shrine presents another example of such an arrangement. Here the ledge or podium at the back of the shrine was rather high and built within a niche in the south wall. Nothing was found on this podium. Across from it was a low bench with a mud-brick back support, probably serving as a seat for an individual worshiper. Around this bench and along the east wall appeared a group of about a dozen clay rhytons, of an oval shape with a pointed base, apparently used for libations. Most of these rhytons were painted with interlinked spirals. Low funnel-shaped vessels, found with the rhytons, probably served as flower pots. Pedestaled cups of another type must also have been ritual vessels, since one of these was decorated with double axes. Two quadrangular sheets of bronze, perhaps for covering a small box, were found near the bench in the adjacent small corridor. These bear an embossed design of lilies terminating above in a papyrus-like form. The stems intersected each other at the center of each sheet.

Bronze box lining with lily decorations, from the Shrine

Stone table for offerings, from a deposit of the Shrine

That the small room with the ledge and bench was the shrine proper is further demonstrated by the presence next to it of a lustral basin, by its direct communication with the repositories to the south through a second corridor, and by the existence in the immediate vicinity of a treasury containing ritual objects. The room of the repositories occupied the south corner of the West Wing before the industrial annex was added on the outside. It was accessible through a small corridor which ran behind the compartments of the Archive Room and the south wall of the small central shrine. Low mud-brick partitions divided the interior into small compartments for the safekeeping of ritual utensils. The floor and the partitions were plastered in white and decorated with red bands. The smallest of the compartments, right next to the shrine, had served for the storage of a round stone table on a tall pedestal, apparently used for offerings to the deity. The wider compartment immediately to the left was used for keeping braziers, some tall with a cross-shaped interior partition, some short and funnel-shaped. One large bronze caldron and one smaller one were also found in the passage to the inner compartment containing large clay pots. At the corner of this last compartment was an installation which resembled closely the latrine in the adjacent industrial annex and was also provided with a septic pit outside the building. It is questionable, however, that there would be a lavatory in the area of the shrine, especially one directly linked with the compartments in which ritual vessels were kept. Perhaps this installation belonged to the sacristy and was used for washing offering vessels or for some other similar purpose.

The Lustral Basin

Next to the small shrine room is a space which, from examples in other palaces and in important mansions in the major Minoan centers, was immediately recognized as a lustral basin. A staircase with eight well-preserved steps descended into the room; it was provided with a kind of balustrade, the lower end of which must have held a wooden column. All such spaces, which are generally located in the areas of the shrines, were strongly believed by Evans to have been lustral basins, where those participating in religious ceremonies purified themselves before entering the shrine, either by bathing in sanctified water or sprinkling themselves. Such purification rites are familiar from Eastern religions and were inherited not only by the ancient Greeks—one example being the Castalian Spring at Delphi—but also by the Christians, who are either sprinkled with or immersed in holy water when baptized. Evans's theory has been questioned by many scholars who observed that such spaces, when located in living quarters, were also used as ordinary baths. However, the similarity in form means only that all the basins were used for cleansing; in the case of lustral basins this took the form of ritual purification.

Findings at Zakros appear to add confirmation for Evans's theory. Not only does the basin area connect directly with the shrine proper, but a ritual vessel, most likely used in a purification rite, was found in frag-

*Staircase leading down to the lustral basin, as first found,
with a saw and hammer that had fallen on the stairs*

ments in the fill covering the basin. The vessel is an amphora made of SEE PAGE 10 polychrome veined marble, the veining of the stone being adapted to the beautiful shape to produce a unique artistic effect. The shape is one hitherto known only from representations, especially on seals and sealings, where such vessels were shown symbolically to contain the water for the rite of regenerating vegetation. The body was spherical and the neck terminated in a double rim. Two large boldly curving S-shaped handles attached to the rim and shoulders made the vessel even more graceful. Apparently this was a ritual amphora also used in purification rites. Its magnificent technique ranks it among the finest stone vessels from the Minoan and Mycenaean world. Its carving was an impressive feat, even though the coiled handles were made of separate pieces of marble attached to the vase by means of tenons. Most surprising, however, is the ingenious adaptation of the natural qualities of the material. Thus a spot with a red nucleus, resembling a spinning floc, occupied the center of the belly, while veins in the stone were adapted to the round foot and projecting circular base ring. Other veins appear vertically on the double rim.

Since the vessel was found in fragments and had probably fallen from the floor above, its use in purification rites, though highly probable, cannot be definitely confirmed. Other objects fallen from above into the basin and the nearby corridor included many clay vessels, also for ceremonial use, such as more than thirty braziers, some funnel-shaped and some with a stand, as well as small bowls of white stone which look like mortars.

A long saw, a kind of anvil, and a curved hammer had fallen on the staircase of the lustral basin from another room above, apparently a little farther east. That same room must have originally contained many other bronze tools which were found in the small angled corridor directly to the east of the staircase of the lustral basin and around the dividing pier from the large Hall of Ceremonies. These tools included SEE PAGE 124 another saw for wood, one for stone, some axes, picks, needles, cutters, chisels, pins, small knives, carving chisels, engravers' tools, and drills—one might say the entire tool kit of the wood and stone worker. We could not determine whether the other saws and tools found in and around the lightwell of the large hall came from the same workshop, though this seems likely, since they also fell from above and were found not far from the rest. Perhaps, however, the latter tools had been taken away from their cabinet to be used in repairs.

Abundant water now seeps through the floor of the lustral basin, but this was certainly not the case when the room was in use. The level of underground water has risen since ancient times, especially in recent years when irrigation was begun in the valley of Zakros. Water now seeps up through all the floors at a low level. Probably in order to save space, the east wall of the basin was constructed as a simple mud-brick partition. The upper part of the south wall, however, was similarly built in order to form a kind of ledge in the interior on which to place vessels used in purification rites.

The three southern rooms of the shrine were reached through the large Hall of Ceremonies, described in the next chapter, by way of a small corridor. These rooms were a vestibule, also used as a workshop, the treasury of sacred equipment, and an interior storeroom. The vestibule-workshop had an angled plan because the corner of the Hall of Cere-

The lustral basin, after partial restoration

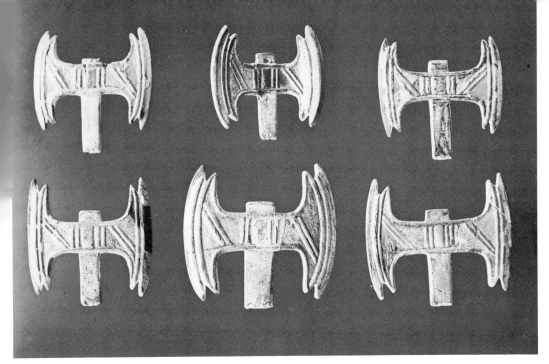

Small ivory double axes, from the workshop of the Shrine

monies penetrated into it. It contained heaps of steatite fragments and cores of red marble or porphyry, which point to industrial activities. Three tiers of irregular stone slabs placed at the corner probably served to support planks on which the craftsmen sat to work. Many utensils used in the workshop were found along the walls. A great many faïence and ivory inlays, mostly in the form of double axes, occasionally combined with the symbol of the sacred knot, are probably fragments left from the disintegration of small inlaid boxes fallen from a floor above, rather than discarded artistic material. With these had also fallen the lower part of the stone rhyton with relief representations, the main part of which was found in the lightwell of the Hall of Ceremonies, as described later.

The adjacent storeroom to the south was apparently built as an afterthought, perhaps at the same time that the small industrial unit was attached to the façade of the West Wing. This is clear from the fact that in both rooms the lower part of the wall of the original façade has a characteristic protruding ledge. The storeroom was found intact, with fifteen pithoi of small and medium size along its walls. These pithoi seem to have contained olive oil, judging from the collecting vessels built under the floor, apparently to receive any liquid that might be spilled while it was being decanted into other receptacles. A peripheral groove on the ground helped concentrate the liquid in case a pot broke. This system is known from other palaces and occurs also in other sections and annexes in the Palace of Zakros. A bronze strainer found in the storeroom may have originally belonged to the system of collectors used to filter spilled oil retaining extraneous matter. Many other pots were found in the same storeroom.

More important, the inner room, accessible through a door from the vestibule-workroom, proved to be the shrine treasury, which was found SEE PAGE 134 with most of its valuable contents intact. The door could shut off the treasury room and thus protect it.

Plan of the Treasury of the Shrine, showing vessels and symbols found

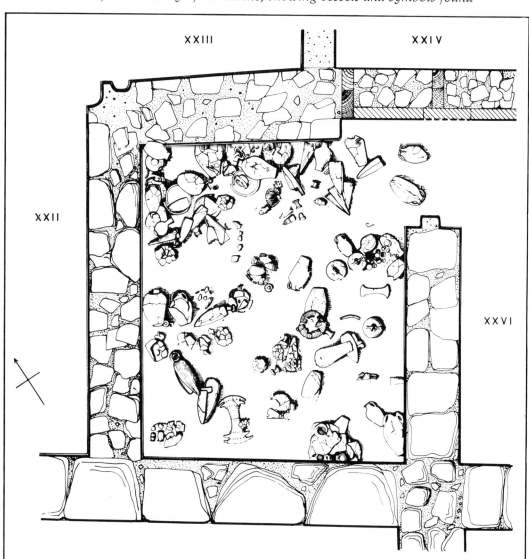

The Treasury

The location of the Treasury behind the central shrine guaranteed absolute security, since the only approach was from the large Hall of Ceremonies through a short narrow corridor and the workshop. There is no evidence that there were windows, and the room must have been lighted artificially. As the earth fill was removed, the excavators were suddenly confronted with an area entirely covered with a multitude of vessels in stone and clay, which took days to extract systematically, after their exact position and appearance had been recorded in photographs and drawings. The clay partitions, which formed the cists in which the objects were kept, appeared only after almost all of the finds had been taken out. The partitions had largely collapsed under the weight of debris from the destroyed upper floor. We ultimately realized that there had been eight contiguous cists built along the walls. Although their exact height is not known, it cannot have been more than a meter. Other objects had been placed in the center of the room against the front sides of the cists and in the corners at either side of the entrance. Large clay pots, especially amphoras, and tall pitchers of the ordinary type would not have been placed in receptacles which could have been more profitably used for smaller precious vessels. Such large pots, except those fallen from above, could also have stood on top of the covers of the coffers. The rest of the equipment, though broken or crushed by fallen debris, was in its original position in the cists. This is the only example of a Minoan treasury found with all its contents *in situ*. In the Temple Repositories at Knossos the receptacles were refilled after the catastrophe, and the objects that could be reused had been removed before the reconstruction of the palace. The absence of vessels made of precious metals from the repositories at Zakros can again be explained by the theory that the people in charge of the Treasury, or perhaps the members of the royal family, had taken these with them in their flight before the catastrophe. Nevertheless, what was preserved in the repositories is still most impressive and gives an adequate picture of ritual vessels and symbols of the Neo-palatial period.

Some of the clay pots in the Treasury at Zakros have remarkable

The Treasury of the Shrine, with ritual vessels as found

The Treasury of the Shrine,
after removal of the contents and partial restoration

shapes and decoration. Impressive is a spherical rhyton with a molded ring decorated with sacred knots around its neck. But especially magnificent are the ritual stone vases with a wide range of shapes and of an exceptionally advanced technique. We can recognize three main categories: libation rhytons and ritual jugs, cups for sacred communion, vessels used in the sacristy. The rhytons are of various familiar shapes— spherical, oval, and conical. There are altogether sixteen examples of the conical type, carved from porphyry, veined marble, white marble, and alabaster. The vertical handles were sometimes carved in one piece with the body, sometimes made separately in the same material and attached by means of small tenons to the rim and sides of the vase. The mouths were emphasized either by moldings or by horizontal grooves. One of the most beautiful porphyry vases simulated the shape of a calyx, terminating on its upper part with a double row of leaves. An alabaster rhyton had lightly curved sides tapering down somewhat in the shape of a horn. The ovoid rhytons, seven in all, are even more interesting, both in shape and in the admirable artistic use of material, such as porphyry, veined marbles, alabaster, and Spartan basalt. They have more or less elongated bodies and often constitute an intermediate shape between spherical and conical types. The curved necks were frequently made of a separate piece, as was also the decorative ring encircling the base of the neck of one specimen, a rhyton made of porphyry with vertical fluting that widens toward the middle of the belly and emphasizes the dynamic shape of the vase. A rhyton of white-spotted green basalt illustrates the Minoan taste for color. Because of the hardness of the material, its carving was a considerable technical feat. In other vessels the adaptation of veining testifies to an artistic imagination alert to the qualities of the material. Thus an elongated oval rhyton of blue-and-white marble combines form and the nature of the stone in a most impressive way: an oval dark spot forms the center of gravity while veins open up around it extending to the pointed end of the rhyton. Finally, a broad dark vein, enlivened by a very fine white one, forms an outline for the entire design. Hundreds of pieces of stone must have been examined before a suitable one was found.

SEE PAGES 6 14 65 139 140

Undoubtedly the most remarkable of all rhytons found in the Treasury, however, is the one made of rock crystal. This vessel had been crushed

SEE PAGE 139

by the weight of debris from above into more than three hundred fragments; its reconstruction by the technicians of the Heraklion Museum is a major achievement. It has an elongated oval shape and a pointed end. Here again the rounded neck was carved out of a separate core, but it is amazing that a piece of crystal quartz large enough to form the body of the vessel could have been found. The craftsman's skill must have been exceptional, since the walls of this precious crystal were made very thin and yet did not crack. In order to give the handle the dynamic and yet graceful curve which is one of the most attractive features of the vessel, the craftsman used crystal beads through which he ran a curved bronze wire. This handle, of which the lower end is coiled, was preserved intact with the beads still on the wire. The green color of the wire was produced by oxidation; originally the wire was perhaps gilded, giving the impression of a golden thread running through the crystal. The movable ring at the base of the neck is made of sections of carved crystal interspersed with small leaves of gilded ivory. This exceptionally elegant vessel must have been one of the most precious ritual objects of the shrine. Very few vessels of rock crystal have been preserved from the Cretan and Mycenaean worlds, and those are in poor and mostly fragmentary condition. A well-preserved and beautifully made vessel in the form of a duck, from the second royal grave circle at Mycenae, is known to be of Cretan origin, carved in one of the royal workshops of the island. The rhyton of Zakros, however, surpasses it in size, technical achievement, and complexity of form.

Another rhyton, this one in alabaster, is more or less spherical in shape and somewhat resembles the ostrich eggs that were imported from Egypt and reshaped as rhytons. A few fragments of such ostrich eggs were actually found at Zakros.

A most elegant ritual jug, similarly used for libations, was made of whitish marble with fine light-blue veins. These wind around the vase and reach up to the top in slanting lines. The shape of the vase is familiar from engravings on seals, where such vases are combined with sacred horns and branches in ritual scenes, probably symbolizing the regeneration of vegetation.

The rest of the stone vessels from the Treasury were also apparently

Ritual libation jug of veined white marble,
from the Treasury of the Shrine

used ritually. Exceptionally important because of their unusual forms and interesting technique are a flask, which looks somewhat like an amphora, made of a stone similar to that of the libation jug, and an alabaster vase in the shape of a half egg, with a wide mouth and with two cylindrical handles. A hole-mouthed vessel, also of mottled porphyritic stone, the SEE PAGE 138 form of which resembles Pre-Dynastic or Early Egyptian vases with their characteristic flattened rim, must have been imported from Egypt and transformed by the addition of a bridge-spout and handles in the Minoan manner. It must have had white inlays filling hollows in the spout to

From the Treasury of the Shrine:
(above) *Egyptian basalt vessel of the Early Dynastic period, made into a bridge-spouted vase;* (below) *basalt vessel with rings for hanging;*
(facing page, top left) *ovoid rhyton of Spartan basalt;*
(facing page, top right) *the ovoid rock crystal rhyton (restored)*

(Facing page, bottom) *Two-wicked porphyry lamp, decorated with a crown of leaves in relief, from the workshop unit of the South Wing*

Conical porphyry rhyton, from the Treasury of the Shrine

*Alabaster vessel in the shape of a pilgrim's flask,
from the Treasury of the Shrine*

imitate the white crystals, but neither these nor the handles had been preserved.

Four cups or calyxes with tall bases used for sacred communion were among the most important ritual vessels found *in situ* in the Treasury. They resemble the chalices used in the Christian churches today for the same purpose. Their conical bodies gradually widen and are based on disk-shaped pedestals. Similar vessels have been found in previous excavations at both Cretan and Mycenaean sites but never attracted special interest, although Evans, basing his theory on a Knossian wall painting, vividly described the ceremony of communion in which he believed they were used. This fresco frieze is the one which includes the famous "Parisienne," apparently a priestess of the palace. The chalices found at Zakros were carved out of hard stone in a characteristically elegant shape. One cup, which had a simple decoration of fine incised lines around the rim and base, was made of semitransparent black obsidian with very fine white

SEE PAGE 144

Faïence vessel in the shape of a nautilus shell, from the Treasury of the Shrine

spots. The only source known for this specific variety of volcanic glass is the islet of Yiali, near Nisyros in the Dodecanese. The manufacture of this vessel was indeed a technical achievement, considering the extreme hardness of the material and other problems involved; finding of a suitably large core must also have been extremely difficult. Only two other comparable vessels are known from the Creto-Mycenaean world: a rhyton from Tylissos, made of unspotted black obsidian, and a vessel of spotted black obsidian (liparite) in the form of a triton, from Hagia Triada.

Another pedestaled cup is made of marble with white and wavy light-gray veins. It is slender in form, and its entire surface is decorated with horizontal grooves. The base was made separately and attached to the foot with a tenon. A third, less elegant cup was made of a conglomerate stone. Last, a fourth chalice was carved out of a veined white-and-blue marble, and its walls were crinkled to produce a four-lobed form. This SEE PAGE 65 SEE PAGE 6 cup stood on an elegant pedestal which undoubtedly simulated a four-lobed altar. An identical pedestal of polychrome limestone, a material also used in Crete for the manufacture of vessels and tools, was found in one of the chamber tombs at Nauplion, but neither its discoverers nor Evans identified it correctly. Evans thought it was a candlestick, comparing it to another stand found in the area of the viaduct at Knossos, which must also belong to a communion chalice. Other chalices of similar shape had previously been found, two in the royal tombs at Mycenae, a fragmentary one from the Well of the Rhyton there, and another from Thera. Recently, fragments of three others were found at Kea, where there must have been a Minoan colony; two of these were of the four-lobed variety.

The craftsmen who produced these stone goblets were undoubtedly imitating metal prototypes, such as the gold and silver goblets represented in a wall painting from Knossos. Among examples discovered are the famous golden cup of Nestor with birds attached to the rim and with its two handles joined to the base with bands, from the royal shaft graves of Mycenae, and a silver cup with an embossed representation of a hunt, from a royal tomb at Midea.

Three lamps, one made of porphyry, the other two of white stone, each with two nozzles and simple decoration, also formed an essential part of the sanctuary's liturgical equipment. Some small basins of whitish stone

Obsidian sacred-communion chalice, from the Treasury of the Shrine

discovered in the Treasury were similar to others used for domestic purposes, but the large number of such bowls from the neighboring room upstairs, also undoubtedly belonging to the shrine, indicate that these were used in the sacristy.

Religious symbols form another category of objects found in the Treasury. Three mace heads of beautiful veined stone were found together in the southwest corner of the room. They have an elegant shape, with a hole at the center for the haft and two flattened ends for hammering. Two similar ones, found in one of the Temple Repositories at Knossos, were thought by Evans to have been left there by the people who broke into the treasury, but there is no foundation for such a hypothesis. The treasury had not been broken open, and in any case maces are religious emblems carried by hieratic personages, as can be inferred both from various representations and from the discovery of actual specimens in graves, as in the Tomb of the Mace Bearer at Knossos. A beautiful mallet-axe of multicolored limestone was also found recently in a cave at Poros in Heraklion.

SEE PAGE 9

The main symbols of the shrine are two large double axes made from a thick sheet of bronze. One of these, artistically the most important of all the double axes from the Creto-Mycenaean world, was magnificently decorated with dense vegetative patterns which covered the entire surface. This decoration consisted of fine small leaves on neatly arranged stems that terminated in lilylike flowers with incurving petals, each enclosing a cut-out circle. There were also two large bronze wreaths, the use of which is difficult to determine. One of them is decorated in relief with a series of compactly arranged double axes with the hafts in a slanting position. These wreaths resemble those which decorate the lips of bronze basins used for washing the hands. Some of these basins are decorated with various motifs, and so are the jugs used in connection with them for ritual washing; there are several examples of these from Cyprus. Certain bronze tools also found in the Treasury at Zakros may well have fallen from the cabinet of tools above.

SEE PAGE 146

SEE PAGE 147

Here, as elsewhere in the palace, were found numerous fragments of ornaments in faïence, ivory, and crystal which had decorated disintegrated wooden boxes. A butterfly in ivory may also have belonged on such a box. Two bronze hinges, with which the lids of boxes were attached, were also

SEE PAGE 148

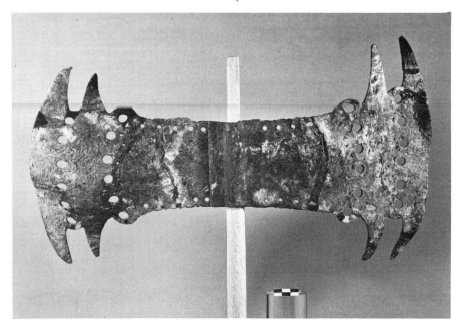

Decorated bronze double axe, from the Treasury of the Shrine;
(below) *drawing showing the decoration in detail*

preserved, as well as four or five clay sealings, with representations of a lion, a monster, and a libation jug.

Certain faïence vessels and ornaments, probably from an altar, are also interesting, though unfortunately greatly damaged by fallen debris and dampness. Among these were a one-handled cup, a cup opening up like a flower calyx, a kind of small offering altar, plants with spearlike leaves, and replicas of fruits. Most important, however, were three molded faïence rhytons, two in the shape of bulls' heads and one of the head of a lioness, and a vessel in the form of a nautilus shell. These preserved traces of light-green glaze and of details added in brown.

SEE PAGE 142

This collection of objects from the Treasury is exceptionally representative and provides invaluable information about rituals in palace shrines. Few other collections of objects found within the palaces and tombs represent more fully and vividly the most advanced stage of Minoan artistic technique.

When these objects were removed, the floor of the room and the

Part of a crown-shaped sheet of bronze, decorated with double axes, from the Treasury of the Shrine

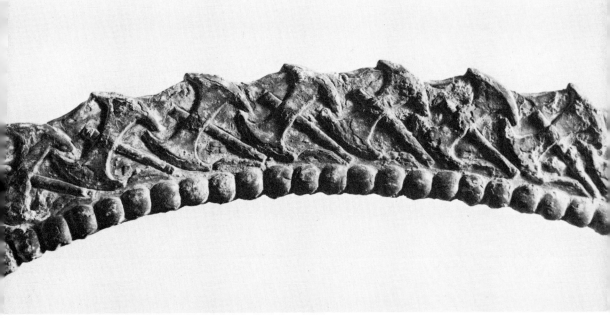

147

Ivory butterfly, from the Treasury of the Shrine

SEE
PAGE
134 remains of the plastered receptacles were revealed. Using the few remains preserved, the cists were partly restored to give a better idea of the original appearance of the Treasury of the royal shrine.

The Archive Room

Directly south of the pantry containing the small pots in the immediate vicinity of the Central Shrine and the Treasury was the Archive Room. Its contents undoubtedly belonged to the shrine. At Knossos also archive rooms and records were connected with shrines; the hieroglyphic deposit there, in addition to records on clay tablets and labels, contained numerous sealings from the boxes in which the tablets were kept, and one

The Central Shrine

Two-wicked lamp of speckled stone, from the Treasury of the Shrine

*Faïence rhytons in the shape of animal heads,
from the Treasury of the Shrine*

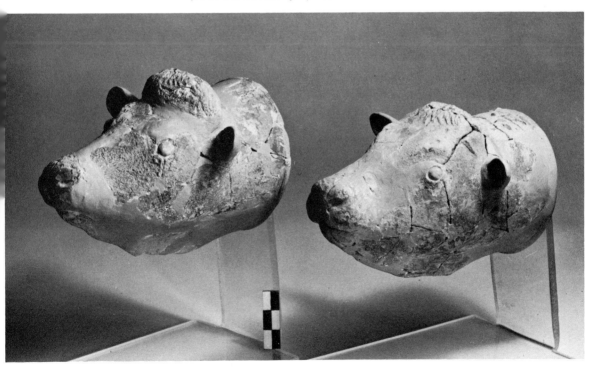

The Palace of Zakros

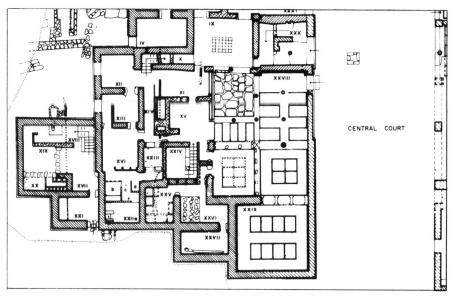

Plan of the Archive Room area in the West Wing

IV   *Storeroom*
IX   *Reception lobby*
X   *Staircase of the Shrine*
XI   *Room with painted amphoras (see also XV)*
XII   *Room of the swords*
XIII   *Pantry of the Shrine*
XIV   *Corridor of the Shrine*
XV   *Room with painted amphoras (see also XI)*
XVI   *Archive Room*

XVII–XXI   *Workshops*
XXII   *Deposit room*
XXIII   *The Central Shrine*
XXIV   *The lustral basin*
XXV   *Treasury of the Shrine*
XXVI   *Workshop of the Shrine*
XXVII   *Storeroom of the Shrine*
XXVIII   *Hall of Ceremonies*
XXIX   *Banquet Hall*
XXX   *Entrance, antechamber, and staircase*

*Niches constructed of mud brick, in which the archives
of inscribed tablets were deposited, and mud-brick partitions
around the deposits of the sanctuary vessels, in the West Wing*

tablet and many clay sealings from another archive were found in the cists of the temple repositories. Perhaps the sealings with a representation of the adoration of the Mistress of the Animals between two lions also derive from archives deposited in a narrow space of the tripartite shrine.

The Archive Room connected with the shrine at Zakros was located behind the west façade at the section where, in the last phase of the palace, a small industrial unit was added directly west of the Archive Room and the repositories. Any windows which may have originally existed on the façade were blocked, and light was provided by lamps.

At the north entrance to the room there were many pots, especially bridge-spouted jugs, cups, and stirrup jars, brilliantly painted in the Marine and Floral styles. With them were two large four-handled amphoras. These pots either fell from above or else are intrusions from the pantry to the north. At the opposite door were found remnants of a small box with ivory bands and spirals, which could well have come from the third niche of the archives. Many stone vessels and part of a beautiful conical rhyton, probably fallen from above, were found near the east wall.

The south wall consisted of a partition strengthened with vertical wooden beams, the hollow beddings of which are visible on the side of the small corridor. Along this wall were built three high niches formed by mud-brick partitions terminating at the front with vertical beams. Apparently wooden shelves rose all the way to the top, holding wooden boxes filled with the clay tablets of the archives; this is inferred from the large amounts of carbonized material, which included clear traces of large beams and boards. Some bronze hinges, probably from the box lids, and some clay sealings were preserved.

The deep russet color of the fill resulting from the disintegration of burned tablets indicated that there must originally have been a great many of these. Only thirteen tablets survived, baked by the fire which reduced the structure to ashes. It is surprising that no more were preserved in this way; perhaps the collapse of the floor above crushed most of the tablets to shapeless masses before the fire spread to the Archive Room.

These tablets and two others found in the large Hall of Ceremonies were thin and rectangular, ranging in size from 0.08-0.14 meter by 0.05-0.75 meter. Some were inscribed on both sides in the syllabic script accompanied by ideograms known as Linear A, which was apparently used exclusively for writing the Minoan language.

The discovery of these Linear A tablets at Zakros has great historical importance, since relatively few specimens of Linear A tablets had previously been found. The largest collection, that from the Summer Palace of Phaistos at Hagia Triada, consists of about 140 tablets, of which nearly a third are fragmentary. They are basically identical in shape, script, syllabary, and ideograms with those at Zakros and were used for writing the same language, in spite of minor differences in individual signs and a less frequent use of composite signs at Zakros. Phaistos, Knossos, Tylissos, Mallia, and Palaikastro have yielded very few such tablets, but some examples from the earlier palace of Phaistos show an early form of Linear A, called Proto-linear, indicating that this type of writing had already been invented in the Proto-palatial period. During Hogarth's excavations at Zakros a unique tablet was found, together with numerous sealings, in Building A–B on the northwest hill; the religious content of the seal impressions suggests that here also may have been an archive related to a shrine. Sporadic discoveries of Linear A tablets at various sites indicates that the same script and the same language were used in both central and eastern Crete at the height of the Neo-palatial period.

Although detailed study of the newly discovered tablets at Zakros has not yet been completed, it is clear that the records were connected with the administration of the shrine. The symbol of the double axes actually occurs on one of the tablets. Preliminary observations, moreover, suggest that the syllabary used at Zakros is closer typologically than that of the Hagia Triada tablets to the Linear B script used during the following period at Knossos, specifically for writing the Greek language. This may mean that a writing system similar to that of Zakros was used at Knossos just before that date, which, if true, would lend further support to the hypothesis of a very close contact between the two palaces.

The royal character of the archives explains why Linear A ceased to be used when Minoan domination ended with the general destruction of the Neo-palatial centers. Linear B, which replaced the earlier scripts at Knossos, is wholly unrelated to older Minoan tradition and in the Mycenaean palaces was used exclusively by a specialized class of scribes.

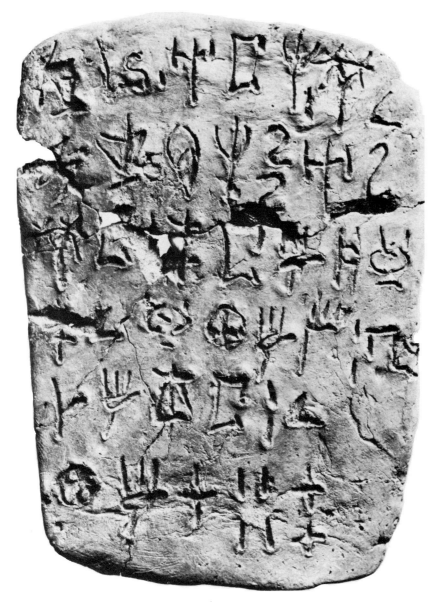

Tablet with Linear A script, found in the Archive Room of the Shrine

Linear A was also used for inscriptions, chiefly on ritual vessels and more rarely in a brief form on grave monuments. Occasionally a pithos is inscribed, perhaps in order to label its contents, origin, and designation. One such pithos, found in a storeroom in the Minoan mansion near Epano

Zakros already mentioned, bears the longest known inscription, consisting of twenty-six signs. Later vase inscriptions of a dedicatory or commercial character, mostly giving names, were written in Linear B and are most often found on stirrup jars, which were frequently used for the transportation of imported and exported liquids in mainland Greece. Most of these jars have a Cretan provenance.

The archives of the shrine at Zakros, like those of other sites, deal with accounts. Almost all the tablets preserved bear numbers enumerating or evaluating objects which were usually indicated by ideograms. The transliteration of these texts can be done with some certainty, for many of the signs anticipate those of Linear B. The meaning, however, still remains a mystery, as does that of other tablets in Linear A.

There has been much discussion about the linguistic origins and affinities of this transliterated Minoan language. Some scholars, such as the American archaeologist Cyrus Gordon, believe that it is of Semitic origin; others, including the English archaeologist Leonard Robert Palmer, think it is Luvian, an Anatolian language with Indo-European affinities; and some philologists relate it to such unfortunately little-known Mediterranean languages as Etruscan, Carian, and Lycian. Perhaps this riddle will be solved and the meaning of the archives revealed if more written records are later brought to light through continued excavation. In contrast to the thousands of texts in Linear B, those known in Linear A number only a few score. For this reason, the fact that even fifteen more have already been found at Zakros has caused great excitement among those concerned with the decipherment of texts in the Minoan language.

14   Ceremony is the physical aspect of ritual belief. It is marked by group participation in rites held in carefully designed and constructed halls.

The Hall of Ceremonies

In the Palace of Knossos chambers undoubtedly used for religious ceremonies were connected with the compartments of the central shrine of the west wing. Of these chambers, some, including the famous throne room, were on the ground floor; others, in the form of columned halls, were on upper stories. All were decorated with wall paintings depicting supernatural creatures such as griffins, or ritual scenes, like that of the sacred communion.

It was therefore conceivable that in the West Wing at Zakros, where the sanctuary was located, we should find halls intended for ceremonial use. Directly east of the shrine compartments, a vast hall, 12 by 10 meters, was uncovered. Its layout and decorations suggest that it was used for formal occasions, probably relating to the shrine, with which the hall communicated directly through three doors. This hall, which has been designated the Hall of Ceremonies, was accessible from the north through a wide opening with a column. The opening originally could be screened by curtains, but in the last phase of the palace it was half blocked up with ashlar masonry and was provided with a door separating it from the square lobby. To the south, triple doors led to another substantial room, also of a formal character. From the Central Court, where religious ceremonies also took place, the hall could be reached through a door with a monolithic threshold having a step in front of it. In size it equaled the main room of the megaron at Tiryns and was only a little smaller than the megarons at Mycenae and Pylos.

The Hall of Ceremonies was of the typical form, with an inner "polythyron"—a system of piers and doors—and a colonnaded lightwell. The latter was actually a small paved courtyard with small columns along each of its three sides, occupying the northwest corner. From it light spread not only to the hall itself, but also through the columned opening to the lobby and through a double window on the west wall to two of the rooms of the sanctuary.

The hall was subdivided into two main compartments. The larger of these, which contains the lightwell, has two small columns along the axis of the east side of the room, in line with another column belonging to the second compartment. The angled arrangement of the polythyron in three and four doors in a connecting series between piers in the second compartment provided the choice of using the interior part as an isolated unit by closing the doors, or as a part of the whole by opening them. The rest of the room adjoined the columned area. This arrangement, though akin to the systems with polythyrons and lightwells in the other Minoan palaces, is quite unlike the others in many aspects.

The magnificence of the room must have been enhanced by the lively colors of the columns and the decorations of walls and floors. Unfortunately there are only scanty remains of the badly burned wall paintings. However, the stucco frames that divided the floors into decorative paneling were well preserved, though the substance that filled the spaces between the panels has disappeared completely. Many guesses have been made as to the nature of that substance. Wooden planks are excluded, since, considering the extent of the fire, they would have left distinct carbonized remains. The presence of wood-working tools such as large bronze saws on the floor led to the suggestion that the planks had been removed shortly before the fire in order to be repaired or replaced. However, the preservation of the stucco frames contradicts such a theory, for the fragile plaster of which these were made would have broken when the planks were removed. Moreover, there is no known case of wooden floors with plaster interstices, the two substances being commonly exclusive of each other in architectural usage. Undoubtedly the lost material was more luxurious than the concrete pavements or the plastered and painted floors which for the most part are very well preserved in the area of the shrine.

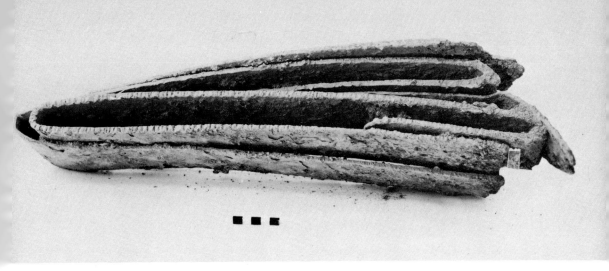

Bronze saws folded one within the other,
from a staircase recess in the West Wing

Possibly a synthetic substance was used, perhaps consisting of a base of wax and resin hardened by the addition of another ingredient, as in the process used nowadays for carnauba wax. Such a substance could not have resisted the impact of the conflagration. A chemical analysis of the earth contained within the stucco frames might solve this mystery.

The conjectured lustrous surface framed by the stucco bands, which SEE PAGE 84 were vividly painted in red, formed an imitation of slab paving, sometimes arranged in a meandering pattern and sometimes as a central panel surrounded by four or six smaller panels. Such a floor must have greatly enhanced the magnificent appearance of the hall. The irregular slab pavement of the lightwell with interstices of red plaster gave the impression of a mosaic framed by the raised stylobate bearing the columns. In both the lightwell and the main space of the hall only the bases of the columns were preserved. Large double windows on the east wall, looking into the Central Court, provided ample light for this area. Their presence is deduced from the holes into which dowels must have fitted to fasten the window frames onto the dressed poros blocks of the façade.

The ceiling of the rooms, carrying the floor of the upper story, was supported by a large central beam which linked one central pier and two end piers as it rested on the pier-and-door partition and the large central column. Smaller beams rested on the columns of the lightwell and on those dividing the eastern section of the hall. The wooden planks of the upper floor rested in turn on rafters based on these beams. The corresponding rooms above must have been reached by means of the staircase starting at the antechamber next to the main entrance to the West Wing from the Central Court.

The peculiar arrangement of three entrances in a row leading into the chambers of the Central Shrine, with two doors on either side of a partition wall built against the east wall of the lustral basin and two very small angled corridors, was intended to connect the shrine individually with each section of the Hall of Ceremonies when the doors of the pier-and-door partition remained closed. In that case the first door led into the north section of the hall, the second one into the confined south section, and the third connected the latter with the workshop, the Treasury, and its storeroom.

The objects found in this hall, mostly fallen from the upper floor, suggest that this unit may have been used for religious ceremonies. The most important of these finds were two stone rhytons, one with a relief representation of a peak sanctuary, the other in the shape of a bull's head, which lay in fragments in the midst of calcined debris fallen within the paved lightwell. These are discussed in detail in the following chapter.

As has been mentioned, some bronze tools from a small storeroom of the upper story were lying on the floor of the hall and had perhaps been brought downstairs for making repairs. Among these were four wood saws, up to 1.7 meters long, with widths ranging from 0.2 to 0.3 meter. All had traces of the attachment of handles on both ends, indicating that they were manipulated by two people. One of the saws is comparable in size to the two largest known saws of Minoan times, one from Knossos and one from Hagia Triada. There were also chisels and cutting tools.

A certain amount of molten lead covered a part of the floor within the panels and the stucco bands of their frames, and this at first led the investigators to believe that sheets of lead had filled the interiors. However, as some of this lead covered the bands, its purpose remains unknown. Various other bronze objects were also found on the floor, such as rectangular sheets, perhaps from the lining of a small box, a short lamp, an ornamented lid, the disk of a mirror, and a hook. Other objects probably belonged to the equipment of the shrine, such as part of a three-legged altar, stone vessels, two ostrich eggs, probably transformed into rhytons, of which only a few fragments were preserved, a terracotta rhyton of the spheroid, pointed-end type, and traces of disintegrated wooden boxes with various types of applied ornaments in glass paste, ivory, faïence, and rock crystal, in the form of flowers, lanceolate leaves, spirals, and bands. There were also bronze hinges and sealings from closed boxes. On one sealing a woman is represented kneeling in front of a stone, while a butterfly is hovering behind her; the stone may be a betyl (from *bet-el*—a stone as domicile of the god). The two clay tablets mentioned in connection with those from the Archives Room were probably kept in one of these boxes. On one of these tablets an ideogram of the double axe is repeated many times. An elongated plaque of ivory decorated with running spirals is perhaps part of the handle of a knife. Among the stone vessels, a one-handled cup executed in alabaster is distinguished by its elegant shape and fine workmanship.

At several spots in the hall, notably within the lightwell, construction materials fallen from the upper floor were altered considerably as a result of the mighty fire. The calcined limestones changed into an amorphous whitish mass, the mud bricks were baked by the fire, and the thick layer

Hemispherical cup of alabaster-like marble, from the West Wing

of russet fill from the disintegration of most of the bricks lay over a finer black stratum of ash and carbonized wood. Some of the pots found within this layer, including the four-handled amphora decorated with double axes, were completely distorted. Carbonized remains of columns and other wooden members of the room lay most thickly next to the preserved column bases, door jambs, and piers.

Precisely what kind of ceremonies took place in this hall and in some of the corresponding rooms above cannot of course be determined. However, judging by the ritual vessels, one may conjecture that on the day of the catastrophe a divinity whom the Minoans must have related in some way to their impending doom was being propitiated with bloody and bloodless sacrifices.

The Bull's Head Rhyton, partly restored (see also page 2)

15   Libations to and with the gods are characteristic ritual acts both
     of the ancients and of modern primitive men. The libation ves-
     sels of the Cretans, rhytons, were and are treasured examples of
     craftsmanship worthy of an honored place in the annals of art.

Two Significant Rhytons

Two of the most valuable and certainly most sacred rhytons for libations were evidently brought out of the Treasury to be used in a ceremony on the palace's last day. These were a stone rhyton with a relief representation of a peak sanctuary and another carved in the form of a bull's head; the chief fragments of both, probably fallen from an upper floor, were found in the lightwell of the Hall of Ceremonies. As these are among the most artistic and important finds from the Creto-Mycenaean world, they deserve detailed consideration. However, a curious circumstance should be mentioned. The fragments of the Sanctuary Rhyton were dispersed at four different spots: the main part of the body was in the lightwell; the lower part was outside the southwest corner of the hall, in the workshop of the shrine; the neck was in the first of the basement storerooms of the West Wing; and the greater part of the decorative collar was at the entrance of the north portico bordering the Central Court. Similarly, though the investigators looked very carefully for missing fragments of the badly shattered Bull's Head Rhyton, part of which was also found in the lightwell, none of these was discovered. Since the West Wing had not been disturbed, both the dispersion of the fragments of the first rhyton and the loss of pieces of the second at first seemed inexplicable. However, both could be explained by assuming an explosion caused by an unknown force. This could well have been part of the sudden catastrophe which struck the palace and which is discussed in detail later.

Both these impressive rhytons are carved out of chlorite. The Bull's Head Rhyton belongs to a large category of carved libation vessels in the form of sacred animals—sometimes the whole animal, sometimes only the head. Those in the form of bulls' heads are the most numerous. Only a few are carved in stone, including the famous one from the Little Palace at Knossos, half of which is preserved and which has one of the eyes, made of rock crystal, jasper and tridacna shell; another from Mycenae, too fragmented to be restored, the bits of which were found in the Well of the Rhyton; a third, said to come from Egypt, which resembles the Knossos example but is of doubtful authenticity; and now the one discovered at Zakros.

SEE
PAGES
2
160
Although pieces of the Zakros example are lacking, particularly on one side near the muzzle, it is nevertheless the most complete of all those that are definitely authentic. It is the smallest and represents a young animal rendered most realistically and elegantly. In particular, the curls of hair, covering most of the face, were treated individually rather than as a decorative whole as in the other examples. The horns, which were probably of gilded wood, are not preserved, but their form has been conjectured on the basis of the silver rhyton in the shape of a bull's head found in one of the royal tombs of Mycenae, which was undoubtedly imported from Crete. The reconstruction of the horns was confirmed by a sketch on the specimen at Knossos—a kind of graffito of a bull's head, probably made by the artist himself as a model for the completion of the horns. In the Zakros example, as in the Knossos one, only one of the ears was preserved; it is attached in a depression by means of a tenon. One eye of the Zakros head was preserved, but without the inlay which gives the Knossian bull its animated expression.

In both examples there is a hole at the nape of the neck and one at the tip of the muzzle, respectively for filling the vessel and for pouring libations. At Zakros the plaque which would fit tightly on the back by means of an indentation was luckily found in the lightwell. Despite the close fit, the vessel could still have leaked, and one must assume that some kind of glue, perhaps the same as that used to join the parts of the ovoid rhyton, was applied to seal it hermetically. As with the Knossian example, only the exterior surface of the plaque was polished. On the underside there are still traces of the drill used to extract pieces of the core to form the indentation for fitting.

In the stone examples from Knossos and Mycenae, rosettes appear on the forehead of the animal. On the silver rhyton from Mycenae a large, many-petaled rosette in gold was added separately, while in other cases a rosette was rendered in very low relief, either as a small wheel with curving spokes or as a barely visible simple rosette in the midst of hair curls covering the forehead. In the rhyton from Zakros the artist apparently tried to create the impression of a rosette by making a whorl-like pattern of small curls with radiating strands around it. This rosette might well have had a symbolic meaning: if the gilded crescent-like horns symbolized the moon, it could have represented the solar disk. In small bronze figurines of bulls used in shrines, such as that at Hagia Triada, the rosettes were rendered as golden spots on the forehead. The gilding of the horns is reminiscent of a ceremonial act preceding the sacrifices of bulls described in the Homeric epics, as, for example, that by Nestor at Pylos.

Besides stone and various metals, other valuable materials were used to make rhytons in the form of bulls' heads. Two such rhytons made of faïence from the shrine treasury at Zakros have already been mentioned, and many similar rhytons in terracotta have been found at various Minoan and Mycenaean sites. SEE PAGE 149

The Sanctuary Rhyton, now restored, constitutes the most complete example from either Minoan or Mycenaean regions of a vessel with a representational relief decoration. Of the two famous steatite rhytons from the Summer Palace of Hagia Triada, only half of the one known as the Harvesters' Vase was preserved, and of the one called the Boxers' Vase there were only a few fragments, subsequently incorporated into a reconstructed version. The Sanctuary Rhyton of Zakros is made of chlorite, a relatively soft stone containing tiny goldlike mica. However, its upper part was dark green, the lower part light brownish. So great was the contrast that the fragments were first thought to belong to two different though similar vessels. The difference in color must have resulted from unequal degrees of burning. SEE PAGE 165

The neck of the Sanctuary Rhyton has concave sides and is marked at the line of its attachment to the top of the oval body by a collar with carved vertical striations. The lips are decorated with a pattern of curls. Small holes for tenons suggest that there was a handle which has not been found. The relief decoration consists of a single representation spread over the entire body of the vase. This depicts a peak sanctuary, most probably the main sanctuary of the palace center. Bits of gold leaf were still preserved on the relief and on the rim, indicating that originally the entire vessel must have been gilded. These traces are supporting evidence for Evans's theory that all steatite vases with relief representations were covered with gold leaf to simulate vessels of precious metals with embossed decoration. This substitution was not due to a lack of gold in Crete, as some scholars have assumed. Most of the golden vessels found in the shaft graves and other royal tombs of the Greek mainland have been shown to be imported from Crete. Besides, objects of gold and silver have been found on the island; the treasure of Zakros described in Chapter 1 is an example. There must have been more such vessels of precious metal both in the shrine and among the king's personal possessions, but these would have been removed when the palace people fled at the time of the catastrophe. The lack of similar vessels elsewhere can be attributed to the fact that no unplundered royal tombs have been found in Crete. Gilded imitations must have been common, however.

Representations of shrines rendered in relief on Minoan stone vases, sometimes in connection with a ceremony, were not unusual, as preserved fragments, especially from Knossos, show. Two or three of these actually represented peak sanctuaries, identified by the lightly built structures set on rocky terrain. In one case a worshiper is shown, bowing, apparently in the process of making an offering of fruit which he places in a basket within the shrine.

SEE PAGE 167 The most complete representation of a peak sanctuary, however, is on the rhyton from Zakros. The tripartite arrangement of the building is clear. The central wing, the large gate of which surmounts the whole, is at the center of the vase. The flanking wings, with columned openings, are crowned with a row of horns of consecration. The panel of the gate is covered with a network of spirals and framed by borders of running spirals. One can distinguish the doorposts on either side of the door, supporting the lintel which is also decorated with a spiral band. Masts with lance-

The Sanctuary Rhyton, found in the Hall of Ceremonies (restored)

shaped ends are combined with pillar-like posts to which are attached square panels, known from other representations of shrines.

On the cornice of the central unit appear two opposed pairs of wild goats guarding a central object which is difficult to identify—perhaps a betyl, which would be a symbolic version of the deity. Another goat climbs the west side of the hill with a most characteristic movement. Above the horns of consecration are two birds, probably hawks, one hovering above the right flank, the other alighted on one of the horns. These sacred birds probably symbolize the presence of divinities.

The parallel horizontal lines across the entrance way must represent steps. A small altar with concave sides rests on the top step, exactly in front of the door. Farther out extends a forecourt with a walled enclosure, also arranged in three sections of which the central one is lower. The enclosure wall is crowned with horns of consecration. At the base and on the left side of the stairway, within the courtyard, appears a stepped altar with a small tree shading it. A third and larger altar occupies the center of the court. Here public offerings would have been made during celebrations. A sixth wild goat strides swiftly over the rocks of the east slope of the height on which the sanctuary stands. The sanctuary was apparently built within a cave or crevice of the hilltop, and the perspective rendering of the overlapping rocks is impressive.

The whole representation illustrates excellently both the naturalism and the decorative, picturesque character of Minoan art at its height. It is also most informative about Minoan sanctuaries, especially those built on hilltops. The wild goat, which is an extremely agile animal, rarely surpassed in speed, used to be common in mountainous areas of Crete, especially the White Mountains and the mountains of Sitia, although today the species is almost extinct, surviving only in isolated areas of the Sphakia district of western Crete. It is natural, therefore, that the goddess in her aspect of Mistress of Animals should have at Zakros wild goats as her attendants. Other evidence of her role as Goddess of Wild Goats is provided by ritual vessels with spouts and handles in the form of a wild goat's head with long, curved horns. These subsequent discoveries confirmed beyond doubt the authenticity of the diadem showing the goddess

The scene represented on the Sanctuary Rhyton

taming two wild goats, which was one of the objects in Dr. Giamalakis's treasure from Zakros.

As mentioned earlier, one of the peak sanctuaries near Zakros was investigated by a member of the expedition. It was at the tip of the mountain called Traostalos, a name which means "enclosure for goats" and is therefore closely enough related to "sanctuary of goats" to have been used to designate the Minoan sanctuary. As in other such sites investigated, there were few architectural remains; what there are date as usual to the first phase of the Neo-palatial period. However, the majority of the terracotta votive offerings, especially those rendering worshipers of the deity and various animals which were either sacrificed or put under her protection, belong to the Proto-palatial period. Naturally, it is not possible to

Detail of the Sanctuary Rhyton, showing a wild goat

determine whether the shrine at Traostalos was the one represented on the rhyton; the artist was not necessarily copying a specific sanctuary. Minoan art contains no representations of actual, specific buildings or clearly defined historical events. This reflects one of the main characteristics of the Minoan spirit, which avoids the concrete, the personal, or the narration of events.

It could not be pure coincidence that parts of the most important ritual vessels of the Palace of Zakros were found within the Hall of Ceremonies, especially as they were accompanied by other ritual equipment. Their presence strongly suggests that the inhabitants were endeavoring to appease the angered deity in the face of imminent danger. The presence of these vessels also supports the theory that the various large halls of the West Wing were used for religious ceremonies, especially since such a function has been attested for columned halls connected with the royal shrines in the other great palaces.

16 The ancient Cretans had aesthetic canons which modern man may well envy. The beautiful motifs with which they decorated their halls were in harmony with the sea and the land from which they had been largely derived.

The Banquet Hall

From the east section of the Hall of Ceremonies, through a triple entrance to the south, one proceeds to a smaller though still spacious room measuring about 6 by 7 meters. Judging from the decoration of its walls and floors, as well as its proximity to the Hall of Ceremonies, this must have been another formal area, probably also used in connection with the shrine. At the time of the excavation we named it the Banquet Hall, because of the numerous vessels for wine that it contained. These vessels were found at two distinct locations. The amphoras, of which there were no less than ten, including one of the big stirrup type, were in the recess formed between the wall and the jambs of the easternmost door, which remained closed. The tiny wine jugs, eight in number, all of the same shape and all undecorated, were found lying in a group near the south wall, where a cupboard for them must have existed at the point where a door leading out into the back yard or garden was subsequently blocked with large stones. While it is not quite certain that this room was used for banquets, it was surely not a storeroom, and the wine containers found in it seem to have been intended for use right there. However, any discussion of banquets or even of simple dinners can be only hypothetical. Wine was used in religious ceremonies, such as sacred communion, in which ritual chalices, ordinarily kept within the shrine treasury, were used. Thus, this room, which received ample light from large double windows facing onto the Central Court, may well have been used ritually.

The Banquet Hall

The floor had received the same type of decoration as that of the Hall of Ceremonies: two parallel lines of panels divided into smaller panels and framed by strips of stucco, here also vividly painted in red, occupied

Plan of the Banquet Hall,
with equipment and the remains of the spiral frieze

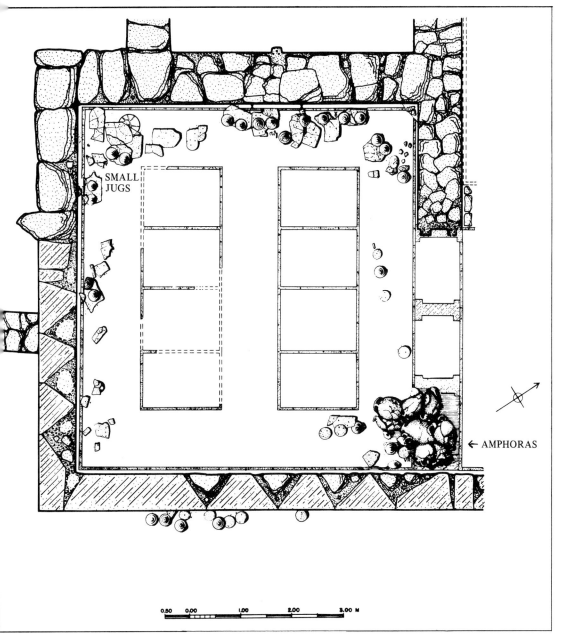

SMALL
JUGS

← AMPHORAS

0.50 0.00   1.00   2.00   3.00 M

the center of the room, creating the impression of slabs or carpets. Here again the substance filling the panels had completely vanished. Another painted stucco strip framed the entire floor. If the room was indeed used for banquets, one can imagine two long tables placed along the two parallel rows of panels.

The walls were decorated with impressive painted stucco reliefs arranged in a frieze running just below the ceiling around all four walls—that is, for a distance of 26 meters. Fragments of the stucco were found scattered on the floor close to the walls. The frieze consisted of large contiguous spirals linked together, rendered in high relief. They were painted in white with a colored rosette at the center of each and were set against a blue background. Unfortunately, the colors were transformed by the fire. Part of the east wall with its frieze had fallen into the Central Court.

Fragments of spirals in front of the triple entrance suggested at first that the frieze was placed very high up above it. The exact position, however, was determined when cuts in the stucco frieze were noticed at regular intervals. Broad and short rectangular cuts corresponded to those in the frieze of the west wall. On the part corresponding to the south wall, on the other hand, there were three deep semicircular cuts in a line, interrupting the row of contiguous spirals. Perhaps this feature was repeated twice on each of the long sides. The interpretation is obvious: the frieze was placed directly beneath the timberwork which supported the upper floor. Two groups of beams, each consisting of three regularly spaced, semicylindrical timbers oriented north to south, formed a kind of grid, supporting rafters arranged in a west-to-east direction. The rafters, cut in the shape of planks, were more closely spaced and formed a base for the flooring of the upper story, which must have consisted of wooden boards or some other material of a perishable nature. Here then is an example of the way Minoans roofed a large palace hall. Another example is provided by the ground floor of the Grand Staircase at Knossos. The method of spanning limited spaces by means of large and small beams is best illustrated in the crypts of the Royal Villa and the South Royal Tomb at Knossos.

At Knossos friezes of spirals appear in wall paintings but not in relief. However, an important relief ceiling decoration consisting of a network of spirals and of rosettes placed within curvilinear outlines was found in a hall in the northwest quarter of that palace, which, from its wall paintings and the ritual objects it contained, seems to have been part of the shrine. A section of the frieze belonging to the west wall of the Banquet Hall of Zakros has been restored by the technicians of the Museum of Heraklion for a length of 6 meters and is now exhibited in the Museum. Of all the decorative friezes preserved in Minoan palaces, villas, and mansions, this is the longest and most characteristic, providing a vivid impression of the way large ceremonial halls were adorned.

Amphoras and part of the spiral frieze, as found in the Banquet Hall

17

True splendor in secular terms is found in the adornment of the physical monarchy, whether in the chambers of state or the quarters for daily living. To this splendor the Minoans gave graphic obeisance.

The Royal Living Quarters

The recognition that the West Wing was occupied primarily by the shrine led to the certainty that the royal living quarters and the government offices should be sought in the East Wing. The narrow, flat land between the two hills broadened progressively toward the sea, from the point at which the main approach to the palace must have started. The terrain on this side was more suitable for the accommodation of living quarters, which would be fairly cool in summer and in winter would be protected from the torrents of water rushing down through the ravine. Aside from these advantages, it was natural that such apartments should face toward the sea, providing easy access to the harbor and direct control of maritime transactions and transportation. It was consequently no surprise when excavations confirmed the conjecture that, as at Knossos, the royal living quarters were indeed located in the East Wing.

Unfortunately, identifying and clarifying the particular features of this wing was, as has been stated, very difficult because of the great damage caused by cultivation and by erosion, the latter due to floods resulting from heavy winter rains. In most of this area there was very little fill, and cultivation, even though no heavy machines were used, had penetrated almost into the pavements of the ground floor, especially where vines and olive trees had been planted. Water channels used for irrigation of the fields cut deeply into the remains, damaging them still further. Finally, the walls of dressed stone that showed on the surface had provided a con-

venient local supply of building material; luckily this had not been exploited to any great extent, since that deserted region of the bay did not
attract many settlers. Only in the north section of the wing, where the
palace was built in terraces on the gently sloping side of the hill, were
any high walls preserved; these were covered by heaps of stones which
had served as retaining walls for the cultivated terraces.

In spite of these difficulties, a comparative study by analogy with
relevant features which are clear in the other palaces made it possible to
trace the plan of the area quite satisfactorily. There are still some problems, but hopefully these will be solved through further excavation. Among SEE PAGES 80-81
the remains could be distinguished the living quarters of the king and of
the queen, with accessory rooms, a magnificent hall containing the unusual
feature of a colonnaded cistern, and certain special structures to supply
water both for drinking and for domestic purposes. Direct communication
between the compartments and interior courts and the chief entrances to
the palace, as well as access to the Central Court either directly or through
corridors, had been brilliantly conceived and planned by a capable and
experienced architect. The execution, of equally high quality, had been
carried out by masons who must have previously participated in similar
construction elsewhere.

Excavation in this section is not complete, and consequently a full
picture of this wing, which must have played a significant role in the life
of the palace, cannot yet be visualized. Moreover, since the east exterior
façade has not yet been exposed, the existence of another main entrance
with a propylon at this side, comparable to those in other palaces, is still
conjectural, as is the total extent of the palace. Nevertheless, the area now
excavated supplies an adequate idea of the grandeur of the royal living
quarters and of rooms used officially for the political administration, apartments all marked by originality and grace.

The arrangement of the façade along the east flank of the Central
Court, with square piers and columns forming a portico much narrower
than the one on the north side, immediately suggested that the royal quarters had been located directly behind this façade. This was confirmed
through the discovery and detailed analysis of architectural remains.

Behind the portico on the east side of the Central Court were two large adjoining megarons—royal rooms—of the type provided with a light-well and a pier-and-door partition which occurs frequently in other palaces. The southern room, oriented north to south, was the larger of the two —a spacious room, about 6 by 9.5 meters, divided into two parts by a poly-thyron of five successive doors, of which only the supporting doorjamb slabs were preserved. The lightwell occupied the southern part of the room, and of its stylobate, on which two columns probably stood, only the underlying slabs of irregular shape were preserved. This room communicated with the one to the north through another polythyron of two pairs of doors. Two other pairs of doors gave access on the east to the great square hall with the cistern. Of all these doors, only the foundations of the jambs and the slabs which supported the thresholds remain. Two single doors, corresponding, like the double doors on the other side, with the two sections of the room, led to the portico facing the Central Court. Both the

Plan of the royal apartments, showing the remains found

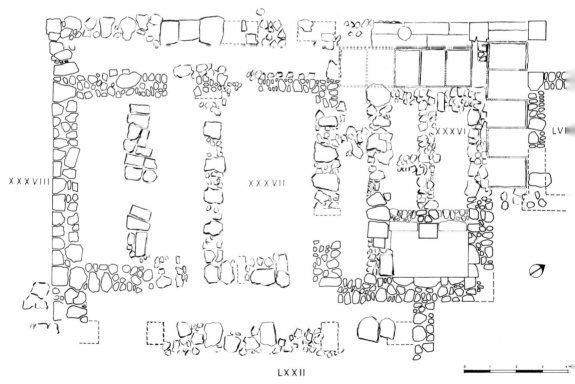

central and side piers of the portico stood on a relatively high stylobate of hard black ironstone. The height of this stylobate in relation to the ground level of the Central Court suggests that the southern room was reached from the court only through a door at the north end of the portico, rather than by climbing over the stylobate. It is logical to assume that wooden benches placed against the east wall made the portico a resting place analogous to the one on the north side of the Central Court.

The northern royal room was oriented east to west and could be entered directly from the Central Court. Its lightwell was at the eastern end. The entrance consisted of a wide opening with two broad steps and

Plan of the royal apartments, showing proposed restorations

XXXVI *The queen's apartment, with portico, inner polythyron, and lightwell*
XXXVII *The king's apartment, with portico, polythyron, and lightwell*
XXXVIII *Corridor to the Central Court*
LVI *Storeroom of the royal apartments*
LXXII *Hall of the Cistern*

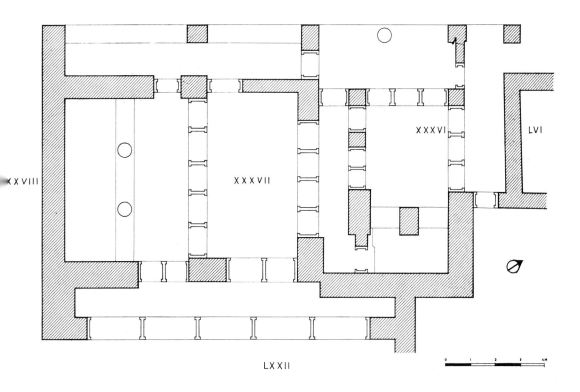

a central column which, together with the square piers at either end, held the architrave. An interior four-sided polythyron, with three doors at each of its three sides, and two openings in the form of windows with a central support facing into the lightwell to the east, permitted the main central space to be either isolated by closing the doors or used as one unit in combination with the surrounding area within the hall. When the doors were closed, the central unit received light only through the lightwell. One could then reach the southern room and its portico by following the angled corridor formed east and south of the isolated central unit. Under these conditions, the front section of the room became essentially an extension of the portico, which must have looked very picturesque with its pillars and central column, an effect enhanced by the similar columnar veranda above. A special entrance, also with two steps, between two square piers led to the north part of the portico. When the polythyron was closed, this entrance led through the corridor thus formed north of it into the interior court. When the polythyron was open, this corridor became part of the interior of the northern room. Another entrance allowed one to enter the portico directly from the corridor.

Beyond the space enclosed by the polythyron the floor had been paved with the same mysterious substance used in the Hall of Ceremonies in the West Wing. Here again partially preserved stucco strips formed meandering patterns and panels which simulated large paving slabs. How the central space was paved could not be determined, since the floor had been destroyed to the point that walls of an earlier building showed beneath it. The lightwell and the bases of the double window consisted of tightly fitting ashlar poros stone, in regular courses, the lowest of which still exist. The floor in this area was lower than that of the rest of the room; two steps led down to it from a door to the south of the lightwell.

Though possessing some of the typical features found in such units, this room is remarkable for its central, separable unit with spaces around it which could be used as corridors and direct access to the Central Court through a columnar vestibule. The only corresponding arrangement is that of the Little Palace of Knossos. There, however, the space with the central polythyron was not recognized by Evans as a living room. He interpreted it as a vestibule of the entrance, when the latter was actually to be sought farther north in the area of the peristyle which served as a light-well. Other comparisons, as will be seen, can be made between the Palace of Zakros and the Little Palace of Knossos.

Judging from elsewhere, there must have been corresponding spaces with similar layout and functions on the second floor. Porticoes were there replaced by colonnaded verandas. Unfortunately, because of the damage caused by cultivation, most of the architectural elements of both floors, such as column and pillar bases, paving slabs, and parts of the balustrades of balconies, were missing. Nor was there any trace of wall paintings or other embellishments to be expected in such important rooms.

That these rooms were used as living quarters by the royal family is indicated by their majestic appearance and their similarity to other such spaces in the great palaces of Knossos, Phaistos, and Mallia, the Little Palace and Royal Villa of Knossos, and the Villa of Hagia Triada, the summer residence of the kings of Phaistos. As in those buildings, the most spacious and easily accessible chamber was intended for the king; the smaller and more private one, which could be easily isolated, for the queen. This identification by analogy should not be considered arbitrary. It would have been further confirmed if the fittings and equipment and the painted decoration of the halls had been preserved, but unfortunately, all these have been destroyed. Two small fragments of a small crystal vase with the hue of amethyst, certain inlays in crystal, and pieces of alabaster give an indication of the precious objects which must have existed in these rooms. It is not unlikely that the three golden objects from the Giamalakis Collection actually came from these royal quarters; as has been noted, they are unquestionably of royal quality.

As elsewhere, the royal bedrooms must have been upstairs, where conditions were more pleasant, especially because of balconies providing a view into the Central Court. The royal family could sit there in the evenings and watch festivities taking place in the court. Walls in the interior of the upper floor were built of mud bricks, both to reduce weight and to provide better resistance against earthquakes. Masses of mud bricks, baked by the fire, and a fill of russet earth covered the ground floor, especially in the area of the lightwell of the queen's living room. As usual, doorjambs, column shafts, door frames, and window frames were all made

of wood. These and the timber used in the construction of the walls fed
the fire which destroyed the palace.

The discovery of a bathroom in the same area confirmed the identification of the rooms under discussion as royal quarters. In both small
and large palaces a small bathroom, usually provided with a kind of antechamber, was found in the royal quarters. These were identified on the
basis of internal arrangement, plus the occasional discovery of a bathtub
and various vessels which could be used in bathing. A similar provision
was made in royal living quarters in Mycenaean palaces.

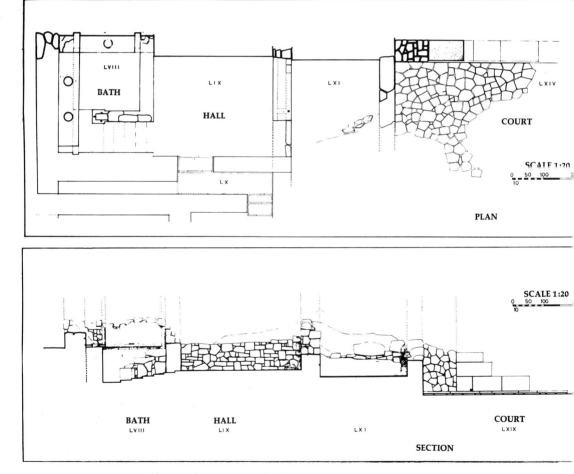

Plan and section of the bathroom and adjoining apartments

At Zakros, the bathroom could be reached from the queen's living room through a corridor. The latter was solidly paved with concrete, but the great part of it had been destroyed by cultivation. The floor of the corridor was perhaps on two different levels connected with steps. The corridor was at a right angle to the north section of the queen's living room, the section which by a manipulation of the polythyron could be changed into a corridor with a separate entrance from the Central Court. Thus the king could reach the bathroom from his living room by going through the portico which faced the court, without having to walk through the women's quarters.

The anteroom was at a slightly higher level than the corridor and was reached through a stepped entrance and a narrow passage separated from the anteroom by a mud-brick partition. This arrangement must have been intended to block the view into the anteroom where preparations for the bath took place. The anteroom received light through a double window on the east wall, which in the last phase of the palace was transformed into a single window in order to allow the construction of a closet within a recess. The masses of bricks which partly filled both the anteroom and the bathroom must have come from interior walls of the ground floor and walls of the upper story. The ground floor had floors of compact clay, which lay immediately above the leveled bedrock.

The bathroom proper closely resembles one in the Little Palace of Knossos. That one, during the Post-palatial period, was changed into a shrine by filling in the inner space and thus covering up its staircase and converting the high podium in the interior that served as a stylobate to a bench on which images and symbols were placed. In its original condition, however, it presented marked analogies to the one at Zakros. The two high podiums were built along two walls, one of which was constructed of stone and the other, which formed a partition between the room and the small corridor behind, was built with mud bricks. The podiums were covered with gypsum slabs on which stood small fluted columns, probably crowned by cornices. A staircase with six well-preserved steps and a colonnaded balustrade descended into the interior, which was paved with gypsum slabs. When the bathroom was changed into a shrine, the column of the back podium was removed, while the three columns of

the other side were incorporated into a clay partition on which were preserved the impressions of the fluted shafts. It is possible that even in the
earlier phase the bathroom had a religious function, perhaps for a lustral
purification, as certain sealings with religious representations were found
in an early stratum within it.

In the bathroom of the Palace of Zakros the staircase was wooden
and only the topmost step at the entrance was plastered. Of the rest of the
staircase only the underlying fill, supporting the wooden steps, and the
foundation of the balustrade terminating with a pier were preserved. A
column originally stood on this pier. Two high podiums at the north and
west walls supported respectively one column and two columns; there are
round cavities in the stucco covering of the podiums in which the shafts
of the slender columns must have been secured while stucco rings encircled
their bases. The stucco covering, imitating slabs, protruded beyond the
podiums and was supported by small beams laid horizontally. The piers
formed on either side thus created a central niche containing the columns.
There was probably a stucco entablature and cornice over the columns.

It is significant that the rear walls of the niches had been painted
with religious themes, consisting of horns of consecration crowning platforms or altars. Unfortunately, these wall paintings suffered heavily from
the fire. In the north niche, the colors, a vivid red for the background and
white for the symbols, were changed to such an extent that the representation is now hardly discernible. The west niche has not yet been sufficiently cleared to know what the theme was. A temporary roof coping
now covers the bathroom in order to protect its fragile remains. A bench
or podium, also lined with plaster, but without columns, appeared against
the south wall of the descending staircase. This wall was apparently
a simple mud-brick screen setting off a long, narrow, empty space behind
it. In the east wall on the side of the anteroom there was a window which
could apparently be screened with a curtain during a bath. This feature
occurs in many royal bathrooms. No vessels which could have been used in
connection with a bath were found; only a few have been discovered elsewhere. Heaps of mud bricks from wall partitions and fragments from the
frames of the niches had accumulated over the podiums and the interior of
the room. With them were many pieces of the concrete floor from the room

above. The floor downstairs was of stamped earth with a thin coating of red plaster. Thus red was the predominant tone of the room.

The twofold character of this suite, serving both as an ordinary bathroom for the royal family and occasionally for ritual purification, solves a contradiction which characterizes Evans's interpretation of such rooms. He describes them as being used exclusively either as simple bathrooms or as lustral basins. The double function is indicated at Zakros, on the one hand by the proximity of the room to the royal apartments, on the other by the use of sacred symbols over altars in its painted decoration. Purification in the lustral basin was probably attained simply through bathing, and since the royal family was considered sacred, such a bath would automatically be considered as a ritual cleansing, which would be necessary for every participation in a religious ceremony. This dual function also explains why certain bathrooms, such as that of the Little Palace at Knossos, were transformed into shrines, and others were installed in the area of the shrines, as in the case of the Shrine of the Double Axes in the Palace of Knossos. Another bathroom of that palace, designated by Evans as the Nursery Room because of its small tub, was also located next to a shrine containing a bench. This shrine is well known for its deposits of beautiful vessels painted with lilies and its storerooms of polychrome pithoi.

In the area of the royal living quarters at Zakros there were a few smaller rooms which may have been used by the royal family, but of which the exact purpose remains unknown. These were accessible from the corridor which led to the bathroom. A door to the west, of which hardly any traces are left, led into two rooms, one serving as a vestibule, the other built at a slightly higher level. A door seems to have been opened in the wall dividing them when the door of the inner room on the side of the north portico was blocked up to make possible the construction of a hearth outside. Numerous clay pots, some of them substantial in size, included a pithos with a discoid lid, basins with spouts, sizable cooking pots, pail-like vessels, and other types. Within a narrow space in the form of a drain along the north wall, there was an interesting stone table with a high cylindrical pedestal and a movable top. The top was fastened by a tenon inserted in a special socket of the base and one in the upper part and held in place by two small wooden pegs going through it. This device made it possible to move the table top without the heavy base. Carved molding decorated both parts. The technique is known from other stone tables and pedestaled lamps—a famous example is a stand from Knossos made of porphyry with a decoration of a spiraling band of ivy leaves—but this is the only instance in which both pieces were found, as well as the tenon that held them together.

Another room, only partially preserved, could apparently be entered from the north end of the corridor where the steps were. A door had existed at this point, though only the carbonized wooden jamb could be detected. The floor was firmly paved with concrete and was on practically the same level as that of the adjacent anteroom of the bathroom. The façade on the side of the interior court was constructed of neatly fitted dressed blocks of poros stone. Because of the vast damage in this area it is not possible to be sure whether there had been another room directly to the south; however, the branching of the drainage system, which must have run directly outside the walls, indicates the existence of an additional long and narrow room, and a small area of concrete pavement is still preserved.

18 Even the most adroit and careful excavator must often speculate about the character of the things he finds. Here is a description of a magnificent room whose function tantalizingly escapes the investigator.

The Hall of the Cistern

Directly to the east of the king's room, and immediately accessible from that through the two double doors, was a most spacious square hall which, judging from its interior arrangement, was one of the most important rooms in the palace—possibly even the king's throne room. In spite of the damage caused by cultivation, foundations for doorjambs and bases for thresholds could be traced and the presence of a pier-and-door partition along the entire west side of the large hall detected. There were seven consecutive doors, the jambs of which must have stood on bases with indentations cut in them to enclose the leaves of the door, a very common system at Zakros and elsewhere. When these doors were closed, a corridor was formed east of the king's and queen's living rooms. The queen could enter the hall directly from her chamber through a door which unfortunately is poorly preserved. The queen's unit projected slightly beyond the king's on the east side, thus creating an extremely narrow space, almost a kind of recess, between her apartment and the polythyron. The presence of a portico rather than a polythyron is unlikely. If there had been a portico, the square area could conceivably have been an unroofed court. Such a solution is not in itself incompatible with the existence of the circular cistern with steps leading down into it, which occupies a commanding position in the center of the hall. Of unique importance for the history of Minoan architecture is the incorporation of the cistern into the palace structure, an arrangement never previously found in any Minoan or Mycenaean palace.

SEE PAGE 223

This cistern is not an ordinary reservoir for storing rain water, but one for retaining water springing from an underground source and keeping it at a standard level. The function of this structure was elucidated by the observation that, from the time it was excavated, water constantly seeped up until it reached a certain height. The water level is today higher than in antiquity. The outer diameter, including the encircling wall, is as much as 7 meters, the inner a little less than 5 meters. The walls are thick and carefully coated on the interior with hydraulic plaster, which is mostly preserved except where parts became detached

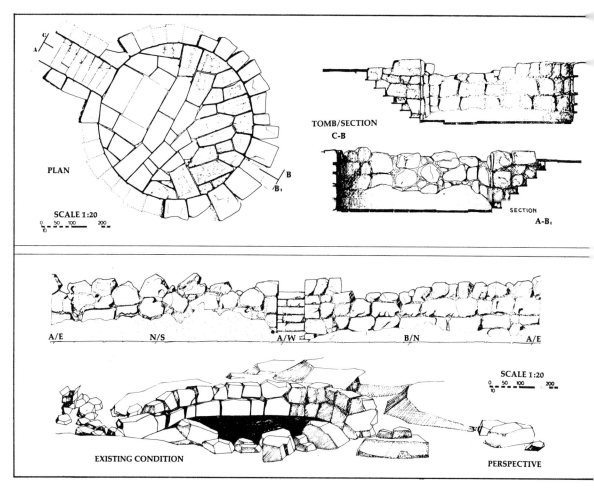

*Plan, section, development, and sketch of the circular cistern
in the Hall of the Cistern*

and fell inside. The masonry, not only in the part underground, but also in the balustrade above floor level, consists of very large stone blocks. Most of the upper blocks, however, had collapsed and fallen inside. From the debris were retrieved two column bases. On two sides of the lower part of the bases, there were cuts, a detail suggesting that they may have been inserted within the superstructure of the round parapet. If this were true, it would mean that there was a colonnade over the balustrade, forming a kind of circular portico and leaving the central area uncovered. There must have been at least five columns. The loss of the other bases and of many of the blocks of the parapet may be due to their removal or displacement by the local farmers. A third base with a comparable diameter, found in the stone heaps to the north, may also have come from the cistern, since the only other columns existing in this area were those of the lightwell of the royal living quarters, and as the bases of those stood on a stylobate, they must have been of a different type.

The discovery of the column bases confirmed our original belief that the hall was not an unroofed space and also that it had an official use. The wooden polythyron in the west side could hardly have been exposed to an unsheltered area—everywhere else in Minoan buildings polythyrons are within rooms or behind porticos. There is other evidence, however. Directly to the north of the hall lies an extensive slab-paved courtyard which in such a case would have been an extension of the unroofed space to the south, separated from it by a wall serving simply as a partition. Such an arrangement, however, would be unorthodox in Minoan architecture. Moreover, the heavy masonry of the intermediary wall, apparently consisting of dressed poros stones, and its great thickness, equal to that of the other walls, hardly suggest a partition wall. The floor itself, paved with delicate plaster which, judging from the successive layers, must have been renewed several times, also suggests a roofed space; normally open courts were paved with slabs, compact clay, or pebbles, or less often with a sort of concrete. A final indication of the existence of a roof is the peculiar form of a drain under the plastered pavement along the north wall in which was concentrated the water from the irregular and far-spread ramifications of the extensive drainage system.

The timberwork of the roof must have been supported by the entablature of the colonnade of the cistern, which thus automatically solved the problem of spanning a wide space. The great thickness of the walls suggests that the roof was very high, apparently higher than that of the royal living quarters. It is unlikely that there was a large hall above with a corresponding central structure. The central area over the cistern would be unroofed, unless we conjecture a kind of circular clerestory with side openings, acting as a lightwell. The latter is rather improbable, however, because of the problems of supporting the additional weight and of covering such a structure.

The hall then would have combined architectural grandeur with the relaxing and picturesque presence of water constantly springing up within the cistern. A flight of eight steps, of which seven are perfectly preserved, led down to the slab-paved bottom of the cistern. Since water could be drawn from above without descending into the cistern, the staircase must have served other purposes as well, such as going down to the water level to swim or bathe. If so, this would be the first instance of a private swimming pool in prehistoric times. Another possibility is that the cistern could have served as an aquarium for local and exotic fish. This possibility was tested by throwing fish into the water, where they survived for many days. The water at present seeps through both the bottom and sides and reaches a level at the fifth or sixth step. In antiquity, however, the coating of hydraulic plaster closed the joints of the blocks of the walls and of the steps. The paving slabs of the bottom, mostly large, were laid in a radiating arrangement. Directly in front of the lowest step was a large slab of poros stone through which the water gushed up and was automatically filtered. This water is somewhat brackish but still suitable for drinking and domestic uses. The spring chamber close by was supplied from the same source. Many segments of a trough-shaped stone conduit were found in the fill within the cistern. This conduit probably channeled away surplus water in order to prevent overflow and keep the water at a standard level. Excavation revealed a part of the conduit drain, built within the projecting base from the east wall of the hall fundament and heading in an easterly direction.

Only one structure comparable to this cistern and dating from the same Neo-palatial period has been found in Crete. This is described in

Evans's monumental publication *The Palace of Knossos* (London: Macmillan, 1921–1935), but it would have to be more completely excavated in order to provide enough information for comparison. Further investigation was hindered by the fact that this structure lay under a modern building in Archanes, a village only 10 kilometers south of Knossos, at the foot of the sacred mountain Iyktos (modern Juktas). At a short distance from it were remains of an impressive building, which might have been the summer palace of the kings of Knossos. This also, therefore, could have been a cistern forming an integral part of a palace. The structure closely resembles the circular cistern at Zakros. It was built of dressed stone, and its measurements were roughly similar. Its floor, which might have been paved with slabs, had unfortunately been completely removed. A small staircase, of which five steps were preserved, led down to the water, which there also seeped through the floor. The conduit system carrying away surplus water was well preserved, but it started at a very low level, directly below the lowest step. The course of the drain was followed recently on the outside by John Sakellaraki, the excavator of the nearby palatial building. Evans believed that the structure was domed above but had no definite proof for this idea. Another very large circular reservoir with a descending staircase was found at Tylissos, but that was the typical kind of cistern with a conduit to supply the water and was not linked architecturally with any particular building. It dates to the Post-palatial period and was constructed after the destruction of the underlying Minoan house.

Because of the constant seepage of water, it was very difficult to excavate the reservoir, and a powerful pump was required. There was a great quantity of fallen stones, burned mud bricks, cornices, and pieces of the drainage system. Various ordinary pots found there must have been used mostly for drawing water. No valuable objects were found, either in the cistern or on the floor of the hall, except for a fragment of a small concave vessel of amethyst-colored crystal, which seems to be different from the fragments found in the royal living quarters.

Whether this beautifully arranged spacious hall was a throne room, used also for official state receptions, or was the main living room of the royal family depends to a great extent on the interpretation of the cistern.

If its main purpose was to add to the magnificence of the space and to provide a picturesque element by the presence of water, then the hall could have been a throne room. If, on the other hand, the cistern was intended for such personal activities as swimming or bathing in the open, then the hall could have been a place where the members of the royal family could spend most of their day, whenever they were not in their individual private apartments. The problem could readily have been solved if any furniture, such as remains of a throne or other mobile equipment, had been preserved. Unfortunately none was. Similarly, it would have been helpful to know what kind of entranceway led in on the east side. Cultivation, unfortunately, had destroyed both walls and floors in this area. Still, the fact that the foundation walls were fairly well preserved along the north and east sides made it possible to trace what one could define as a large rectangular entrance hall or, more appropriately, as an enclosed unroofed introductory space, 6.5 by 12.5 meters. A very small part of the concrete floor was preserved in the northwest corner. From certain dressed poros blocks preserved *in situ,* both on the exterior east façade of the Hall of the Cistern and in two walls of the entrance space, we can infer that the entire entrance system was built in ashlar masonry.

A rectangular groundwork, chiefly of poros blocks, here projected beyond the façade of the Hall of the Cistern. This foundation, which had partly subsided and become detached from the wall, had apparently supported a small propylon leading into the grand square hall. The stately entrance suggests a formal character for this hall, which was apparently directly accessible also from the other main entrances of the palace. At least the approach from the main northeast gate, across the slab-paved court and through a door at the southeast corner leading into the entrance hall would seem the regular entranceway. However, such a formal character would not exclude the possibility that the hall could also have been used by the royal family and their personal retinue when it was not needed for official purposes.

South of the polythyron of the great hall, and exactly opposite the staircase of the cistern, which was oriented diagonally, pointing to the southeast corner of the room, there projected a rectangular structure with neatly laid ashlar masonry at its south end, which was first considered to be the lobby of the main entrance. Further excavation, however, revealed here the main installations of the spring of water, thus excluding the possibility of an entrance from this side. These installations were underground. The projecting rectangular space was then thought to have been used as a storeroom, and certain clay and stone vessels, loom weights, and a three-stepped pyramidal base of a double axe were believed to have fallen from it. This hypothesis, however, seemed less plausible on the discovery of poros-stone steps which had slid from their original position and fallen into a slanting position within the lower chamber. It then seemed more likely that this structure was the well of a staircase consisting of two flights and leading up to the second story of the royal apartments. This staircase could have terminated in a kind of veranda, perhaps colonnaded, occupying the area above the adjacent space. An upper corridor corresponding to that on the ground floor could have branched off from the small veranda and provided access to the royal apartments of the upper story and the other rooms of the southeast quarters. No other plausible location in this area has been found for the staircase which was undoubtedly necessary.

19   Ancient man was expert in the handling of problems in hydraulic engineering. Modern engineers are often surprised to view the skillful planning and execution by which the ancients solved such practical problems as water supply and sewage disposal.

Spring Chamber and Spring Wells

The basement room under the conjectural stairwell in the area of the royal apartments proved to be the main chamber in which the water sprang up and collected, as it still does abundantly today. The excavation of this space presented great difficulties, but its essential features and its function were eventually clarified. Two superposed massive stones occupied one third of the total space of the room. At first we thought that the stones formed a platform from which water could be drawn, but the discovery of a covering floor precludes such an interpretation. The evidence for a staircase makes it much more likely that the platform actually supported the second flight of steps of the staircase previously mentioned. The well chamber communicated with a tunnel running underground along the south wall of the Hall of the Cistern, through which accumulated silt could be removed from the chamber. The entrance to the tunnel has not yet been definitely located, since investigation of the area has not been completed. Cuts to hold the lintel of a small door in the passage appeared on two dressed stones on either side of the tunnel at the point where it joined the chamber. The abundant spring water was channeled SEE PAGE 119 into a well, designated the Well of the Fountain, which was constructed south of the Spring Chamber. This could correspond to the "built fountain" mentioned in the *Odyssey*.

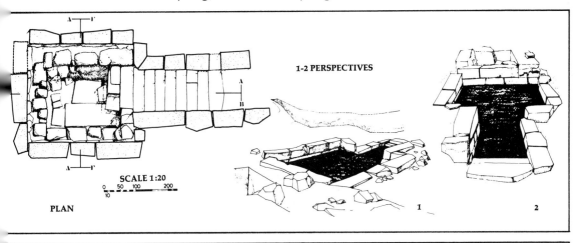

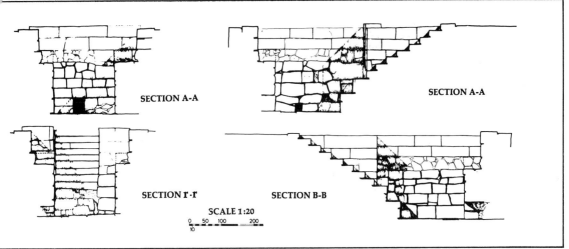

Plan, section, and sketches of the Well of the Fountain

The upper walls of the Well of the Fountain were carefully constructed in ashlar masonry of poros stone in regular courses on top of a base projecting inward for 0.6 meter, thus limiting to 3 by 4 meters the basin for collecting water. A flight of fifteen hewn steps, of which eleven are perfectly preserved, led down to the basin. The staircase started outside the chamber and was flanked by two walls of ashlar masonry. The lower part of the chamber, paved with irregular slabs, was apparently always covered by the water which flowed from the source through an opening at the base of the north wall. This outlet was 0.55 by 0.35 meter, but there was a smaller one at the base of the east wall. This hole channeled water from another underground artery. The projecting ledge on the four sides of the chamber is difficult to explain. It could not have been used for people to stand on to draw water, especially when the chamber was flooded; moreover one could get down to the water easily by means of the staircase. If the roof of the central space had been supported on the projecting base, the roof would have been too low. Perhaps the only purpose of this base was to reduce the size of the draw basin. To compensate for the narrowness of the interior, the superstructure was beautifully constructed and very impressive. Ornamental flower pots might have been placed on the ledge. The whole system for the provision of water was impressive and is certainly the most characteristic example of installations for water supply in Minoan times.

A comparable structure was found at Knossos, but outside the palace, near the Caravanserai and the viaduct which bridged the Vlichia stream. In this, there was a neatly constructed chamber 2 by 1.6 meters in size, which contained the spring and also a small central rectangular basin into which the water bubbled. Three steps led down into the spring chamber, the floors and walls of which were lined with gypsum slabs. A small niche in the rear was for idols, while two high ledges flanking it were perhaps for ritual symbols and implements. The spring chamber consequently served as a shrine; its contents indicate that it was used until the latest Minoan times. One figurine of a goddess raising her hands was shown in her abode, a small circular clay hut. Numerous dishes, conical cups, and braziers indicate that the chamber was used for sacred offerings just before the destruction of the palace at the end of the second phase of the Neo-palatial period. Among the food offerings were olives, which survived in charred condition.

Similar offerings, also including olives, were made at the contemporary Spring Chamber in the Palace of Zakros, and offerings of food, described later in this chapter, were also found in another spring well nearby, built in a chamber at the southeast corner of the Central Court. Indications of the sanctity of the area are part of a sizable pair of horns of consecration, found directly outside the spring, and a stepped pyramid, discovered in the spring well itself, which could have supported the symbol of the double axe. By analogy with the Fountain House at Knossos, the ledge at the back wall of the Spring Chamber at Zakros could have also held ritual symbols and idols.

In addition to many vessels for drawing water, fragments of a stone conduit—perhaps the one that carried away surplus water from the circular cistern—were found in the fill of the Spring Chamber. One of these stone segments was actually built into the north wall of the spring, and its orientation suggests that it may have been linked with the conduit of the circular cistern. Surplus water from the latter could have been channeled into the Spring Chamber. However, further investigation of this system is needed.

The area surrounding the Spring Chamber was level with the highest step of the staircase. No walls appeared in this area; if there had been walls which were destroyed they could still have been recognized by foundation courses or trenches. The Spring Chamber, then, was in an open area, perhaps a court contiguous with the rectangular enclosed area east of the Hall of the Cistern. The Central Court could be reached directly through a corridor in the northwest section of this area. A large door gave entrance to a small anteroom and to the corridor on the west side. The large sandstone slab serving as the threshold of the intermediate door was still preserved. There also seems to have been another small anteroom at the west end of the same passage. The large, broken pair of sacred horns made of stucco, already mentioned as having been found in the Central Court in front of the end of the corridor, had probably fallen from the cornice crowning the façade of a corresponding corridor in the upper story. The inner façades of the Palace of Zakros seem to have been crowned at certain points with horns of consecration, as were those at Knossos. As Evans pointed out, these indicate the sacred character of the Minoan palace.

Directly south of the corridor was a long, narrow unit, divided into two rooms with doors on the side of the Central Court. The use of the northern room remains unknown; the southern one, as mentioned earlier, contained the installations of the second well. Little is known of the interior arrangement of the first room. During the last phase of the palace, a clay partition was built in its south end, apparently a water closet constructed like the one in the industrial unit of the West Wing with a drain terminating in a septic pit outside the east wall in the interior court.

The room containing the well could be entered through a door exactly at the southeast corner of the Central Court. One walked down two steps and then turned south to six more steps which lead down to a platform from which water could be drawn. The circular well was contained in a small rectangular enclosure, the north wall of which was joined with the balustrade of the staircase. The water must derive from a spring, for the depth of the well from the drawing platform is no more than 2 meters, and the bottom itself is paved with slabs. Water springs up in great abundance today, not only filling the well but overflowing most of the steps. Here again the installation was provided with a conduit to carry off any surplus water. One segment of this was found within the east wall, pointing in the direction of the interior court. Traces of wear from passing feet appear on the stairs, but a small depression on the platform must have been made intentionally to hold round-bottomed water pitchers. The timber of a hoist was satisfactorily preserved, as it had remained constantly in the water. The hoist was secured on the pier of the balustrade and on the south wall of the room. The cuts for its adjustment were still visible in the wood.

An important fact gradually became clear: during the last phase of the palace—perhaps on the very last days in awareness of impending doom—special offerings to the deity were made within this well. Remnants of offerings in ordinary cups and dishes were found. One cup actually contained olives, but olives were also found scattered about, along with other cups. An amazing aspect of this discovery was the degree of preservation of the olives, which had even retained their fleshy parts. When the olives first came out of the water they looked as if they had just been picked from the tree, a fact recorded in the excavation photographs. Unfortunately, after a few minutes, the skins wrinkled rapidly, and, despite many attempts to preserve them, the olives never regained their original appearance. Grape seeds, and small branches, probably from aromatic shrubs, were also collected; these too were evidently from offerings made to propitiate the deity. Pieces of pumice,

*Offering cup containing olives,
as found in the built well in the East Wing*

certainly of volcanic origin, found in handleless cups, may also have been
offered because of their relation with the source of the coming catastrophe. Certain other pots found in fragments in the well must have been
used for drawing water and left there when they broke. Animal bones,
most of which were burned, may have been remnants of sacrifices or of
pieces of meat included among the offerings. Fragments of three-legged
offering tables, plastered and painted, also indicate ritual activity. Only
one animal figurine was found here. These last-mentioned objects, however, were found in the fill of the well chamber, together with fragments
of a thick concrete pavement, apparently fallen from a room above, where
religious ceremonies may also have taken place. Behind the east wall of
the well was a small storage space which could be reached by passing
through the wall partition.

The well built in the East Wing to provide spring water,
in which were found offerings to the goddess,
including the cup containing olives

The built well constitutes another example of the adaptation within a building of a special installation for the provision of water, with a staircase leading down to it. Ordinary wells are, of course, known from Minoan sites, but these are always independent of buildings, being located in courts and other unroofed, open areas, and water was drawn from them by means of a rope lowered from above. The problem of water supply, then, found a special solution at the Palace of Zakros, and this fact is of great significance. The Palace of Knossos was supplied through terracotta water pipes, those of Phaistos and Mallia by means of cisterns or reservoirs. At Zakros, for the first time in a Minoan palace, special provision was made to assure a water supply directly from the source by the ingenious architectural installations described here.

20   The interior court with its surrounding rooms was the center
       of much of ancient urban life, whether in a public structure, a
       palace, or a modest home. Here one could rest, eat, and gossip
       in a harmonious and comfortable setting.

The Court at the Main Entrance

SEE
PAGES
80-81

Directly north of the Hall of the Cistern and its vestibule extended
a spacious interior court paved with slabs. A little farther up and at the
northeast corner of the court is the main entrance to the palace, described
earlier. The entrance, the court, and certain small adjoining rooms and
enclosures played a vital role in the daily life of the palace. Fortunately,
despite the great destruction inflicted on this area, the layout and organization could still be traced. The court is roughly square, with a small
projection toward the queen's apartment and the corridor leading to the
bathroom and south of a long, narrow room with a concrete floor. A fairly
good picture of the original appearance of the court can be obtained from
its northwest corner, which is the only well-preserved part. The enclosing
walls were neatly constructed in ashlar masonry of poros stone laid in
regular courses. The pavement consisted of irregular slabs, in the northern
section resting directly upon the leveled bedrock and farther south on a
fill of small stones and earth which had been dumped there to level the
ground. A drainage system with several branches occupied the southern
half of the court.

Earlier structures, which are described later, appeared under the
pavement. The eastern enclosing wall was an extension of the east flank
of the passage of the northeast entrance. In this area the excavators were
greatly confused, not only because of all the damage caused by agriculture,
but also by the rubble retaining walls for the cultivated terraces on the

slope of the hill, which ran across those of the Minoan remains in quite different lines. The situation was aggravated by the fact that a large quantity of blocks had been removed from the ancient building.

Certain rooms could be entered through a door, now mostly destroyed, at the east wall of the court. Only one of these rooms, and that only partially preserved, has been excavated. A drain, apparently starting at the northeastern corner of the court, ran under the concrete floor of this room. The fragments of stone lamps with two wicks, of stone grinders, and of clay pots that were found here did not help to identify the purpose of this space. One of the finds was a clay kernos of curious form with a religious use. It consisted of a three-legged caldron of which the feet were attached to three small, interlinked wheels in a triangular vertical arrangement. Little birds sat on the wheels. Unfortunately, the vessel was fragmentary and badly worn. Directly east of the room there were many potsherds forming rubbish heaps analogous with others found elsewhere outside main rooms. In this particular case, perhaps these shards had been dumped from a higher area north and east of the gate. This area was limited on the north side by an enclosing wall bordering the road. It was undoubtedly unroofed and contained several small structures serving various domestic needs. A hearth of stone slabs, found with pots on it and probably used on the very day of the catastrophe, appeared at the southwest corner. Farther north there was a deposit space roughly made of small flat stones, set against the eastern wall of the gateway. It contained a great many small ordinary housewares, especially handleless conical cups, dishes, and small jugs. SEE PAGE 91

Other structures appeared in the eastern section of the enclosure. An irregular, trapezoidal enclosure having its entrance on the eastern side was probably used as a workshop. Next to it was a smaller, square structure which may have been a water closet. The interior of the latter, accessible by two steps, was separated by poros slabs from a slab-paved underground pit. Its identification as a water closet is fairly certain since a drain has recently been found.

Behind these structures is a recently discovered unroofed space which evidently was a lapidary's workshop. Its purpose is indicated by a large quantity of small prismatic pieces of steatite and bits of lapis lazuli and some bronze tools. In an earlier phase of the palace this area had a different arrangement. It had a bench built against one of the walls and was closed on the western side by a partition running perpendicular to the road. Its slab-paved floor was at a lower level than the later one. Perhaps certain movable offering tables made of painted plaster, found in several fragments in the lower stratum, are indicative of the function of this space, but nothing more can be ascertained at present.

21 All available evidence indicates that among the citizens of ancient civilizations were cooks whose range of culinary production was limited only by technology and the availability of foodstuffs. The kitchens of Zakros hint at sophisticated menus.

The Kitchen Quarters

Next to the main entrance from the Central Court to the West Wing SEE PAGES 80-81 another entrance led into a corridor, which was certainly used primarily as a service entrance. Those wishing to reach working areas would not have gone through the main entrance but instead would have followed this corridor either to reach the storerooms of the West Wing or, through a door on the north with steps leading to it, a very wide apartment which apparently functioned as the kitchen. From the same corridor and through an opening which was walled in during the last phase, one could reach a small storeroom under the wooden staircase of the main entrance. Many clay pots were stored there, as well as two large disk-shaped lids, each with four tongue-like pierced projections by means of which they were attached to the mouths of the pithoi; a grid on small feet, with a cooking rack of fishbone pattern; a lamp with a curving handle; cooking pots and numerous domestic wares, such as pitchers and various types of cups and dishes. The walls of the staircase, of which the north one formed the south wall of the service corridor, were made of mud bricks with a stone base. A corresponding corridor upstairs was decorated with attractive frescoes consisting of large multipetaled rosettes of varying sizes in four colors, perhaps arranged in spirals. Similar stucco fragments with rosettes which were collected in the small paved northwest courtyard had probably been dumped there during some renovation of the painted decoration of the palace.

The "kitchen" to the north of the corridor was one of the largest rooms of the palace, c. 9 by 12 meters, only slightly smaller than the Hall of Ceremonies. Its roof was apparently supported by six wooden shafts in the form of pillars set on large irregular stones. The casual construction, the presence of accessory space on either side of the room, and the types of objects found clearly indicate the room's practical purpose. Three steps against the west wall could not have led upstairs, for there is no space for a landing. Nor is there any support provided for a staircase running along the wall. The most likely explanation is that these steps led into a wall closet, a hypothesis which is further supported by the great thickness of the wall at this spot. A stuccoed ledge along the east section of the south wall must have been the supporting base of a sizable cupboard, as its height precludes its having been a bench. A door with partially pre-served wooden jambs originally communicated directly with the West Wing storerooms but was later blocked.

The hypothesis that this spacious room was a kitchen was first sug-gested by the discovery of great quantities of bones of small and bigger animals, indicating the preparation of meat dishes. These were found at several spots, but especially in the northwest corner. Another accumula-tion of bones of small animals and birds was found in a kind of small enclosure formed within a sort of screen wall close to the west wall of the room and blocked on both sides. Finally, on a hearth in the northeast corner, where there was a passage ascending to the northern apartments on the hill terraces, there was a large three-legged pot, apparently used for cooking.

The kitchen identification gained support when the neighboring subsidiary rooms to the east, reached through an entrance with two steps, were found full of cooking utensils, placed along the walls. Some of the vessels at the west side of the inner room had been crushed by a mass of large mud bricks from a wall which collapsed into the room. One could distinguish clearly the successive lines of large bricks which had fallen in a slanting position and been baked by the fire which reduced the kitchen area to ashes. This is one of the best-preserved examples of mud-brick masonry in the palace. In the area of the service rooms the entire con-struction was of mud bricks placed above a stone base. Consequently the

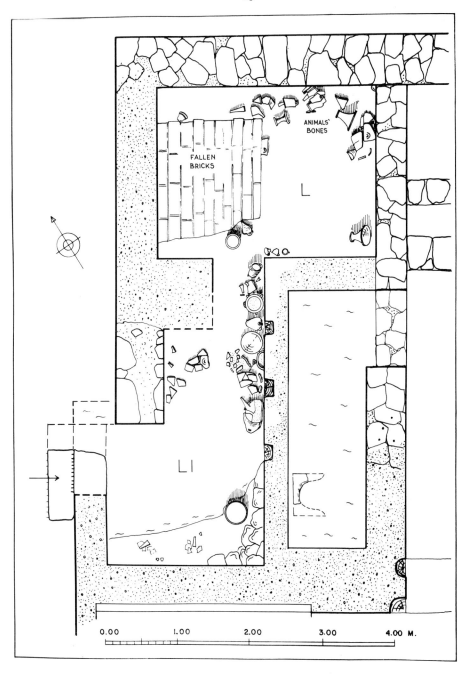

FALLEN
BRICKS

ANIMALS'
BONES

L

L I

| 0.00 | 1.00 | 2.00 | 3.00 | 4.00 M. |

Plan of the service rooms of the Kitchen,
showing equipment and the crumbled mud-brick wall

Service room of the Kitchen, into which an entire mud-brick wall had fallen

whole complex of rooms was designated as the "mud-brick rooms." The bricks were c. 0.6 by 0.4 meter each. The domestic ware kept here consisted of amphoras with elliptical mouths, low wide-mouthed jars, braziers with a high stand and an interior cruciform partition, tripod hearths, grills, bowls, and cups with one or two handles. With these was lying a three-legged mortar made of trachyte with a semicircular hollow for rubbing or grinding various substances. Numerous animal bones found with the pottery, probably from animal meat stored there or about to be used in preparing food in great quantities, formed a thick layer.

In the northwest corner of the first subsidiary room a kind of hearth was installed in a niche with a ledge, probably as a support for a cupboard, against its south wall. From this ledge a whole collection of miniature vessels, tiny versions of large ones, had apparently fallen. These might have contained spices for the food. A three-legged pot, also used on the day of the destruction, was found on the hearth. Other kitchen utensils and domestic pottery lay at several spots in the large room. Large pots and

Service room of the Kitchen, with culinary vessels as found

small pithoi were stored in the fairly large room to the west of the kitchen. The fragments of some pithoi lay along the north wall.

It is quite possible that this spacious room also served as an informal dining room. Large wooden tables could have been placed between the three pairs of supports for the use of palace servants and minor personnel. Two double-nozzled lamps made of stone and one single-nozzled clay lamp were probably used to provide light for dinners at night, and for additional light during the day, since the window placed high on the south wall facing the Central Court would not have let in sufficient daylight, especially on cloudy days. Even today, large dining rooms in Orthodox cenobitic monasteries are not well illuminated.

The large columnar hall above the Kitchen must have been the dining room for the royal family and guests. Professor J. Walter Graham, who studied the architecture of Minoan palaces and in particular that of banquet halls, concluded that such halls were usually located in an upper story, had sizable dimensions, were provided with a series of columns, and were connected by stairways with subsidiary rooms downstairs where food was prepared. This section of the Palace of Zakros, which he cites as an example, conforms closely to the pattern he describes.

The well of the ascending staircase was found directly east of the first subsidiary room. It could be entered from the slab-paved portico at the north side of the Central Court. The bench of the portico, where people could sit and rest, had its back against the mud-brick south wall of the subsidiary room, and next to it, to the right, the door, with a carefully laid threshold, opened into the staircase. The sign of the double axe was incised on one of the dressed blocks of the entrance. Further evidence for the existence of this staircase was the fact that the bedrock rose gradually within the stairwell; the fact that it was wooden was inferred from the carbonized remains. Typically, the staircase consisted of two flights with an intermediate landing. Horns of consecration had fallen into the west compartment of the stairwell. Perhaps these had been dumped there later, along with stones used to level the ground above the bedrock. Two adjacent communicating rooms farther east were used for storage. Behind and a little to the north of the first flight of stairs a kind of closet was constructed. Some pumice was stored in the front room which probably communicated with the portico.

Starting at the east end of the portico, a long passage in the form of a ramp with sloping level steps led up to the apartments built on the slope of the northern hill. Bedrock appears here also, ascending within the passage toward the north, a clear indication that it was not a corridor on the ground floor. A door on the right at the beginning of the passage led into two communicating rooms already described in connection with the royal apartments in the East Wing. Apparently during the last phase of the palace changes were made, for this door was blocked and a partition wall built in front of it blocking the passage, where a hearth on a dais was located. The hearth consisted of upright slabs with a diagonally set opening for feeding the fire. A great quantity of ashes was found inside it. Next to it and in front of the partition was a ledge on which vessels could be placed.

It is not clear whether the hearth was used for practical or for religious purposes, but the fact that the ramp passage was later transformed into a storeroom for small domestic pottery seems to support the first view. At least three hundred pots filled the entire long, narrow space. They consisted of various cups, dishes, three-legged cooking vessels, braziers on tall and low stands, lids, jugs, pitchers, and amphoras. Perhaps they were used in the adjacent kitchen and at the hearth. On the other hand, the theory of a religious function for the hearth could be supported by the fragments of small transportable offering tables, both rectangular and round, with polished surfaces and vividly colorful decoration, which were found lying nearby.

22 Most ancient rulers had as a part of their retinue a corps of craftsmen whose products either found their way into the palaces or were sent as gifts to foreign princes. Or, as indeed is very probable in the Minoan case, the objects were sold, thus providing a dependable source of income. Craftsmen were regarded with much pride and shared their ruler's quarters. The clamor of manufacturing was apparently a typical sound in the palace environs.

The Workshops of the South Wing

A complex of rooms at the south side of the Central Court, delimited to the west and south by passages, has been designated the South Wing of the palace. Excavation showed that this wing was mainly used for technological processes, with a few areas reserved for storage. The façade on the court, built in ashlar masonry, was in harmony with the other interior façades of the Central Court. At the center of the façade a door with a threshold of hard limestone about 2 meters long led into a small vestibule, from which the other rooms could be reached either directly or by way of a narrow corridor. To the right of the door there was a wooden staircase leading up. It was not difficult to trace the foundations of this staircase. A small passage under a second flight of stairs led from an exterior door in the façade of the western passage to the main entrance hall. This corridor had been decorated with wall paintings which depicted delicate plants. The upper part of the composition is lost, for the corridor was preserved only up to a meter above floor level. The fragments of paintings were removed and taken to the Heraklion Museum for cleaning and restoration.

Under the first flight of stairs there was a small storage space entered from the west end of the corridor. Next to the lobby was a spacious room

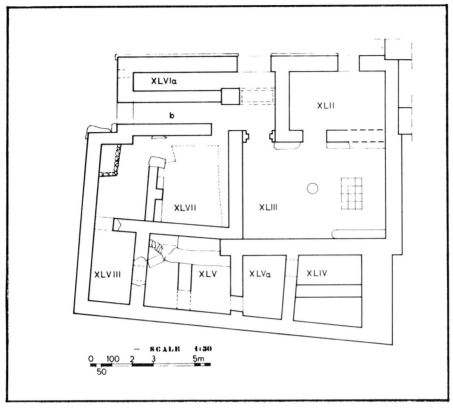

Plan of the workshop unit in the South Wing

XLII *Storeroom*   XLIII *Sitting room*   XLVI *Staircase*   XLVII *Workshop*
XLIV, XLV, XLVa, XLVIII *Cellars, workshops*

with a concrete pavement decorated with a carpet-like square of tile laid on either side of the column supporting the ceiling. Plastered benches appeared along the north wall and in the southeast corner. A small bronze tripod rested on top of the one in the corner. Several pieces of sheet metal, some from double axes, fallen from the upper floor, suggest that the room upstairs was used for bronze working. The ground-floor room might have been used as a sitting room for the craftsmen. Some blocks of porphyry may have been raw materials. The room directly to the north had been used for storing large vessels, mostly pail-like or hole-mouthed pots, of which about twenty were found. Some flat lids with semicircular handles were also preserved. A large animal jaw found in one of the pots

211

Incense burner, from the workshop unit in the South Wing

suggests that food also was kept in these. A bronze caldron with three legs must have been used for cooking. Many other clay kitchen utensils were found here, including large plates, basins, braziers, strainers, cooking pots, and pot lids with a perforated hemispherical partition.

Another storeroom, divided in two by an interior partition, was accessible from the same small corridor. A great quantity of pots were found in its western part, mostly along the partition wall but also on the bench of the southern wall and in a deposit space at the northwest corner where there were a large number of cups and other ordinary wares. The pottery here consisted chiefly of large, wide-mouthed, pail-shaped vessels of the same type as those of the northern room. Small jars had two or four handles on the shoulders and a decoration simulating ropes, which were rendered by strips of applied clay with impressed finger marks. A relief pattern of crosses, one shaped like a swastika, appeared on the shoulders of one of the jars. A pot of the pithamphora type had painted decoration. Most of the other pots were either for cooking or for special technological processes. There was a whole group of braziers with perforated stands and openings for putting in coals, incense burners with a slablike handle and a curving one to protect the hand from being burned, other similar ones on high stands with an interior cross-shaped diaphragm similar to that in the vessels found in great numbers in the deposit spaces and storerooms of the West Wing. With these were also some unusual objects which, for lack of a better identification, are described as lids for cooking pots. These have fluted edges and a central hemispherical partition, with another partition below pierced by many small holes and a large hole at the center for the insertion of coals, as in similar vessels found elsewhere. No pots were found with which these so-called lids could have been combined. A suggestion that these utensils were used independently for extracting essences from aromatic herbs led to the hypothesis of a workshop here for the production of perfume from local plants. This would not be unlikely, for both in the Mycenaean palace at Pylos and in the annexes of the palace at Mycenae there was evidence for such a royal industry. Written tablets from these two sites and from elsewhere refer to the availability and the processing of such aromatic substances as mint, coriander, fennel, celery, cumin, cress, laurel, and myrtle. Some other vessels of an odd shape found in the same storeroom might also have been used in this process, along with the braziers and strainers. Spherical pots with a perforated partition separating the pot from its conical stand and cylindrical ones with similar partitions were found both in this storeroom and in other rooms nearby.

If there was a perfume laboratory it would have been installed in the wider eastern part of the room. Two extremely large three-legged kettles were found at the base of the southern wall, with a few small vessels next to them. Most of the other pottery was on another narrow ledge along the east wall. Several small pipkins and numerous small, conical, handleless cups were found upside down, chiefly in the north section. Three-legged pots of various sizes, normally used for cooking, could also have been used for extracting aromatic substances from herbs. Certain other pots, mostly of a fine texture and with diverse decoration, fell from a room upstairs. Some of these, now repaired and restored, seem to bear affinities in shape and decoration with Mycenaean pottery from the main-

Vessel with interior strainer, from the workshop unit of the South Wing

land. Some fragments of a very large basin and of a terracotta grill with a grate having fishbone-shaped openings were found along with these pots, while other similar fragments were scattered in the passage to the west of the complex.

From the storeroom of the workshop one entered a room at the corner of the complex. Judging from a kind of cupboard made of slabs which had collapsed into the basement, and from a rectangular stone basin, this room may have been a subsidiary work space. Its communication with the three consecutive rooms occupying the entire southern side of the complex is not clear. Unfortunately, all the floors had been utterly destroyed except for strips of red stucco along the edges. All these rooms had basements, probably entered through trapdoors. Housewares found here, partly fallen from above at the time of the destruction, partly resting on the floors,

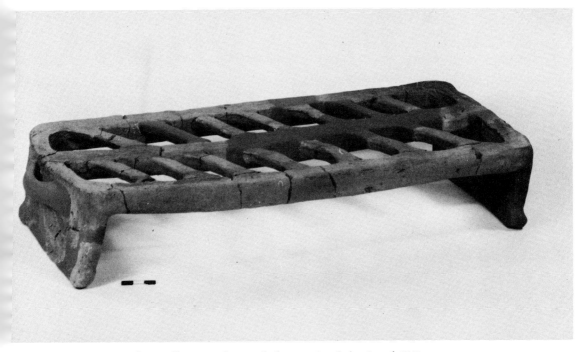

Clay grill, from the workshop unit of the South Wing

show that the area was used until the very last phase of the Palace. The basement rooms communicated by means of openings which were ultimately blocked in order to prevent the walls from collapsing. Earlier walls appear to have been reused in these basements as partitions to separate the spaces. Early walls were also traced under the "perfume workshop," but there were no basement rooms.

On the ground floor were various workshops: one for the manufacture of objects in crystal, ivory, and faïence; another perhaps for the production of bronze vessels; still another for an unidentified process in which grinding stones and grinders were used. Probably there was a lapidary workshop here. A door giving access to the compartments from the southern passage had been blocked up during the last phase of the Palace. The room at the left had a bench at the north side, built like other wall benches at Knossos and Phaistos, which had partly subsided because of the presence of the basement below. Some clay vessels were resting on a low ledge close by; an opening underneath indicated the probable existence of a hearth. The large curved grinding stones and grinders found at the northeast corner suggest some kind of manufacturing; a partially preserved large pithos in the southwest corner may have contained raw materials.

Some elegant vessels in various shapes, carved from various kinds of stone, had fallen into the basement. These were a small spherical vase of spotted white-and-black stone with a horizontal fluted decoration, a wide cup of brownish-red stone, a tall funnel-shaped goblet of gray marble, a cylindrical pyxis with two rings in relief, a nest-shaped vase of dark-green stone, and a bridge-spouted vase with hollow protuberances used as handles. Perhaps these beautiful vases had just come from the workshop, but this is doubtful, since this area contained no evidence of tools or raw materials which could be connected with their manufacture. Clay vessels were quite numerous also. Important among these for dating purposes are certain slender, tall amphoras with a narrow high neck and a molded foot with a protruding ring. Similar amphoras were found in the room at the east corner of the same complex. Important for chronological correlation with mainland Greece was an interesting Helladic vase of characteristic form decorated with a foil pattern filled with network resembling that of a tennis racket. Some small pieces of ivory may belong to inlay decoration from a pyxis.

The next room, originally immediately accessible from the south passage, was much smaller. It contained a large stone mortar at the southeast corner and fragments of large stone vases, in addition to a number of clay pots. Its most significant contents, however, were several bronze vessels, sheets of bronze, and parts of vessels, such as legs and handles of caldrons. Evidently this was a workshop, either for repairing metal objects or for their manufacture. There was an interesting brazier, with the part that contained the coals brilliantly decorated with a continuous band of ivy leaves and the wooden handle held by a bulbous bronze tube firmly fixed to the vessel. The only known comparable brazier, of pleasing form but not so exquisite in decoration, was found in the royal tholos tomb at Vaphio in the Peloponnese, where the two famous golden cups with scenes of the capture of bulls were found; these cups are undoubtedly of Cretan origin and of the same date as the treasures of Zakros. In the work-

*Drawing of a decorated bronze incense burner
found in the workshop unit in the South Wing*

shop were also a small bronze jug with a fine handle, a larger one with a strap handle and a ring around the base of the neck, a shallow caldron with three legs, the legs of another caldron, and the handle of a ladle. A nearby room contained many sheets of bronze fallen from the upper story, adding to the evidence for a metal-working shop in this area.

The room at the southwest corner, however, held chiefly samples of fine artifacts, in such decorative substances as ivory, rock crystal, and faïence. These, and the cores of raw material also found, clearly show that this room was a workshop. Most impressive was a very large core of rock crystal, from which a whole vessel could be carved. Other smaller crystal cores were suitable for the preparation of small ornamental objects of the kind actually found in the room—spherical heads for long pins and

Core of rock crystal, found in the workshop unit of the South Wing

mushroom-shaped heads, perhaps for ornamental hairpins. Other objects were carved of steatite. Small strips, bands, plaques, and disks, partly decorated, must have been intended for inlay decoration of caskets and furniture. There were also artifacts of faïence and paste, but there is some doubt that the room was also used as a workshop for those materials, since pieces of melted glass found there could have resulted from the fire that enveloped this area. However, certain objects in faïence, of a flattened conical shape resembling the skirts of the Snake Goddess of Knossos, suggest that manufacture was carried on here. The discovery of a small fragment of a faïence hand, in which the fingers could be distinguished, points to the same interpretation. Unfortunately, because of the dampness caused by underground water, these objects were in very poor condition.

A quantity of stone vases, some unfinished, points to the possibility that stone carving may also have been done in this workshop. The most

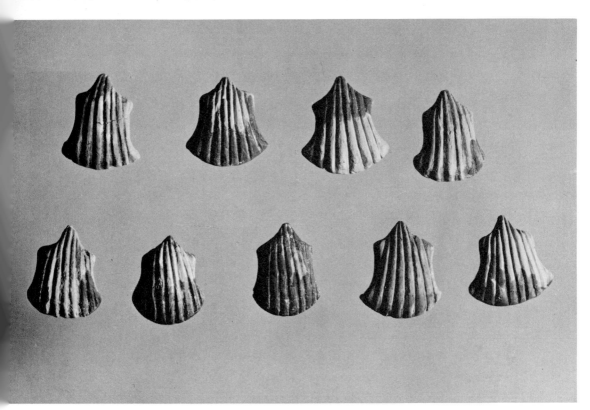

Small faïence shells, from the workshop of the Shrine

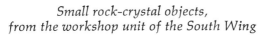

Small rock-crystal objects,
from the workshop unit of the South Wing

noteworthy products were an elegant small triton of chlorite, a cylindrical box with a lid of blackish stone with red veins and decorative rings in relief on the rim and base; bird-nest vases in dark stone, a beautiful two-wicked lamp of porphyry with an ornamental wreath of carved leaves, a kernos consisting of three interlinked pots, and part of a cup of lustrous black stone with a handle similar to those of the golden cups of Vaphio. In some of these drill marks are still visible. Perhaps the graceful stone vases of the adjacent workshop might have been finished here first and transferred there for storage. Other objects found in this room included a three-legged bronze caldron, bronze tools, probably used in the workshop, and an abundance of clay pots, also presumably used in the manufacturing processes, such as a brazier with a central depression, pots with strainers inside, a tripod-shaped pot with three legs, vessels with a long bridged spout, and tall, slender amphoras with long necks and rounded bodies. A whole group of small oblong stone weights and other discoid and biconvex terracotta weights must have come from a loom upstairs.

How far the South Wing extended beyond the manufacturing complex and the passages coming from the west and south sides cannot yet be determined. Further excavation is needed to clarify the situation.

Chlorite triton, from the workshop unit of the South Wing

Vessel found in the workshop unit of the South Wing;
it is provided with an interior strainer

Another view of the chlorite triton shown on page 220

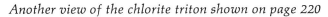

23   The relationship of sewage to disease does not appear to have been unknown in ancient times, for evidence is accumulating that an awareness of that correlation was in part the motivation for the construction of drainage systems.

The Drainage System

Excavation at Minoan sites has demonstrated the high degree of technical perfection achieved in drainage systems in houses and palaces. Evans has described extensively the systems used in the Palace of Knossos. He distinguishes two types, a converging one and a peripheral one in which the water channel passes through a series of interior unroofed areas and terminates at a larger drain that carries the water to the river banks outside the palace proper.

The drainage system in the Palace of Zakros has been traced, except SEE PAGES 80-81 for sections which are covered by the floors of rooms; to study those without destroying the floors would be very difficult. In the East Wing, the system could be followed to a great extent because most pavements had been destroyed. In the West Wing three branches of a drain, consisting of short and narrow U-shaped clay conduits, were traced. One of these ran through the west side of the industrial unit in a north-to-south direction. Another passed under the deposit spaces of the rooms of the shrine containing the pithamphoras, under the shrine itself, and under its Treasury. It was perhaps a branch of this drain which emptied near the septic pit outside the room with the deposits. The third branch ran under the concrete floor of the square lobby in the area of the shrine. There was also a broader built drain running under the floor of the Banquet Hall with an outlet in the enclosed unroofed area to the south. The lightwell of the Hall of Ceremonies was drained by an open stone channel running along the north wall.

In the industrial unit of the South Wing two drains, one lined with stone, the other of stone cut in the shape of a trough, carried water toward the eastern and southern approaches. Since there were no unroofed interior spaces here, the water must have been used in the workshops for manufacturing purposes.

In the area of the well a built drain carried water into the open area to the east. As mentioned earlier, all water closets were provided with drains which emptied into septic pits outside the walls. This indicates that water was specially provided for keeping the water closets clean and for washing by the people using them.

Another built drain ran under the floor of the lightwell of the main

The East Wing, showing the circular cistern
and the Well of the Fountain

royal apartment of the East Wing and had an outlet in the southern open area just outside the corridor leading into the Central Court. The rain water falling into the lightwell of the smaller royal apartment was channeled into the interior court directly north of the Hall of the Cistern. In SEE PAGE 223 this same court, where most of the slab pavement had been destroyed, the most characteristic example of a complete drainage system of the converging type was revealed. One branch started at the north but its collecting basin was some 4.5 meters from the north wall of the court and almost 3 meters from the west wall. This joined another branch which ran along the north wall of the Hall of the Cistern and emptied into the unroofed enclosed area to the east. Two other branches join at a common drain which, at the end of the first branch, joins the first drain which runs along the north wall of the hall. These branches started from two points, one directly outside of the room which projected into the courtyard, the other close to the east wall of the queen's living room. It is obvious that the water collected at these two points through vertical conduits from the roofs of the upper stories of this wing. A much deeper branch passing under one of the other drains in a west-to-east direction most probably belongs to the earlier phase of the Palace. A rectangular structure paved with concrete, found next to the last drain and under the court pavement, goes back to the same date. Pottery both in the structure and the drain indicates that these went out of use at the beginning of the last phase.

The drains of this section were well constructed of dressed stone and while the initial branches were narrow and shallow, the terminal ones were of larger proportions in order to drain larger masses of water brought from various directions. These larger channels were also built of closely fitted poros stones. The drains were covered over by slabs, some of which were quite large, especially at the points where they covered more than one branch.

Another, perhaps independent channel, drained the apartments east of the court. Still another drain, running perpendicularly to the area where the harbor road terminated, carried water through a small opening down to the level of the pavement of the same interior court. The road was bordered by a ditch where another branch of drain descending from the upper terraces might have emptied. This drain, in its upper course, was covered with slabs and passed between the extensive annex of the palace and the building east of it. Still another drain, starting from an inner room of the latter building, joined with the channel just described.

Two more drains have already been mentioned, one bordering the north side of the small northwest court and descending between two units of the quarters on the northwest slope, the other conducting drainage water from the roofs of the West Wing into the West Court as it passed under the central terrace section of the latter. The first drain apparently served the buildings on the upper terraces of the hill during the last phase of the palace, for a section of it was discovered at a relatively high level in the rooms of the northwest sector, running over the layer of shards which had been used for leveling the floors of the adjoining rooms to the south.

The drains described here undoubtedly constitute only a small part of the complex network which extended in all directions under the floors of rooms, courts, and unroofed spaces. Drainage toward the sea must have been easy, since the ground slopes downward. Despite all the measures taken, it is questionable whether the system could have disposed of all the surplus water during heavy rainfalls. The precautions against overflow in the water installations of the circular cistern, the Spring Chamber, and the built well have already been described. Perhaps analogous measures were taken against possible floods in the interior of the palace. The technical skill shown at this early date in all kinds of hydraulic engineering, drainage, and hygienic installations is amazing, especially when one considers the neglect of such hygienic measures in relatively recent times —for example, at the palaces of the French kings at Versailles.

24   Rulership needs more than just a ruler, for that institution's well-being depends on those loyal to it. Near the palace were other smaller but elaborate buildings. Were these for the ruler's family, for his nobles?

Palace Annexes on the North Slope

From the first it was evident that the palace stretched north to the hill slope, since some passages starting at lower rooms and courts led in that direction. Moreover, it was considered extremely doubtful that there would have been private buildings on the slope and top of the hill, over-looking and dominating the palace. Further excavation proved that the buildings there were annexes, serving purposes related to the organized life of the palace. Naturally the discovery of these annexes presented new problems requiring interpretation. The principal one was to clarify the plan of this section during the last phase of the palace, for most of the remains belonged to earlier periods. The different orientation of some of the complexes indicated that blocks of buildings older than the palace had been incorporated into the palace annexes with quite new plans. Very careful study of the stratigraphy has helped to clarify the whole evolution, which was several times interrupted by geological destructions.

SEE PAGES 80-81 One of the principal annexes extended north of the small north-western paved court, whose level at the last palace phase was raised by placing a trodden-clay layer over the original pavement. A drain was constructed to descend between two annexes through the northeast corner and along the north retaining wall under the floor of the court. One could easily distinguish the two constructional phases of this quarter: the retaining wall was rebuilt, and farther toward the west two walls, carefully constructed of ashlar masonry, met at right angles, closing the passage that had formed the entrance to the annex, now filled in. Evidently in the last phase only the upper part of this building was used, after terracing, but it is possible that the new terraces were transformed to terrace gardens, as was done in the Palace of Knossos. The filling of the basement rooms preserved intact important material of the first palace phase (1600–1500 B.C.), a circumstance rarely found at the other Minoan palaces.

A narrow staircase of ten fairly well preserved steps, flanked by balustrades, led up into a medium-sized slab-paved room with a central column, and farther to the west to other terraced spaces not very well preserved. On either side of the staircase unroofed enclosed areas were formed, each having at the rear a high podium or broad ledge, on which flower pots may have stood. The back wall of the platforms was lined with slabs. Much pottery was found in the fill of these areas or lying on the pavement. The rest of the complex consisted chiefly of basements used for storerooms or workshops, as the utensils and tools found indicated. A wooden staircase led down to the principal one of these. The floor of the foremost rooms was formed by leveling a fill of shards and broken clay and stone vases, most valuable for the study of the furniture of the first palace period.

This building abutted on the north side against a massive wall terracing a higher level in this direction, where there extended another complex, named from its orientation the Oblique Building. As the pottery found in the lower layers showed, this building, at least in its main lines, was already in existence at the Proto-palatial period (1900–1700 B.C.). It was evidently incorporated in the new construction and reused after a rather radical transformation. Part of it was discovered and investigated by Hogarth in 1901, but he did not suspect that he was within the limits of the palace area and interpreted the building as two adjoining houses, which he designated D and E. The whole of this complex was excavated SEE PAGE 26 during 1968 and 1969, and the principal problems were solved. That it did form a palace annex is clear; this explains its sturdy and careful construction in a technique quite similar to that of the palace itself, with which it communicated by a main road artery and a secondary branch.

The Oblique Building may be considered as having been divided into two parts, a western and an eastern one. The rooms of the ground floor, most of them simple basement rooms approachable only through trapdoors from the first floor, were in use only in the earlier phase and were later filled in. The upper floor was then reconstructed and used as the ground floor, having an entrance directly from the west-east branch of the road. The larger rooms of the original ground floor were at the foremost part. One had a concrete floor under which a small collecting jar was built, probably for use in connection with a wine press, pots of which were discovered by Hogarth. A second room had a central pillar supporting the floor of the upper story. Between these rooms an angled staircase, found by Hogarth but since destroyed, led to the upper story, and behind it a small storeroom was found with seven jars along its walls. Two narrow passages with wooden staircases led from this room to apartments in the upper story, but the main entrance was from a lobby some steps higher with a long staircase descending to it, the upper steps of which were renewed with poros stone.

The floors of the upper story, reconstructed in the last palatial period, were destroyed, except those of a central lobby giving a direct approach from the road. The threshold of ironstone was very well preserved, and one can distinguish the same type of paneling with stucco interstices that was found in the official rooms of the main palace. Presumably great halls extended on both sides, built over the filled-in basement rooms. The broad and sturdy threshold of the eastern room was near the long staircase, which probably descended to the terraced gardens. It would be difficult to define the exact use of such a building; perhaps it was the dwelling of some high official.

Beyond the branch of the road, on a higher terrace, was a complex unfortunately poorly preserved and not yet completely explored. The discovery of ritual utensils and two repositories built at the foot of the rock seems to indicate the existence of an unroofed sanctuary, which was first used in the Proto-palatial period, as the pottery of polychrome Kamares style showed. On the top of the hillock two other complexes were partly explored by Hogarth, who called them houses G and H. The last one is intersected by another complex, which is in process of being explored. An extensive quadrangular room, with a central column supporting the roof, and two small flights of stairs, one ascending from a lobby, the other

SEE PAGE 27

connecting with building H, seems to have been a workshop, judging from the utensils found and the existence of some manufacturing installations. In the corner of the lobby a big jar was lying upside down. A series of deposits, oblong or quadrangular, full of pots for culinary use, were found near the large room. Two bronze knives were lying in the same area. A series of other rooms was connected with the area of the south façade; this façade was strongly built in cyclopean masonry. It seems probable that a sort of bastion supported a veranda giving a view of the whole palace area.

At the other side of a paved lane ascending the hill, another palace annex was found. This, because of the sturdy construction of its exterior walls, was named the Strong Building. It consisted of at least fifteen rooms, with two or three corridors connecting them. Three main entrances at the east façade gave access from different terraced levels. The middle one was approached by an ascending ramp, which was transformed to a narrow

The northwest sector,
showing rooms belonging to the first phase of the palace

exterior staircase at the last palace period, during which the building seems to have remained in use. The spacious main room was quadrangular in form, with a column in the center supporting the roof. Its cemented floor was laid on a filling of shards, a fact which has helped in dating the reconstruction to the years around 1500 B.C. Separated from the main room by a corridor were two small rooms with collecting jars built under the cement floor. Four small storerooms in the immediate vicinity were quite full of jars and various pots, most of them of culinary use, and all in their original positions although smashed by material from an upper story. The existence of such a story was attested by the presence of small, nicely decorated vases which had fallen from it. Some stone vases were also found dispersed in the ground floor, among them a unique piece imitating on a minor scale a multihandled jar encircled by cords forming zones; twelve handles distributed in four tiers are rendered by tongue-shaped projections.

South of the quadrangular room on a lower level was another system of storerooms, containing a great quantity of pottery arranged systematically according to types. Handsome decorated vases of the Floral style were found, as well as large three-legged cooking pots, stored along the bucket-like pots, amphoras, and pitchers. At a corner of the lower lobby was an angled bench.

To the east of the Strong Building, separated from it by an ascending lane branching from the main road leading to the harbor, extended another complex, named the North Annex, whose well-constructed south façade followed the line of the main road, leaving a broad space in front of the northwest entrance of the palace. This annex is not yet completely excavated, and the system of walls already brought to light forms an inextricable complex, owing to the fact that they belong to different successive buildings, dating from the Proto-palatial to the last palace period. At the last phase a strong terracing wall supported the fill of the higher terrace to the north. The leveling of the rooms at its base with a fill of shards and broken vases of the first palace phase provides the possibility of studying the furniture of the complex at that time. But what proved extremely important from the scientific point of view was the discovery, at the lower layer, of rooms of earlier buildings of the Proto-palatial period

(1900–1700 B.C.), with their contents of large jars and various pots intact —the first such discovery in the region of Kato Zakros.

Finally, another complex was brought to light immediately to the north of the Kitchen and auxiliary rooms of the main palace; the connection by two ascending ramps or wooden staircases demonstrates the relationship to the palace proper. In this annex the same three successive periods were recognized: the first belonging to the period preceding the construction of the palace; the next two to the two palace phases. Polychrome pottery of the Kamares style was discovered at the lower layers. Presumably part of the earlier buildings was cut away to allow for the construction of the Kitchen. The strong terracing wall was renovated at its upper part with poros blocks taken from the destroyed section. Some of these have masons' marks, principally the double axe. At the same period a well-constructed angled staircase connected the more spacious room to some small, newly built apartments to the north. Between the strong, obliquely laid western exterior wall and the northwest annex, the new drain already mentioned descended to the small paved court. In this sector some workshops can be recognized by their installations and furniture.

Further exploration may determine more precisely the nature of the annexes on the north slope. Their size and careful construction, their dominating position, and their immediate proximity to the palace strongly suggest that they belonged to it, in the same way that the Armory and the Royal Villa belong to the Palace of Knossos. Annexes of similar character existed at the northeast section at Phaistos; the northwest building at Mallia with its basement crypts and large slab-paved courtyard is also regarded as a palace annex. The high quality of the furnishings discovered at different points of the buildings on the Zakros north slope is consistent with their character as palace annexes. Consequently, it is not impossible that further exploration will bring to light deposits of archives and sealings. Such significant materials were discovered in the A–B complex excavated by Hogarth on the same north slope, somewhat isolated toward the northwest.

SEE PAGE 26

Mycenaean centers contain comparable annexes around palaces, but all scholars do not agree on their palatial character. On the eastern section of the acropolis at Mycenae, for instance, there are the so-called House of the Artists and the Metal Workshop which is combined with a shrine. Lately, the House of the Columns at the same site was recognized by Professor George Mylonas as a part of the palace itself. At Thebes some annexes were discovered not far from the Palace of Cadmus—the Armory, where many bronze weapons and archive tablets were found, and the Ivory Workshop, which contained a rich collection of carved ivory works.

Other architectural remains of dressed poros stone south and east of the Palace of Zakros may also belong to annexes or may ultimately prove to be part of the palace itself. If the latter is the case, that palace would be no smaller than those of Phaistos and Mallia. The evidence thus far, however, suggests that the Zakros palace was inferior in size and grandeur, though certainly not in refinement and elegance.

Palace and Town

Archaeological reporting is not limited to a catalogue of finds and their immediate meaning. In the end the question that archaeologists must strive to answer is: "What does it all mean?" It is the larger picture that is required. The excavator must give his own interpretation for oddly there is a feel to the past that only those who have recovered its remains can sense. It is a mystique, if you will, but whatever it is, the archaeologist is compelled to put that intangible into this reasoning interpretation.

233

25 A critical archaeological question is concerned with origins. In this case the evidence for an older settlement which might have provided the foundation for the later settlement is reviewed.

Older Minoan Remains

Since excavation in the region of Kato Zakros is still going on, any attempt to trace the development of the Minoan settlement and the palace is still premature. On the palace, very few stratigraphic studies have been made, and those specifically in areas where earlier remains came to light. Only the actual finds to date can therefore be discussed now.

There are no traces of Neolithic habitation around Kato Zakros. While two or three Neolithic axes were found in Minoan strata in the palace, these had probably been brought from elsewhere and kept in use because of the magic power they were believed to possess. However, Neolithic settlements existed farther away, chiefly on the plateau of the mountain range west of Zakros, at such sites at Karydi, Magasa, and Xerolimne.

The small natural caves of the Gorge of the Dead were used for burials from the beginning of the Pre-palatial period—that is, about 2600 B.C.—as is shown by datable pottery and funeral gifts, and from the existence of these burials a settlement on the bay of Zakros at that early date can be inferred. South of the bay, clefts by the sea were occasionally used for burials, as at the Black Ditch. Most of these burials date to the second and third phases of the Pre-palatial period—from 2400 to 1900 B.C. The beautiful stone pyxis with a dog carved on the lid, mentioned earlier, was found in a cave burial at the valley end of the Gorge; as was attractive pottery of two styles, one with incised decoration, the other mottled—the so-called Hagios Nikolaos and Vasiliki styles.

The earliest buildings discovered under the ruins of the palace, some

SEE PAGE 32

SEE PAGE 69

under the Kitchen and the corridor south of it, some under a room of the northwest sector, also date from 2400 to 1900 B.C. Some of the pottery found in these was an advanced stage of the Vasiliki style, utilizing spiral and other curvilinear patterns against a dark ground, and some a predecessor of the Kamares style, in which the beginning of polychromy is apparent. Buildings being uncovered in deep strata under the West Court and beyond the south approach to the palace may also belong to the same period.

Under part of the main shrine there are remains of a Proto-palatial building with a series of rooms. It does not seem to have been extensive, unless part of it was built on higher terraces and leveled off when the palace was constructed. Proto-palatial walls came to light also in the area of the Spring Chamber of the East Wing, directly south of the corridor leading to the Central Court. The date is again based on the pottery found, which is characteristic of the Proto-palatial period; part of it is in the polychrome Kamares style but differs from the corresponding style in central Crete in conservatively retaining many of the features of the preceding stage. In 1970 an extensive Proto-palatial building was revealed east of the inner court of the Northeast Entrance to the palace.

More Proto-palatial buildings were found where the palace extends onto terraces on the north hill. As has been mentioned, both the building first investigated by Hogarth and designated by him as Houses D and E and certain rooms above the Kitchen and its annexes were in use during the Proto-palatial period, as pottery in the deeper strata indicated. An extensive Proto-palatial building, also previously mentioned, was found, intact with its furnishings, under Neo-palatial remains of the northeast slope sector. A problem here is to determine whether these various structures were originally interconnected to form a continuous extensive building of which the parts built on the terraces were leveled off to make space for the palace. This does not seem altogether unlikely, since the retaining wall delimiting the main room of the kitchens in the North Wing cut through Proto-palatial remains. If there was such a building, the next question is whether it could be considered an earlier Palace of Zakros, comparable to the earlier palaces recognized under the later ones at Knossos, Phaistos, and Mallia.

Traces of the first phase of the Neo-palatial period (Evans's Middle

Minoan III A) are few and dubious. Only one house under the original floor of the West Court seems to belong to the time before the palace (or at least its final form) was constructed; its date, based on pottery found in the foundations of the west façade, was the beginning of the second phase of the Neo-palatial period—that is, around 1600 B.C., or, in Evans's chronology, the end of Middle Minoan III.

View toward the north sector, currently being excavated

237

26   The stages of growth in a building can sometimes be revealed by probing foundations. The various later plans owe their character to the place and form of the original structure.

Stages of the Palace's Construction

The palace during its first stages (1600 to 1500 b.c.) had basically the same form as in later times, but many details of the interior arrangements were different. Some sections had not been built; other areas then in use were later covered over with fill; some floors were at a lower level. The West Court sloped and was paved with slabs. The workshop unit which projected into this court had not yet been built. From the north section of the West Court a small staircase led to the apartments of the northwest sector, which were built in terraces. These rooms were covered over at the end of the first stage, perhaps to be replaced by gardens. The small northwest court was also slab-paved, and along its west side there was probably a road leading to the northwest sector and to the rooms of the northern terraces. The main complexes of storerooms, shrine compartments, and ceremonial halls had already been created, but the arrangement of the internal partitions subdividing them was probably different. Certain changes at the beginning of the next stage are clear: in the antechamber of the entrance at the side of the Central Court a new floor was laid and the base of the staircase partly covered. Two doors were blocked, one between two of the northern storerooms, another between the Kitchen and the storerooms. A door was created on one side of the columnar lightwell of the Hall of Ceremonies. In the Banquet Hall a door was blocked. Some floors were repaired. The ramp ascending from the north portico of the Central Court to the apartments of the higher terraces was transformed into a storeroom, and a hearth was built where the ramp had begun. This change necessitated the blocking of a door.

In the East Wing the royal quarters, the bathroom, and the Hall of the Cistern assumed their final form. The Spring Chamber was probably filled in, though without affecting the supply of water. A few alterations were also brought about in the entrance space of the Hall of the Cistern, since a tub of a type found elsewhere, resembling present-day tubs on a smaller scale, was discovered in a deep stratum at the northeast corner. Similarly, a large pithos lay upside down outside the fountain in a layer much lower than that of the floor of the entrance space. These discoveries indicate a change in the level of the floors, but the high level of the water that seeps up through the ground makes it difficult to investigate the earlier floors. The drainage system in the interior court of the East Wing was constructed at the beginning of the last stage, but an older system was detected lower down. A rectangular oblique structure paved with concrete which also appeared under the court floor was probably an extension of the large Proto-palatial building.

The construction of the northeast gate, a little to the west of the original entranceway, also dates from the beginning of the last stage. The extensive building north of the royal road, built at the beginning of the first stage, was apparently reused during the last palace period after some alterations of its interior arrangements.

The renovations of the South Wing appear to have been more radical, since the buildings found under the later floor were quite different in form. As has been mentioned, some of the earlier rooms along the south side were reused as basement storerooms. The approaches from the south were also rearranged, and new walls built over a layer of potsherds which had been used at the beginning of the last stage to even the level of the ground.

After the final destruction, the area of the palace was not reoccupied. Houses of the first phase of the Post-palatial period were found only in the town area on the south hill; these had been built on a much restricted scale over earlier remains.

27 Trade was vital to the Minoan economy and it was clearly far-reaching. Even the Egyptians who had a cultural anathema for things foreign found in Cretan manufactures much to covet—as indeed did the Cretans in Egyptian works.

Maritime Commerce

The establishment of a palace at Zakros and the transformation of the rather unimportant settlement into a palace center must have been motivated not so much by the need to utilize vital local resources as by a desire to create a well-organized harbor from which to control maritime trade and strengthen commercial relations with the East and Egypt. The initiative seems to have come from Knossos, judging from affinities already mentioned between the two palaces in architecture and in various crafts such as stone carving, metallurgy, ceramics, and the production of artifacts in ivory and faïence. Also, as has been mentioned, the Linear A script of Zakros is much closer typologically to the Linear B of Knossos than is the corresponding script of the region of Phaistos. It is possible, therefore, that Knossos established a harbor and a trading post at Zakros for its own benefit but permitted autonomous development under kings or princes who were probably of Knossian lineage.

Closer contact was thus established with Asiatic and Egyptian ports, since their ships did not have to circumnavigate the eastern end of Crete, a feat that is still risky, because of the promontory called Samonion in antiquity and now known as the Accursed Cape (Aphoresmenos) because of the shipwrecks that have occurred around it. In addition, the establishment of special palace workshops producing artifacts of exceptional quality made it easier to supply the Eastern markets where such products were in great demand.

There is ample evidence of trade with Egypt. The splendid jug with

The eastern Mediterranean area

SEE
PAGES
106
107

a decoration of painted nautiluses found there, and now in the Museum of Marseilles, was almost certainly made in the Palace of Zakros, probably by the same artist who produced an identical jug discovered in the store-rooms of the West Wing. Zakros must have been the point of departure of the Kefti embassies, shown in wall paintings in the tombs of high Egyptian magistrates of the reign of Queen Hatshepsut and Thutmose III, carrying gifts to the pharaohs. Many of the objects borne by these envoys are identical with examples found in the palace treasuries—namely, rhytons, molded vases, marvelous jugs, kraters, necklaces, bronze ingots, and so forth. The most representative scenes are those in the tombs of Senmut, User-Amon, Rekhmire, and Menkheperreseneb. In the first two tombs, the Kefti, who are now generally considered to have been Minoans, were clad in the typical Minoan loincloth. In the third tomb, which dates from the mid-fifteenth century B.C., this attire, including the codpiece, was subsequently painted over with the representation of a kilt which covered the hips and was folded over in front, terminating in a long, oblique point. This type of kilt was worn at Knossos primarily during its Mycenaean period (1450–1380 B.C.) and resembles the kilt used later at Mycenae. This change by superimposed painting to a costume of Mycenaean fashion has been interpreted by some scholars as reflecting the replacement of a Minoan by a Mycenaean dynasty at Knossos. Further evidence for this theory is found in the fact that in the tomb of Menkheperreseneb, dating from the latter half of the fifteenth century B.C., the Kefti were painted wearing the new fashion. These changes in style of dress, together with the typology of the objects brought as gifts, provide corroborative evidence for dating the final destruction of the Minoan centers at 1450 B.C. and the last phase of Mycenaean rule at Knossos to the years between 1450 and 1380 B.C. The final date was recently verified by a comparison of the latest pottery in the destruction levels of the Palace of Knossos with the definitely dated Minoan pottery at Tell el Amarna, the capital city of the reformer pharaoh Akhenaton (Amenhotep IV). The discovery, in a tomb in the harbor town of Knossos, of an alabaster vase with a cartouche of Thutmose III, along with pottery of Palace style, further demonstrates the correctness of these dates, which were first determined by Evans.

The dispatch of artifacts to Egypt as gifts must have been a disguised form of commercial exchange, as the deputies would bring back to Crete such valuable materials as gold, alabaster, basalt, and diorite, presented as gifts in return. Ivory may not have been imported directly from Egypt, since not only the Kefti but also other ambassadors, probably from Syria, are shown carrying elephant tusks. That commerce could assume the form of gift exchange is attested in the correspondence found at Tell el Amarna, dating from the second third of the fourteenth century B.C. These texts show the king of Alasia (Cyprus) to have sent copper as a gift but to have persistently demanded the dispatch of gold in exchange.

Any doubts about the identification of the Kefti as Cretans arise from the fact that they are occasionally depicted with Asiatic people, quite often wearing similar clothing, or are shown carrying objects of Oriental derivation. Thus various scholars believe that the Kefti came from Cilicia, from the Syro-Phoenician region, or from Cyprus. Those depicted in these circumstances, however, might conceivably be immigrants from Crete living on the Asiatic coast or in Cyprus. The Kefti are also reported as transshipping cedar wood from Lebanon to Egypt, where this indispensable material was used in architecture, as well as in making various housewares, sarcophagi, and river boats. The Minoans may also have acted as intermediaries in the transfer trade in bronze and elephant tusks, the former from Cyprus, the latter from Syria. This would account for the materials that the Kefti in the tomb paintings carry in their hands or over their shoulders.

Since lumber was in such demand in Egypt, exports from the bays of Zakros and nearby Palaikastro would be expected to include trunks of huge cypresses, of which great forests have been proved to have existed in Crete. That such forests were abundant in mountainous Sitia is evidenced by the extensive use of wood, mainly cypress, in the construction of almost all the buildings of the Neo-palatial period, and of the palaces in particular. Among the ten saws for cutting wood found in the Zakros Palace itself the longer ones had handles on both ends so that the sawing could be expedited by two people working together. Certain vast rectangular structures on the south coast of the bay could have been used for temporary storage and partial preparation of logs before they were loaded onto the vessels. Part of a quay probably used for loading wood was revealed on this section of the coast after a fierce storm many years ago. Logs could have been brought down from the mountains by rolling them into the torrent that rushed down through the ravine.

Oil and fine wines were produced in great quantities in the region of Sitia, as is indicated by the numerous storage pithoi found in the palace and also in other buildings of the harbor, and these liquids must also have been exported. Special jars with a narrow mouth that could be sealed would have been needed for their transportation, and the popularity of the so-called stirrup jar which began in the Neo-palatial period must be attributed to the fact that this container met the requirements. With the growth of trade in the Minoan Post-palatial and the Mycenaean periods these vessels were more widely used than any other type of container. Equally widespread was the use of another vessel for wine—the kylix or stemmed drinking cup.

Aromatic oils from herbs native to Crete were in great demand in Egypt and the East. These were prepared in special workshops like those in the South Wing of the Palace of Zakros. The Egyptians applied these oils to their hair and bodies, using special utensils often represented in Egypt. In Crete perfumes and aromatic oils were also used in bathing (this perhaps explains why water was not directly channeled into or drained out of bathrooms). However, extracts of herbs were used in Egypt mainly for their sterilizing properties in the embalming of the dead. Another substance indispensable in embalming was resin, which was derived from either cedars or pines and which, according to Egyptian sources, was brought by Kefti ships. The existence of cedars in Crete in early times is attested by the name Kedros (cedar) applied to a branch of the mountain ranges of Ida. Pines must have been more common, as they are today in the region of the Aegean, and would have been the source of great quantities of resin. The possible use of resin in the preparation of a synthetic substance for coating floors in the Palace of Zakros and elsewhere has already been discussed. Other exports must have included honey, the quality of which still depends on the types of aromatic herbs in the region where the bees are raised, and also wax of superior quality.

Definite evidence for the importation of raw materials was provided by the discovery of six ingots of bronze and three elephant tusks, which SEE PAGE 61 were apparently stored in a small room on the upper floor of the West Wing. The ingots are of the older type with slightly curved sides familiar from examples found at Hagia Triada, Tylissos, Mochlos, and elsewhere, and dating to the fifteenth century B.C. In later Mycenaean times the shape changes: the short sides curve deeply and the long ones are almost straight with the four ends sharply projecting. Such ingots were found in Cyprus and in a vessel shipwrecked off Cape Chelidonia, near the coast of Cilicia. A special workshop for manufacture of bronze objects appears to have been set up in this small vessel, for it contained anvils, hammers, fire tongs, and other tools, as well as quantities of tin. The theory is that the boat stopped at various points along the coast to supply the inhabitants with the bronze objects that they needed.

Recent studies have shown that ingots did not represent a currency unit with a fixed weight acceptable without further checking, but rather a standardized shape of the bronze as raw material, obtained from molds in a smelting establishment. The curved shape simplified transportation of the ingots on a man's shoulders and was convenient for storage. The weight ranged between 26 and 33 kilograms, and the ingots could sometimes be divided into halves or quarters. Though bronze could be used as a unit in trading transactions, it was also a raw material out of which utensils, tools, weapons, and other objects could be manufactured.

The largest and best-preserved of the tusks was about 0.7 meter long and probably derived from an elephant of the small-sized species, which was found in Syria but not in Africa. This explains why such tusks were imported to Egypt by sea. In addition to Zakros, whole tusks have been found at Ugarit and in some other Syrian sites; comparisons show clearly that all ivory found in Crete was imported from that area, mainly, it appears, through the harbor of Zakros. Elephant tusks from Syria were also used later for the manufacture of artifacts in Mycenaean sites, as is shown by a vessel with a representation in relief, carved out of part of a tusk, which was found in one of the chamber tombs at Mycenae.

Of the harbor installations which must have certainly existed, no traces have yet been discovered, but no special investigation has been undertaken except for a simple survey over the shallow area of the bay.

The area has been radically altered by subsidals in the coastal zone which have occurred at various times since antiquity and also by the silt accumulated at the mouth of the rivulet. Attempts to trace such installations in other harbors have also met with great difficulties, but at least the location of the harbors is known; these include the harbors of Knossos at Amnisos and at Katsambas, that of Phaistos at Matala, and that at the small bay of the settlement of Mallia. Harbors for transit trade were established at the small island of Pseira and the peninsula of Mochlos.

Another reason for establishing a palace center at Zakros was undoubtedly to provide at that vital position in the trade with Asia and Egypt a base from which to control the sea. The bay at Zakros, because of its location and its safety, was ideal for the establishment of a maritime base. These factors were especially important in the light of prevailing conditions of navigation and the potentialities of the ships, which had the two-fold function of carrying goods and of providing defense if need arose.

The term "maritime base" naturally did not have the connotations it has today. The first maritime bases in Venice and Genoa were adapted to the needs of armed ships which also carried merchandise. At the peak of Minoan power there was no real threat from the sea. Egyptian ships had no reason to come out of the Nile, and their sailors probably lacked the temerity to do so. The various Asiatic peoples had no ambition to spread over the eastern Mediterranean. The Phoenicians did not become sea-oriented until after the Minoans were settled on their coasts, especially at Ugarit, and relations between these two peoples seem always to have been peaceful. Minoan penetration into the Cyclades was achieved in a peaceful manner and provided no ground for warlike action on the part of the Cycladic fleet, which in any case was inferior to that of Crete. The Minoans' only serious rival was the constantly growing power of Mycenae. Even there, however, the Minoans, who had colonies on the mainland at least until the palace centers were destroyed, maintained a cultural supremacy. Their peaceful penetration, according to Evans, was aimed primarily at transmitting the products of their civilization. Essentially, then, the functions of the Minoan navy were to supervise sea traffic and trading posts and to protect the Cretan coasts against pirate raids. Zakros harbor as a maritime base must have served these purposes most successfully.

28 The situation of a Minoan palace was directly related to its proximity to the urban community that made possible the commerce on which the local rulers depended.

The Town of Zakros and Its Road System

Since only isolated houses were found on the north slope during Hogarth's exploration of Zakros in 1901, it was impossible at that time to visualize a continuous town with its road system. Later a Minoan settlement of Palaikastro was discovered at a near-by bay on the east coast of Crete. There a dense and continuous town plan in extensive blocks, with a developed system of main roads and branching lanes, gave a clear idea of a Minoan harbor town. The houses first found at Zakros were too widely separated to make a comparison with the Palaikastro settlement possible. Now, however, we can be sure that the harbor town of Zakros had a similar system of town planning, with fine houses situated in a dense system of blocks connected with a developed net of roads and lanes.

Because exploration was concentrated on the total disclosure of the Zakros palace, large-scale excavation of the town has not yet been possible. However, from the quarters brought to light in the first two years of the excavation (1962–1963) and the further disclosure of the buildings on the north slope from 1967 on, one may draw important conclusions about its form. The general layout was the same as at Palaikastro, with the houses forming extensive blocks, each consisting of three or four dwellings connected in a complicated system, with the façades along the main arteries or the lanes branching from these. But the need to adapt the arrangement on the hill slopes and then in the flat area extending toward the beaches gave the town as a whole a different pattern, surely extremely picturesque in its variety of houses descending the slopes and dominating the zone of the main harbor. The famous Town Mosaic found at Knossos, with its variety of multicolored façades, very characteristically represented in the numerous small faïence tiles, provides an indication of such a town.

From the other palace centers one can infer that the largest, most important, and best-constructed houses formed the immediate environment of the main palace building. Some of these were designated as dwellings of high officials of the palace or of members of the priesthood. The upper classes evidently preferred to live in the vicinity of the palace. This assumption explains why, at Zakros, as at the other centers, the houses nearest the palace are larger and more magnificent than those some distance away. The number of the rooms, distributed on two or more stories, was considerable. Judging by what was preserved of its ground floor, one of the houses of the south hill must have had thirty to forty rooms.

Of the system of roads of the town of Zakros, only a small part has been revealed, but its main lines are beginning to be evident. Certainly the artery that led from the north beach of the harbor at a slightly oblique angle to the general orientation of the palace was one of the most important. Only the last section of this, near the main entrance on the northwest, has been disclosed. Its pavement was renewed every time partial repairs were needed, and the repaving has obscured the original arrangement with a *kaldirim* (the term used for the irregular slabbing of the Turkish roads on the island of Crete) framing a central passageway of regular slabs of white stone. An older pavement came to light under a destroyed part of this artery. The road continued its course to the west beyond the entrance, probably reaching the point where the original entrance existed. The buildings on both sides of this harbor street were entirely adapted to it, which gave them the oblique position in relation to the palace already mentioned. From two points, one just opposite the entrance, the other at its end, lanes of steps descended. These lanes, mentioned in Chapter 24, passed between three of the palace annexes and are not yet entirely explored. From the plan it is clear that they were stepped ramps or short stairways turning at right angles. The existence of a third lane, passing between two blocks of houses, is inferred from a broad oblique step between two corners, near the northeast room of the complex at the north of the palace's kitchen area. Presumably this lane met the east-to-west lane passing in front of the Oblique Building. The latter lane, with part of its pavement of irregular slabs excellently preserved, has its beginning at a principal artery, more than 3 meters wide, ascending the north slope from south to north and passing along the west side of the whole northwest quarter. Although not entirely disclosed, the artery seems to have proceeded from this point by means of a stairway of ten steps and then by broad, stepped ramps. Probably it started much farther to the south, where it would have served to connect the different terraces of the West Court.

The system of roads among the houses on the south hill was similar. Small lanes ran between the blocks of houses, ascending the slopes by steps or ramps terminating at level sections on which the entrances of the houses usually faced. The façades of the buildings, broken in angles according to the usual Minoan system, made the lanes of unequal width, and the narrow streets often led to impasses, where a house blocked the way. Some of the lanes were peripheral, surrounding the top of the hill. One or two of these were sectioned by transverse walls during a period of reoccupation and thus transformed into corridors or oblong apartments.

We can assume that there was a main artery leading west from the entrance of the East Wing of the palace to the main part of the harbor zone, though further excavation is needed to confirm its existence.

29 The palace was a city in miniature, the center of activity, and the hub of the Minoan world.

Daily Life in the Palace

Like other Minoan palaces, that of Zakros was the center of an intense political, social, religious, economic, and private life, but its control over the harbor gave life there a special character. The palace participated in the activity of the harbor, which provided constant communication with the outside world. From the upper floors and apartments of the stepped terraces of the north hill people could easily watch the arrival or departure of boats, see who the newcomers were, follow the loading and unloading of the merchandise, and estimate the success of fishing expeditions. Since trade was essentially under royal control, the king himself or supervisors appointed by him could directly oversee all operations. Products stored in the palace would be packed in special places, and the loading of material stored outside the palace could be ordered promptly through the king's representatives or functionaries. Imported products and raw materials would be deposited temporarily in appropriate areas near the entrances and later distributed to special storerooms. The palace scribes would be ready to record the imports on clay tablets which would be subsequently filed in systematically organized archives. In the Palace of Knossos a hypostyle hall near the north entrance, from which a road led to the sea, was described by Evans as the "Customs House," a place where imported goods would be kept temporarily in order to be checked. In the Palace of Zakros the interior court next to the northeastern harbor gate, as well as roofed spaces nearby and the wide rectangular enclosure leading to the Hall of the Cistern, were probably used in a similar way.

The embassies carrying gifts to the courts of Egypt and the East must have been prepared with great solemnity. Archives from the palace of Mari, a city-town on the middle Euphrates, record that the artistic products of the Kaptaru (Cretans) were in great demand; in Egypt, too, the magnificent convoys of the Kefti were eagerly awaited. They must have been very impressive in the meticulous appearance of the participators, their elaborate hairdos with long strands and short curls, the shining belts of precious materials decorated with curvilinear designs, the embroidered kilts, the many attractive jewels. The envoys came from all the palace centers of Crete, and each group must have been distinguished by special characteristics. Many were probably of royal lineage. The references in Egyptian inscriptions to "The Great Kefti," the men arriving from the "Isles of the Green Sea," indicate the respect given them. Sometimes the embassies had more than one destination: they could stop at the ports of Cyprus and of the Syro-Phoenician coast, obtain bronze ingots and elephant tusks, leave some in Egypt in exchange for other precious materials, and take the rest back to Crete when they returned. They would also sometimes visit the royal courts of the large states in Asia and subsequently sail along the coast to the harbors of the Nile delta.

The craftsmen at Zakros must have been kept busy producing the luxurious pottery, stone vessels and tools, objects in metal, jewelry, seals, and artifacts in ivory and faïence. Many looms were in use, chiefly in rooms of the second floor, for the production of woven materials, which, judging from what seem to be dyeing installations, would have been richly colored. Murex shells provided one of the main organic pigments. Many such shells were found in the area of the Zakros palace, but their utilization for industrial purposes was shown long ago by the discovery of heaps of perforated shells on the island of Leuke (modern Kouphonisi) off the southern cape of Crete. Elaborate examples of embroidery are represented on wall paintings. One of the most beautiful of such patterns appeared in a painting in the Minoan villa near Epano Zakros. A design consisting of systems of linked rosettes forming spirals, which is shown in a wall painting of the palace, may also have been a common motif in embroidery. To these products may be added perfumes, also produced at the palace; the workshops for their preparation have been described.

Many women, including some of the royal family, must have participated in all this production in the palace. Even queens and princesses performed such tasks, if one is to be guided by Homer's descriptions.

The importance of religion in the life of the palace, which is discussed in detail in the next chapter, suggests that much of the artistic creativity was motivated by the need to produce objects suitable for offerings to the deity or use in rituals. Such objects, however, could have also been exported or sent as gifts to monarchs.

Religious ceremonies carried on mainly in the palace provided occasions of entertainment for the inhabitants of Zakros and the people in its vicinity. Whether bull games took place there, as they did at other palaces, is not known. Evidence from representations on sealings is not conclusive, because many of the sealings were attached to packages or objects imported from other regions of the island. For various reasons, however, bull games at Zakros seem unlikely. The narrow valleys of Epano Zakros could not have been suited for breeding the huge bulls, and the difficulties of bringing them over the mountains from other regions would have been enormous. Moreover, the bull acrobats, in addition to natural agility, required extensive training with the bulls. However, the people of Zakros could have gone to the big cities to attend such games, as people do today in Spain, where bullfighting, as has been suggested, may have been inherited from Minoan outposts in the Iberian peninsula.

There is no information on the type of hierarchy that existed in the palace, but the number of apartments indicates that many officials lived within its confines to be available as the king's retinue and to serve as functionaries in charge of political, religious, social, and economic affairs.

As head of the state, the king received high officials, the deputies from other palaces, and ambassadors from the great kingdoms of the East and Egypt in his formal throne room. This, as suggested previously, may have been the Hall of the Cistern. The wide entrance area, the presumable existence of a small porch on the poros-stone crepis projecting beyond the eastern side of the Hall, and the easy access from north and east make this identification even more likely. The throne must have been placed to the right of the entrance—that is, against the north wall, as was the case in the sacred throne room of Knossos and later in the throne rooms (megarons) of the Mycenaean palaces. Similar royal reception halls existed in the three other Cretan palaces. At Knossos a wide staircase led to a colonnaded antechamber and next to it a hall with an interior peristyle which was decorated with scenes of facing griffins, each pair attached by a cord to a column, and of various athletic games, all rendered in painted stucco relief. At Phaistos the hall had an antechamber with a peristyle. From this, one could enter the main hall through a polythyron, as at Zakros. At Mallia the hall was accessible by means of a very broad staircase; its interior arrangement, however, is unknown. The extensive destruction of these halls unfortunately prevents definite conclusions about their interior decoration. At Zakros the relatively better state of preservation allows the formation of a more complete picture. However, the destruction of the floor in the area where the throne might have been placed makes it impossible to decide definitely that this was the throne room.

The royal family must have spent most of their time in their own living quarters. The good organization of these apartments, their adaptation to the purpose for which they were built, their connection with service or subsidiary rooms, and their appropriate decoration must have made them comfortable and pleasant to live in. The special architectural form of the Minoan megaron, provided with a lightwell, polythyron, and side porticoes, devices which were first developed in the palaces, was admirably adapted to a semitropical climate. The adjacent chambers for the king and queen, as arranged on two successive floors, allowed easy communication and at the same time a degree of independence. Well ventilated and lighted through the lightwells and the many openings on the side of the porticoes and colonnaded terraces, these rooms could at will be interconnected, connected with the area immediately outside, or completely isolated. Thus, depending on the wish of the royal persons, the apartments could form one unit with free interior communication or could be reached easily from outside, from the Central Court, or from the Hall of the Cistern. It is reasonable to assume that the bedrooms were installed on the upper floor in corresponding chambers provided with colonnaded verandas. Unfortunately, nothing is known about the furniture and other fittings. Balconies and porticoes provided resting spaces which were open and yet protected, an example being the north portico with its built-in bench for reposing and with a corresponding veranda above.

The Hall of the Cistern, which communicated directly with the royal apartments, though probably intended mainly as a throne room for formal receptions, could have been also used by the royal family on ordinary days, as it offered the great advantage of the cistern, always supplied with plentiful water from the spring and easily accessible by means of descending steps. The use of this hall as a women's abode of the type of an Oriental harem is completely ruled out: there is no evidence for the presence of a harem surrounding the monarch, and this, moreover, would be incompatible with what is known about the Minoan social order. Court ladies might have attended the queen, however, and young female companions the princesses. The children might have played in the hall under the supervision of nurses. Further speculation, however, is not warranted, since there is not enough actual evidence to reconstruct the whole life of the palace.

A special bathroom with a characteristic layout, in direct access to the royal quarters, has been encountered in almost all the palaces. Such installations must have been considered indispensable to assure the amenities of cleanliness and comfort. The anteroom must have been used for preparations for the bath, as the clay screen blocking the view into the bathroom suggests. Perhaps the room directly to the east of the anteroom, unfortunately partially destroyed and with none of its equipment preserved, was a dressing room. Next to the bathroom there may have been a water closet, for part of a drain was preserved outside in the interior court.

The conclusions drawn here about such installations are based on analogies with Knossos, where the queen's dressing room had a water closet that could be reached from the queen's hall by way of a corridor. At Zakros, too, a corridor led into the rooms just described.

Water for drinking and for ordinary domestic purposes derived, as previously explained, from special installations, such as the Spring Chamber and the well next to the royal apartments. We can visualize the young serving women of the palace walking down the steps to the water with pitchers and jugs on their shoulders. Water was carried over to the living quarters and service rooms, especially the Kitchen.

In the Palace of Zakros, for the first time on Crete, extensive special installations for the preparation of food were found. The large Kitchen was also used as a dining room, an arrangement similar to that found in Orthodox cenobite monasteries. The three-legged cooking pots were on the fire. Meats from large and from small animals had been carved separately. The nearby larders were full of provisions, and many culinary utensils, ready for use, were found in adjoining storage spaces. In the same kitchen formal meals for royal banquets were prepared. Dr. Graham ingeniously suggested that these banquets were held in the colonnaded hall above the Kitchen, reached by a special staircase through the north portico. A provisional kitchen seems to have been installed near the northeast entrance.

The assumption that there were extensive gardens on the higher terraces of the hill is a matter of guesswork rather than of factual inference, since these terraces, although supported by carefully built retaining walls, contained no remains of buildings. These gardens would correspond to what Evans described as hanging gardens on terraces on the eastern slope of the hill of Knossos, where the palace building extended. The eastern slope of the hill at Phaistos may have been similarly laid out. At the Palace of Mallia, it is generally accepted that a fairly large garden extended in front of the porticoes of the royal apartments. Scenes in wall paintings suggest that the colonnaded balconies and porticoes were also adorned with vases filled with beautiful flowers. Clay flowerpots found at Zakros and at Knossos have an attractive typical decoration and a small opening at the bottom for draining.

The location of functionaries' and servants' rooms is not quite clear. They could have been in various annexes, such as the extensive north building and the obliquely oriented northwest structure, but this cannot be stated definitely until the quarters on the north slope have been completely excavated. As has been suggested, these annexes could equally well have been workshops or buildings for special purposes, analogous to the armory next to the royal road near the Palace of Knossos.

Some spaces near the entrances may have been used as guards' rooms, and the royal guard undoubtedly checked all approaches and watched over the royal apartments. Nowhere, however, was there any evidence of an organized military force or of preparations against the threat of invasion. Neither at Zakros nor at the other palaces are there signs of fortifications the people of Crete appear to have ignored the danger of attack. At Zakros the organized power of armed merchant ships was considered strong enough to protect the city in case of a sudden incursion, which, considering what a rich and exposed city Zakros was, indicates that Minoan thalassocracy was a real fact.

Yet while the Minoan peace embraced the entire island, all its people lived under the threat of a terrible doom, the nature of which they knew from bitter past experience. Time and again they had rebuilt their ruined settlements, destroyed, as they believed, by the recurring wrath of underworld powers. Ominous signs of another impending catastrophe were evident in the last days of the Zakros palace, and the people must have tried desperately to appease the angry divinities. Yet in the intervening periods the Minoans would not think about the catastrophes of the past but in the fervor of new achievement optimistically assume that nothing of the sort would happen again.

30 The true character of Cretan religion is so far largely unknown. Yet what we do know indicates that the ancient Cretans had an intense pragmatic religiosity linking nature and man in an effective bond.

Religious Life

Sir Arthur Evans's theory of the theocratic organization of the Minoan state and his interpretation of the palaces as sacred precincts have often been considered to owe more to his lively imagination than to actual evidence, although all scholars have recognized that religion played a special role in the whole of Minoan life. However, new evidence from Zakros now seems to confirm Evans's view that the primary function of the palaces was a religious one and that they played an important role in the religious life of the people.

Worship was carried out chiefly in the palaces, with the west wing essentially given over to the shrine and other chambers devoted to cult. Ceremonies were held in specially designed halls, but, at Zakros as well as the other palaces, the public witnessed them from the courts and the spaces of the enclosures. On such occasions the small altar in front of the main entrance to the West Wing was used. Religious structures were crowned with symbolic horns of consecration, and sacred double axes were mounted on stepped bases; many of these have been preserved. The small shrine, where images and sacred symbols were placed for ceremonies on a high podium within a wall niche, was accessible only to the priesthood and to the king who headed the religious hierarchy. Purification of those taking part in a religious ceremony, probably with the sprinkling of holy water, would have taken place in the lustral basin and in the bathroom with the colonnaded ledges and the niches decorated with painted sacred horns.

Religious rituals required considerable equipment. Some was used in preliminary preparations, including braziers and incense burners to perfume the spaces, little basins and sprinkling vessels for purification, flowerpots for decoration, and so on. Vessels used for offerings included ritual jugs and rhytons of various forms for libations, fruit stands and kernoi for first fruits and produce, and special incense burners. For blood offerings, cone-shaped pails known as "samnia" were used, as well as transportable altars. Examples of all these were found at Zakros.

One of the many rituals was the transmission of the sacred communion in special chalices. Four of these vessels, beautifully shaped and carved from valuable stone, which were found in the shrine Treasury, have already been described. A general idea of the communion ceremony is provided by representations in wall paintings and on seal stones. The ritual, moreover, was preserved in later mystery cults—chiefly the Eleusinian mysteries—and survives in Christian liturgy today. The fragmentary wall painting at Knossos depicting the scene of the sacred communion (called by Evans the Camp-Stool Fresco) shows parts of the bodies of priestesses—the "Parisienne" among them—and of priests in feminine attire, carrying the holy cup, which was made of either gold or silver and in various shapes, to other figures which presumably represent deities. This is also deduced from the representation on the bezel of the famous golden ring from Tiryns, where the goddess is seated on a stool, with a bird behind her, and holding the sacred chalice, while a procession of daemons bring her the liquid of the sacred communion in ritual jugs.

The exact nature of this liquid is not known. Perhaps it was a mixture of many liquids, like the Eleusinian *kykeon*. This term is derived from a verb which means mixing by stirring but the liquids which constituted the mixture are mostly unidentified. The representation on the Tiryns ring also suggests a mixture, since several jugs are shown. The main ingredients may have been milk, honey, and the blood of the sacrificed animal, perhaps a bull. There are many traditional tales about the dire effects of drinking bull's blood, especially in cases when the person who drank was polluted or unclean. The idea of testing purity by having an accused person drink holy water has been preserved in Byzantine and medieval tradition, and even in some Christian churches today receiving Holy Communion without previous bodily and spiritual cleansing by fasting and confession is believed to have terrible consequences. The use of bulls' blood as a communion liquid would account for the rhytons in the form of bulls' heads; the blood would come out through the muzzle. In the Christian Holy Communion the conception that the wine is the transubstantiated blood of Christ is an essential element.

Perhaps the Minoan ritual included the consumption of a part of the sacrificial bull which represented the male deity, thus securing temporary participation in his divine essence. Such a ritual is familiar in Dionysiac worship in the so-called tearing-asunder rite (*diaspasmoi*), when the victim, who was identified with the god, was torn to pieces and a part consumed by the frenzied maenads.

The equipment used in various ceremonies is illustrated by the contents of the shrine Treasury and its repositories and storerooms. The ritual itself is illustrated by various representations, especially in miniature art on seal stones and ring gems, and their imprints on clay sealings, examples of which were found at Zakros, especially in the older excavations, and also in other palaces. In these representations, the priests hold double axes and double hammers, beautiful examples of which, made of stone, were found in the shrine Treasury.

Naturally it is difficult to specify the exact rituals conducted in the large formal halls of the West Wing. However, the fact that two of the most valuable ritual vessels—the Bull's Head Rhyton and the Sanctuary Rhyton—were found in the largest of these, the colonnaded Hall of Ceremonies, cannot be considered as lacking significance. The identification of one of the halls as the Banquet Hall does not preclude its use for ritual purposes; sacred banquets and dinners are known to have been related to ceremonies during which parts of sacrificed animals were consumed and sanctified wine was drunk. The drinking of wine is closely related to Dionysiac worship, the roots of which are now being sought in Minoan Crete.

Zakros, surprisingly, does not contain crypts with a central rectangular pillar, which were found in all the other palaces and in which worship took the form of bloody and bloodless sacrifices. However, the absence of such crypts does not necessarily imply any fundamental difference in ritual. The underground areas where water seeped up, such as the Spring Chamber and the Well of the Fountain, may have served the same purpose. Remnants of sacrificial offerings were actually found in those areas, although it is not clear whether the offerings were part of a standard ritual or indicate emergency rites of propitiation held when the threat from the underground world aroused alarm. Worship in the crypts in any case seems to have been connected with chthonic (underworld) deities, if the faïence images of snake goddesses found at Knossos in the shrine repositories, next to the pillar crypts, represented such deities, as Evans believed.

SEE PAGE 167 The tripartite peak sanctuary shown on the Sanctuary Rhyton is undoubtedly a representation of a royal structure, judging both from its impressive effect and from the artistic quality of the vessel on which it appears. Peak sanctuaries built on heights near the other large palaces also seem to be royal. Such are the shrine on the sacred mountain Iyktos (modern Juktas) near Knossos, and that on the hill of Prophetes Elias near the Palace of Mallia. The peak sanctuary of Zakros, described in Chapter 4, must have had a definite relation to the religious life of the palace. Apparently pilgrimages from the palace to the sanctuary took place on certain fixed days. These may have been combined with processions of worshipers carrying offerings, like those depicted on carved stone rhytons from Knossos. Unfortunately, those vases are too fragmentary to convey a clear impression. Analogous pilgrimages must have been directed toward the sacred caves where chthonic deities were believed to abide, but about these deities and their worship very little is known.

Only a few images recognizable as probably representing divinities were found at Zakros, but a few general conclusions about the nature of the deities can be drawn from other representations. Religious scenes appear on a series of sealings, most of which were found during Hogarth's exploration of the site in 1901. These scenes make it clear that the religious pantheon of Zakros is identical to that of other Minoan sites of the Neo-palatial period. The only difference is in the representation at Zakros of a more varied daemonic world, which seems to be the product of a nightmarish imagination. Some scholars believe that this variety was

intended simply to make seal designs difficult to repeat, but this is unlikely, since the types of daemons seem to be reflections of common
religious beliefs among Minoans.

The Minoan pantheon evidently consisted of only a few divinities
which were portrayed in various forms. Birds flying over or sitting on top
of horns mark the epiphany of two deities in their divine form. The earth
goddess who controls the animal kingdom appears in the form of the
Mistress of Animals taming wild goats, the swift and undomesticated
animals of the Cretan mountains. On the gold diadem in the former SEE
Giamalakis Collection the rule of the goddess in this form over sea life PAGES
also is suggested by the presence of octopuses. Attendant animals included 262
lionesses and wild cats, the heads of which are copied in certain rhytons
in faïence and terracotta. No representations of the goddess with snakes,
reflecting her chthonic character or her role as a protectress of the house,
have been found at Zakros, but their absence is probably due to a pure
accident of preservation.

The sacredness of the bull, which is probably a manifestation of the SEE
male fertility divinity, is shown by the rhytons of chlorite, faïence, and PAGES
terracotta in the form of bulls' heads. A very small male figurine seems 149
to have horns, like the bronze statuette of the Horned God from Enkomi
on Cyprus.

The cycle of vegetation is reflected in such representations as the
sacred tree shading an altar on the Sanctuary Rhyton and an "altar of SEE
vegetation," with a bull's head above it, shown on a seal stone. Certain 93
ritual jugs and amphoras with curved handles appear in identical form on
seal stones in scenes showing the revival of vegetation through watering.
A dense design of vegetation is used as a symbolic decoration on the
beautiful double axe found in the shrine treasury. Floral motifs of faïence, SEE
some cut for inlay and others in relief, used for the decoration of the 146
altar, were found with the other religious equipment in the treasury, as
was corresponding plant decoration in the Temple Repositories at Knossos.
These may relate to the goddess of vegetation.

In general, it appears that life at Zakros, as in the other palaces, was
deeply imbued with religious feeling. Faith, which provided a strong link
between man and nature, was the main base on which political and social

life were organized. Under such conditions a theocratic system would have best guaranteed harmonious relations among the deities, the rulers who acted as divine representatives, and the subjects. The new evidence at Zakros on the matter supports Evans's theories. Many obscure points still need to be elucidated, however, before there can be a clear understanding of the way this system really worked out. The decipherment and interpretation of the texts of the tablets from the shrine of Zakros in comparison with the much more numerous ones from Hagia Triada may provide further information.

Small terracotta rhyton in the shape of a lioness's or wild cat's head, from the area of houses on the southwest hill

Destruction and Memories

Where there is a phenomenon which marks the time and place significantly the archaeologist must seek explanations which resolve the reasons for its presence. Few riddles have puzzled archaeologists as much as has the question of the cause of the eclipse of Minoan civilization. Foreign invasion? Changing climate? Plagues? Natural catastrophe? This section deals with cataclysmic happenings which bewilder the mind. That they did indeed occur is its premise, and the evidence presented is convincing.

31

Nothing in nature is more awesome than earthquakes and volcanic eruptions. As island in the sea is never more vulnerable than when its earth is shaken and the sky is dark with ashes blown from beyond the horizon.

The First Catastrophe

Archaeological investigations have shown that the palace center of Zakros suffered two catastrophes of great scale, and that the second destruction brought to an end the life of the city as a palace center. After it the palaces were not rebuilt and the city was abandoned for a long time. Eventually sporadic habitation was resumed at places where ruins of houses had survived. After the first destruction, on the contrary, the palace, as well as the houses of the town, was rebuilt without substantial alteration of the original plan and life continued as before. In the palace, sections were filled in in order to rebuild on a higher level or to extend the royal gardens. The chronology of the destructions was determined by the discoveries of pottery on the floors of the houses with the remains of the level that had been destroyed in the first catastrophe. In many instances these remains were sealed, so to speak, by floors later constructed above them in such a manner that the successive layers can be clearly distinguished. The pottery found in the destruction layer was characteristic of that prevalent during the years around 1500 B.C., as described by Evans (his Middle Minoan III–Late Minoan I A) and by other scholars and dated on the basis of typological correspondence and contemporaneity with Egypt and the Orient. The first palace, therefore, had not had a very long life. The pottery in the destruction layer belonged to the transition phase between the Middle Minoan Kamares style and the Late

Minoan naturalistic style, indicating that the palace had been built about 1600 B.C.

It has now been established that the first destruction at Zakros had occurred in the same period during which the other Minoan centers were destroyed. Such a widespread destruction is generally considered to have resulted from a single cause. Not only were all the Minoan palaces destroyed at the same time, but all were rebuilt immediately afterward with only minor changes. Though the destruction was general, it was apparently not on so great a scale as the one at about 1700 B.C. which had destroyed the older palaces and other centers; at that time there was probably no palace at Zakros. Some farmhouses, such as those at Amnisos, Vathypetro, Metropolis of Gortyn, the four of the Sitia area, and others, were not rebuilt, but at the other centers life continued in the reconstructed buildings of the cities, palaces, and farms. Analogous phenomena accompanying the destructions and the reconstructions have been confirmed for all the centers. This makes absolutely inadmissible the idea that many similar catastrophes could have occurred in a short space of time, as the result of such circumstances as fires, internal disturbances, pirate raids, or enemy invasions. Far more probable is the explanation that the destruction of all the centers had the same cause. The most plausible theory is that this cause was geological in nature, and earthquakes immediately come to mind. This hypothesis, however, could be confirmed only by detailed and assiduous investigation of the phenomena accompanying the catastrophe and the available facts. Unfortunately, the extensive rebuilding has created difficulties both in checking and in interpretation, especially during the period of the first great excavations, when methods of study and recording were imperfect.

Evans himself tried by supplementary study and observation to determine the causes of destruction. After the earthquake of 1926, which struck central Crete especially and during which he was at Knossos, he expressed the opinion that the principal destructions were due to geological causes—mainly to earthquakes. He produced a whole series of evidence, including displacements, great stones hurled a considerable distance, the collapse of walls in a manner that could be explained only by the force of seismic shocks. Analogous evidence from many other Minoan buildings destroyed at the same time as the palaces tended to confirm Evans's view. In some instances, however, there was difficulty in determining which of the successive seismic destructions resulted in the burying of certain deposits. According to Evans, at Knossos the deposits of the Temple Repositories, as well as those of the Deposit of the Lily Vases, of the Houses of Fallen Stones, and of the Sacrificed Oxen near the southeast corner of the palace resulted from the destruction of the years around 1600 B.C. But new criteria and the comparison of the pottery of the deposits with other more accurately dated groups, which include the transitional styles from the Middle Minoan to the Late Minoan period, make the destruction in 1500 B.C. more probable.

The subject is especially important, because upon this chronological distinction depends the accurate dating of the great rebuilding of the New Era at Knossos and the other palace centers, a rebuilding which followed a catastrophe of wide extent. On the basis of Evans's chronology, the destructions of other buildings have been dated by analogies. For example, the villa in the harbor town of Amnisos contained wall paintings showing lilies on triple stems exactly like those on the lily vases of Knossos, as well as cooking implements similar to those found in the northeast storeroom of that palace, which were destroyed, according to Evans, by the earthquake of 1600 B.C.

In the Villa of the Lilies at Amnisos, the excavator, Professor Spyridon Marinatos, found that huge blocks of poros stone, forming the lower part of walls, had been dislocated, but other phenomena that he observed caused him, for the first time, to connect the destruction with a volcanic eruption on the island of Thera (Santorini). He verified that, immediately above the fill which covered the ruins, there was an abundance of pumice, of which the volcanic source was indubitable. While this material did not compose a whole layer, as the excavator with some exaggeration described it, the quantity of pumice found in the fill was considerable, and a significant amount of the same material was found deposited in the strange tower-like building near the villa which was identified as a beacon station, a kind of primitive lighthouse. In any case so much pumice on the shore of Amnisos could only be explained as being carried from Thera, more than 100 kilometers away, by a tidal wave immediately after an eruption of the volcano there. According to Professor Marinatos, it was the size and violence of the volcanic tidal waves which caused the devastation not only of Amnisos but of the whole north shore of Crete and for a great distance inland.

After studying the destructive phenomena of the analogous eruption of Krakatoa in the Sunda Strait in 1883, Marinatos supplemented his theory and dated the extensive volcanic destruction of the Minoan centers at about 1520 B.C.

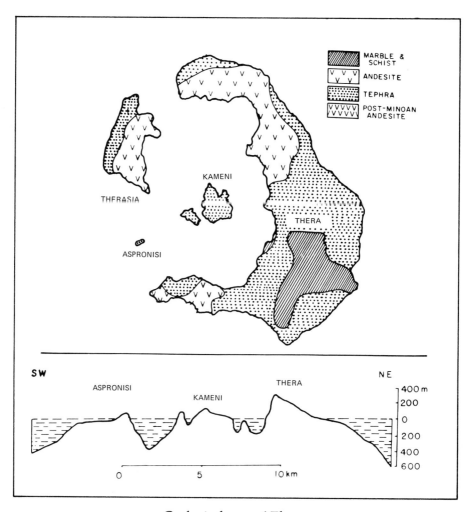

Geological map of Thera

32 Thera, also called Santorini, is an island built by volcanic action. As it was created, so it can be destroyed, and with it much more.

The Thera Volcano
and the Buried Minoan Settlements

Thera is the southernmost of the Cyclades Islands and thus the nearest of these to Crete, which is about 120 kilometers distant. The volcano continues to be active; the most recent eruption, happily not very severe, occurred in 1925, but smaller outbreaks took place in 1928, 1939, and 1950. No one, however, would have supposed that eruptions of this volcano could have had destructive consequences for Crete and the region surrounding the south Aegean, if geologists had not found it to be a volcano of the caldera type, which had periodic eruptions in prehistoric times with unimagined destructive consequences.

Originally the island of Thera was circular, disk-shaped, with small elevations composed of metamorphic assemblages of marble and schist which are still discernible in certain areas. At the end of the Tertiary period, it had been reshaped by successive eruptions and had gradually become covered with lava. In some regions fertile soil developed and these areas attracted settlers who built houses at various points on the island. The remains that have been found show that the settlements were Minoan and that they prospered and acquired wealth from trade.

But in the depths of the earth the burning fluid bubbled, ready to be hurled as soon as it found a passage through the crust of the hardened lava. When at last the eruption came, the magma was hurled to an unimaginable height, and pumice and ash covered the island in a layer 30 to 60 meters thick. The ash carried by the wind was dispersed over an immense expanse around the island and gradually fell into the sea or on neighboring land. Not long after came the greater destruction. The enormous subterranean cavity emptied itself of molten material, causing the vault to collapse under the pressure of the overlying land. The greater central portion of the round island was submerged, with the result that today's caldera was created with its broken circle of islands—Thera, Therasia, and Aspronisi, with an extent of 83 kilometers. The collapse of so enormous a mass of earth created an astonishingly high volcanic wave (tsunami) which moved with such speed that it maintained most of its crushing power when it reached the shores of Crete.

Early Investigations on Thera

The general date of the Thera eruption had been confirmed much earlier by ceramics found in the buildings under the volcanic ash on that island. The buildings themselves had emerged in the 1860s when French engineers were extracting white volcanic ash from the quarries of Therasia, a smaller island near Thera, to use in making cement for the construction of the Suez Canal. Since no one was at hand to note the significance of the find from an archaeological viewpoint, many valuable remains were lost, but care was taken to preserve many others in good condition, some of them buildings with their complete equipment. Wooden beams there were also preserved, still charred, in position, and in some cases trees of the gardens surrounding the buildings could be distinguished, with their branches and sometimes their leaves.

Finally, the remains aroused the curiosity of the owner of the quarries, a Mr. Alaphousos, who brought them to the attention of Dr. Nomikos, a lawyer from Thera, and Dr. Christomanos, a professor of chemistry at the University of Athens, and then to that of scholars of the French School of Archaeology in Athens. The importance of the ruins became obvious, and in 1863 a suitable investigation was put in hand. This, however, proceeded extremely slowly, against insuperable difficulties caused by the collapsed material and the fact that the buildings were found to be under a 30-meter layer of pumice.

Soon after 1866 there was a quite considerable eruption of the vol-

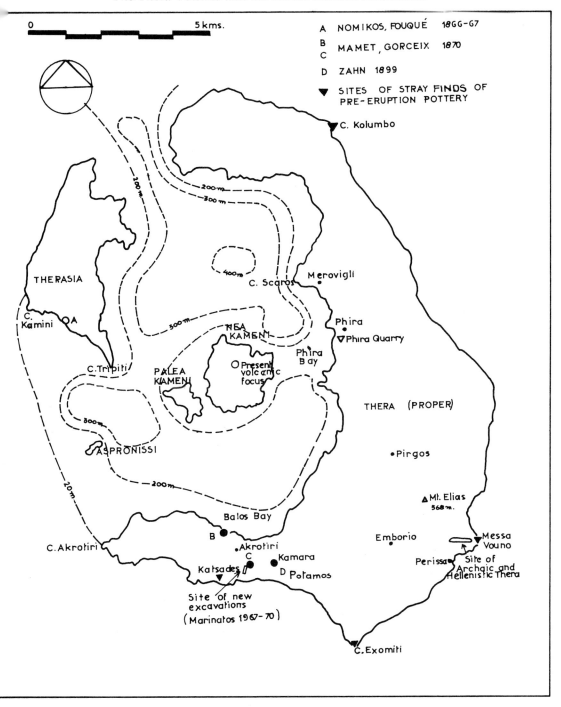

Thera, Therasia, and Kameni, showing sites excavated
(Palaea Kameni emerged from the sea 196-157 B.C.;
Nea Kameni between 1701 and 1711 A.D.)

cano, which continued to be active for some years. The French geologist
Ferdinand André Fouqué was sent immediately to make a scientific study
of the eruption and to carry on observations. He realized the great importance of the ruins for providing chronological evidence of the eruption
that had buried them. At that time, however, there was no one in a position to date the buildings and finds. Exploration on Therasia, where the
first houses were found, was considered by Fouqué to be very dangerous.
The site Akroteri on Thera itself, where archaeological remains seemed
to exist, was also buried under the volcanic ash but seemed well suited for
investigation because of the erosion of the layers occasioned by the waters
of a stream. In the bed of this stream it would be easy to reach the layer of
the buildings. Fouqué himself, in unsystematic digging, extracted some
pots and also collected two gold rings. Since he was not an archaeologist,
he asked the French School in Athens to undertake more systematic
investigations.

Archaeologists Mamet and Gorceix began excavations on Thera
at a time when the volcano was somewhat less active. They discovered
three rooms, built on corroded lava, which belonged to the original floor
of the island before the enormous eruption in which the houses had been
buried. The walls of these buildings reached to a height of about 2 meters
and were relatively well preserved. On the ground was found a plentiful
supply of pots, tools, weaving and fishing equipment, lamps, and other
objects, as well as quite a quantity of stored food—cereals and vegetables.
There were many bones of domestic animals. The investigators progressed,
not without danger, through tunnels in the disintegrated layer of pumice.
In one passage they found wall paintings, representing lilies and irises in
vivid though partially burned colors. The first discovery of early wall
paintings in the Creto-Mycenaean world thus came to light in these strange
excavations under the ashes of the eruption. In another place, at the little
harbor of Balou, they discovered houses suspended on the precipice, part
of which had been cut off by the submersion of a portion of the island.
Charred doorposts and wooden beams inside the walls were discernible.
One house was recognized to have had two stories. A row of large pithoi
was found in place, and many cooking vessels and other equipment still
contained remains of food. Some of the pots were decorated with white

lilies on a dark ground and others with leaves in a dark color on the open polished surface.

The condition of the remains suggested a prehistoric Pompeii, but only when the excavations by Heinrich Schliemann at Mycenae produced their brilliant results a few years lated did it become evident to how remote a period those remains emerging from the volcanic ash belonged. The more accurate correlation with the Minoan civilization was not made until long after the latter had been discovered. In 1922 the French archaeologist L. Renaudin published a report on the pottery and other objects from Akroteri, which had been stored since their discovery in the French School in Athens. The evidence that the buildings and the finds belonged to the Minoan civilization and were to be dated to the sixteenth century B.C. showed that the buried settlement was part of a Minoan colony and had been destroyed about the end of that century. This was further confirmed by other discoveries made in 1899—one year before Evans began his excavations at Knossos—again in the same region, the site of Potamos on Thera, during a short investigation carried out by the German archaeologist Robert Zahn. On one of the pithoi then discovered there was an incised inscription which was subsequently proved to be written in the Linear A script. From the time of the first excavations by the French School a whole century was to pass before the investigations could be renewed on a wider scale and with new methods. Meanwhile, the theory that the successive destructions of the Minoan centers were caused by repeated eruptions of the volcano of Thera had been more clearly articulated.

The Krakatoa Parallel

Clues to the consequences of the great eruption on Thera are provided by the Krakatoa eruption in 1883, the only similar eruption about which detailed information is available. Through a succession of eruptions the volcanic island of Krakatoa was changed into a prehistoric caldera. After being inactive for about 200 years, the volcano suddenly erupted again in August 1883, after a smaller preliminary eruption in May. For two days it poured forth lava, ash, smoke, magma, vapors, and gas. Strong roaring and vibrations of the air accompanied the eruption. The ashes and vapors, evil-smelling from a mixture of sulfuric acid, covered the great part of the neighboring islands, Java and Sumatra, and the sky there for two whole days was completely dark. The ground was covered by a layer of ash and pumice to a depth of 0.3 meter. A small part of the layer consisted of rocks from Krakatoa. Two thirds of that island, 28 square kilometers, collapsed into the cavity created under water and was submerged. The submersion created a volcanic wave 35 meters high, which swept the shores of Java and Sumatra, destroying 295 settlements and drowning 36,000 people. The phenomena, moreover, were observed over much of the terrestrial globe. The tidal wave became perceptible in all oceans, and roars from vibrations in the atmosphere were estimated to have been audible over a third of the earth's surface. Houses of settlements in an area 800 square kilometers around Krakatoa suffered damage. Revolving land winds swept the light ash over the sea.

The Krakatoa region, showing areas flooded in the eruption of 1883

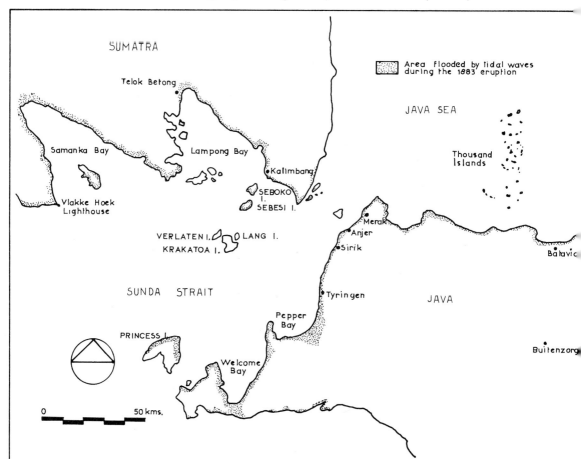

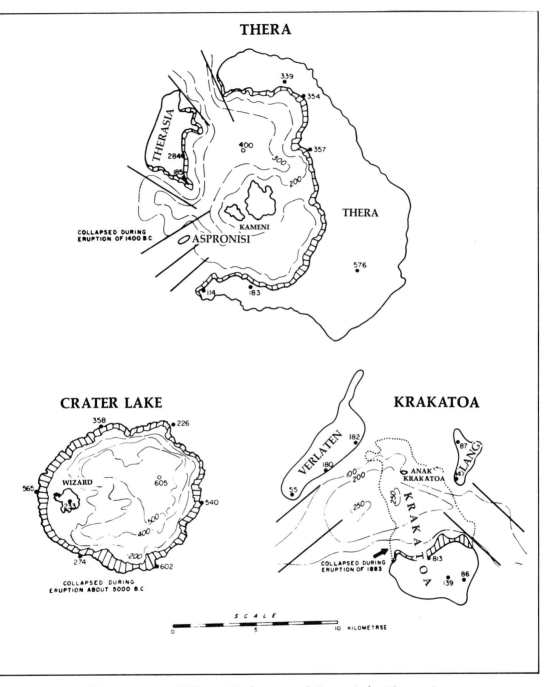

THERA

THERASIA

339

354

400

357

300

200

KAMENI

THERA

COLLAPSED DURING
ERUPTION OF 1400 B.C.

ASPRONISI

2844

185

576

114

183

CRATER LAKE

358

226

WIZARD

605

565

540

233

500

400

200

274

602

COLLAPSED DURING
ERUPTION ABOUT 5000 B.C.

KRAKATOA

VERLATEN

182

180

LANG

87

ANAK
KRAKATOA

141

55

100

200

250

250

K
R
A
K
A
T
O
A

COLLAPSED DURING
ERUPTION OF 1883

813

86

139

SCALE

0   5   10 KILOMETRSE

The volcanoes of Thera, Krakatoa, and Crater Lake (Oregon),
with submerged parts indicated

By comparing these phenomena with those of the Thera explosion it can be deduced with relative certainty that the latter was of multiple power, at all events not less than four times as great. At Thera the area submerged was 83 square kilometers, there were three cones of explosion, and the layer which covered the ground exceeded 30 meters in thickness. The volcanic wave, resulting from a much greater displacement of water, was incomparably larger and was transmitted with greater swiftness, the speed depending on the depth of the sea, which between Thera and Crete is 1500 meters. The height of the wave is estimated to have been 70 to 100 meters and its speed to have exceeded 350 kilometers per hour, so that in 20 to 30 minutes it would have reached the shores of Crete which it would have literally swept. Observations which have been made on islands near Thera, such as Anaphe, showed that a layer of pumice 5 meters thick was deposited in a region lying in the depth of a valley 250 meters above sea level. Moreover, the tidal wave would have reached the shores of Syria, Tunisia, the Nile Delta, and Palestine-Syria about 3 hours after the eruption. At Jaffa (ancient Joppa, now part of Tel Aviv), a layer of pumice was found 5 meters above sea level. The roaring would have been heard far beyond Scandinavia, central Africa, and the middle of the Atlantic Ocean. Earthquakes would have preceded and followed the eruption, first because of the movement of the crust of lava and later as a result of the vast collapse. The general strength of the eruption has been estimated as equal to that of hundreds of hydrogen bombs. It is thus possible to gauge the effects on the Minoan centers, which lay at a relatively short distance.

Dating the Eruption

One fact that remained curious was that, while the remains on Thera confirmed that the catastrophe occurred in the years around 1500 B.C., in Crete in that period, though most of the Minoan centers suffered, the destruction seemed to have been less terrible than would be expected and to have had no irreparable effects. The Minoan centers were rebuilt, without substantial alteration, and life there continued for at least 50 years, until the final destruction, of incomparably greater extent, resulted in the complete ruin of the areas. It seemed plausible to assume two successive eruptions, the second of which was the one which caused the submersion of the greater part of Thera with the consequences already described. For the clarification of the whole subject, supplementary investigations by both archaeologists and geologists were needed.

The geologists proceeded first to tracing the ash fallen to the bottom of the sea. In 1947 and 1948 a Swedish mission with a special oceanographic ship, the *Albatross,* and in 1956 and 1958 an American mission with the ship *Vema* took samples of sediment by drilling. These were long cylindrical cores, twenty-one in all, removed at different points in the eastern Mediterranean. The cores were examined to determine whether they contained layers of volcanic ash. Two such layers were found, showing dissimilar patterns of layering. In both types, the ash layers were thicker in the cores taken nearer Thera, the source of the volcanic ash, thus confirming its provenance. Only five of the cores, however, contained both layers. By determination of the refractive index of volcanic glass in each layer and the recognition of a sapropelic layer (sediment consisting chiefly of organic matter) succeeding the lower layer of ash the two sorts of layers were easily distinguished. This analysis showed that there had been two eruptions with enormous climaxes, chronologically far apart, depositing ash composed of different materials and differently distributed according to the prevailing wind that transported it. The first type of ash layer was identified by a thin intermediate layer of foraminifera as being previous to Post-Pleistocene times and by the sapropelic sediment as preceding the early post-glacial period (c. 10,000 B.C.). By the carbon 14 method of dating, computing on carboniferous sediments, the date of the first eruption has been calculated as about 25,000 B.C. Since there was a wider dispersion and a thicker layer of ash shown by the cores collected northeastward of Thera, the prevailing winds were presumably eastern and thus the eruption probably occurred in winter.

The second type of ash layer, on the basis of an accompanying layer of pteropoda, was dated by the same method as later than 3000 B.C., thus providing a clue to the date of the second eruption. But the only large-scale eruption of the Thera volcano after that date was the one that buried the Minoan settlement on the island, and these remains provide a means of dating the eruption more accurately. Thicker layers of the upper tephra were found in the cores collected between the northeastern shore of Crete and the island of Karpathos. Thus the dispersion of this volcanic ash, which was less extensive than that of the lower layer, was from northwest to southeast—that is to say, with a northwest wind, which most probably prevailed in summer. The dense cloud of the ash presumably did not reach Egypt, but it covered most of Crete except for the western part. These observations have confirmed the hypotheses already proposed concerning the power and radius of activity of the volcanic eruption. More

Distribution of volcanic ash during the eruption of the Thera volcano about 25,000 B.C. Points where cores were taken by the oceanographic ships Albatross *and* Vema *are indicated*

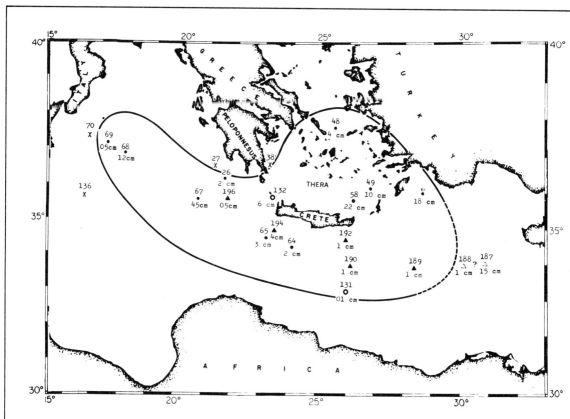

accurate examination of the layer of upper ash on one of the cores, however, has confirmed that the eruption occurred in three successive stages, since three alternating layers of coarse or finer ash have been distinguished. This means that the volcano continued to be active for a long time and that it had three successive eruptions separated by some years. The second one caused the destruction of the settlements and the consequent devastation of the island, but the last was the one which caused the submersion of a portion of it. The three layers of ash were also distinguished on Thera. The charred wood of a pine tree discovered in the stratified tephra 30 to 60 meters thick, covered immediately by the thick layer of pumice, could be dated by the carbon-14 method to 3370 years ± 100, thus provid-

Distribution of volcanic ash during the Thera eruption of c.1450 B.C.

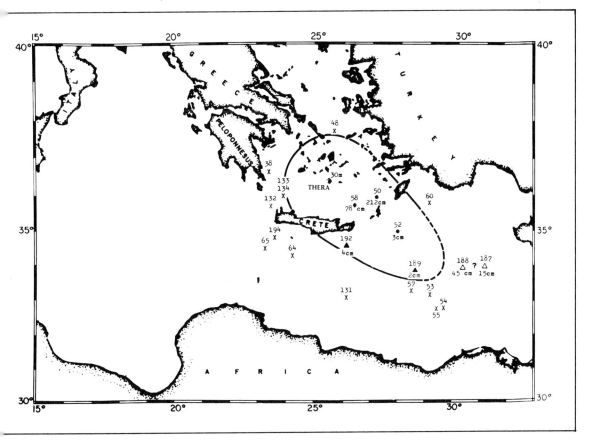

ing a date between 1500 and 1400 B.C. for the eruption. This chronology coincides with the archaeological data relating both to the destruction of the Thera settlements and to the last destruction of the Minoan palace centers.

The Recent Excavations on Thera

In 1967 Professor Marinatos began new excavations at Akroteri in the area where the layers with archaeological remains had been rendered accessible by erosion. There the original layer of lava was visible, above this a light layer of soil, and then a layer of pumice and of crystalline ash. This last was very thick, averaging about 30 meters, but at certain points reaching 60 to 70 meters.

The pumice has been and is still being intensively exploited by digging large and long tunnels in the lower strata. The volcanic glass, which is a suitable material for the preparation of hydraulic cement, has also been exploited. Because of the elasticity and compressibility of the material and the limited penetration of moisture into the lower layers, Marinatos thought that archaeological exploration could be continued by tunneling, in such a way as to disclose the archaeological remains under cover, without having to open the area from above. By this method the material found would be relatively undisturbed, and after excavation would give an impression similar to that conveyed in the most recent excavations of Pompeii and Herculaneum.

Akroteri's position exactly opposite Crete, and its relatively well-protected bay, made it a natural choice for a Minoan settlement. The little bay of Balos on the other side of the peninsula, where Mamet and Gorceix made one of their investigations, had abruptly descending sides created by the collapse of the central part of the island. However, the exact location of the early excavations, except those made by Zahn, could not be determined. These had presumably been made in the ravine, toward its eastern part, in the same region where Marinatos has begun testing by means of trenches at different points on both sides of the ravine, only a short distance from the south bay.

Almost at the beginning, at a shallow depth, buildings began appearing, accompanied by characteristic pottery of Cycladic-Minoan style, belonging to the transition period from Middle Minoan to Late Minoan. Excavation has been continued in the succeeding years, always with great success. Many complexes of buildings have been disclosed, with all their furniture in its original position, and gradually the excavator arrived at the conclusion that the settlement must have been a Minoan colony of palatial character. The marvelous construction of a series of excellently preserved walls in ashlar masonry strongly suggested a palace, but as yet this is only a working hypothesis.

One of the main complexes, now called Sector A, is at the more northern point of the area under excavation. It consists of a series of storerooms, with special installations for different kinds of products in jars of various dimensions or in pots. The rooms were lighted by broad windows; the sills and ledges for the adjustment of the wooden frames were well preserved. In the first storeroom a whole series of jars and pitchers was discovered in position along the south wall. Most of these were decorated with interconnected spirals and rope patterns. A great quantity of loom weights of lenticular form, fallen from the story above, indicated the existence of a weaving installation. In several of the pots there were curious cracks which must have resulted from a fire of considerable intensity. Volcanic stones were found, intermingled with pumice and pieces of furniture, indicating that the destruction had resulted from a volcanic eruption. A column base was found *in situ* in the middle of the chamber and another came from the room above. Along the south wall of the same storeroom, on a kind of low rectangular hearth, was a series of culinary vessels—heavy conical vases and three-legged cooking pots. An elliptical stone basin was embedded in the floor near the hearth. A three-legged stone mortar and some other utensils of clay or stone completed the furniture. A small bridge-spouted spherical vase decorated with light flowers on a dark background must have been imported from Crete.

North of the first storeroom on the ground floor were two others, narrower than the first. These contained some peculiar installations and an astonishing amount of pottery. Most of this was lying in its original positions, but several pots had fallen from the upper floor or from shelves and were found smashed; some were only partly preserved. Partition screens of mud bricks separated groups of large jars. Here also several pots had been cracked by the excessive heat of the fire. Some of the smaller vases were of stone and had served the kitchen or workshops. One group of small jugs and other utensils came from a shrine on the upper floor; with these there was an important clay rhyton molded in the form of a lion's head. A part of the floor of the upper room was found still in position. On it were an offering table and a nippled ewer decorated with barley motifs, which could have been used in the rites of a vegetation cult. To the same shrine probably also belonged a conical clay rhyton, a jug decorated with a vetch motif, a small clay chest for the storage of aromatic substances, and a beautiful small elliptical basin and a polychrome jug decorated with flying swallows. Some small three-handled jars had elegant decorations of connected spirals, plant motifs, branches, and an imitation of veined or mottled stone. The room was lighted from two windows; on the ledge of one of these was found a whole series of attractive vases, including three nippled ewers. Some of the vases were obviously imported from Crete.

The third storeroom was literally stacked with jars and smaller pots heaped together. Some of the smaller ones had fallen from the floor above. The jars were decorated with rope patterns and concentric circles. The general disorder showed clearly the force of the disaster. The forms of the vases showed great variety; there were bottles for aromatic oil, fruit stands, strainers, dippers, incense burners, and others. Among the most important vases was a cylindrical jar decorated with lilies and a dark background. It contained an organic substance and a small figurine of the goddess.

Some smaller rooms, immediately to the west of the three storerooms and also containing a wealth of material, have recently been investigated. Their well-constructed façade, with an admirably preserved door and window, was excavated by tunneling. A road ran past these rooms. In a corridor at the south of this building and in the building nearby were beautiful frescoes of Minoan style, one fragment showing a palm tree and part of a man. A sanctuary was also represented, with columns whose capitals had vegetable motifs and horns of consecration. In front of the sanctuary was a monkey of the species *Cercopithecus callitrichus* in a ritual position.

Other parts of buildings, in ashlar masonry, have been discovered at the south and southeast of the Sector A. Although they are not yet exposed they seem to belong to a very important complex, which may well, as the excavator believes, have been a small palace. It is interesting to follow in this sector the terrible effects of the earthquakes which seem to have accompanied the disaster.

Fifty meters farther south another complex has proved to be a principal quarter of the settlement. It was a very difficult task to disclose this extremely complicated system of buildings, transversed by a paved road—named by the excavator the Telchines road—which had several right-angle turnings and led to more spacious unroofed areas or courts. The high façades of the buildings on both sides remained, with their entrances and windows; some of the latter, located just at the level of the road's pavement, surely belonged to basement rooms, which are not yet excavated. The existence of such rooms is proved by the partial sinking of the pavements of the rooms above them. Complex B to the east, only partly investigated, was extensive and included rooms on two different levels, those on the upper floor having floors either of flagstone in regular arrangement or of beaten clay. One of the principal rooms, quadrangular in form with a central column, had a rich supply of jars and smaller pots on its half-sunken pavement. Among the finer vases were a nippled ewer with flying swallows as decoration, a boat-shaped bowl with a decoration of swimming dolphins, a big strainer with a trail of ivy, and a cylindrical vase with a light-on-dark decoration of crocuses or caper flowers. The next room to the north had a double entrance of Cretan form. A winding staircase of ten steps led from the ground floor to these upper rooms. Two small rooms near by were full of fresco fragments, fallen from above, showing subjects very reminiscent of the well-known frescoes representing gardens and monkeys from the House of Frescoes at Knossos. These provide further confirmation of a close relationship to Minoan Crete. In Sector C, on the other side of the Telchines road, were other important buildings, not yet excavated. Exploration of a small area toward the southwest seems to confirm the theory that after the destruction of the principal buildings, squatters reoccupied parts of them and used them as workshops; for security they blocked some of the openings and the entrance of a staircase. This reoccupation shows that the definitive catastrophe which submerged the central part of the island had not yet happened. Two successive eruptions fifty to sixty years apart, the second of unimaginable violence, would best explain the archaeological and geological evidence discovered on Thera and Crete. The date of the first catastrophe—around 1500 B.C.—is clearly determined by the furniture found. The second was surely that of the final destruction of the Minoan centers, around 1450 B.C.

33 Throughout time, **man** has felt that prosperity tempts fate. In the end a judgment follows—perhaps as an obliterating act of raw nature.

The Final Destruction

The detailed and systematic excavation of the Palace of Zakros, as well as of the houses of the town, has clearly demonstrated that the final destruction was sudden and complete. Everywhere there is unmistakable evidence that the life of the city ceased because of a catastrophe that caused widespread destruction. The storerooms were found full of pithoi and pots containing supplies and provisions. In the shrine areas, the contents of the treasure rooms, the deposits, the archives were in place; in the ceremonial rooms equipment was found where it had just been used for ceremonies. In the kitchens, kettles and cooking pots were on the hearths; many utensils were ready for use; quantities of meats and other foods were in process of being prepared for meals. In the auxiliary rooms there was evidence that the service personnel were carrying on their duties, and in the workshops that artisans were occupied in skilled work of various kinds, the nature of which was eloquently attested by the raw materials, the half-finished objects, and the tools.

The abrupt interruption of the flow of life in Zakros recalls the corresponding condition revealed in the recently discovered Minoan settlement of Thera, described in the preceding chapter, and, even more, the much later destruction of the cities around Mount Vesuvius in the eruption of 79 A.D. For the elucidation of the causes, however, the available evidence must be examined in some detail.

Both the first investigation by Hogarth and the more recent exploration showed that the catastrophe struck the whole city as well as the palace at the same time, and that it was accompanied everywhere with extensive fires, in which the buildings were consumed. Dating the event was made easy by the great number of objects found—especially the characteristic pottery. The naturalistic Marine and Floral styles were both at their height, and a precursor of the Palace style had begun to appear. This evidence suggests a date of about 1450 B.C.

The absolute chronology has been verified, as we have seen, from the representations in the tombs of Egyptian officials, mostly from the reign of Thutmose III (1481–1447 B.C.) where the Kefti were portrayed bearing gifts entirely analogous to objects found in the Zakros treasuries.

The exact fixing of the chronology has particular significance in determining the nature of the catastrophe. There is definite proof that nearly all the later Minoan palaces suffered a similar general destruction at the same time. For a time specialists were doubtful as to whether the date of the final destruction of the palaces was about 1450 B.C. or about 1400 B.C. Lately, however, the problem of the exact chronology seems nearer solution. The palaces and other important centers in central and eastern Crete, Knossos included, were simultaneously destroyed about the middle of the fifteenth century B.C., apparently as a result of the same causes. Knossos, however, and only Knossos, was rebuilt as a palace a few years later, but by a Mycenaean instead of a Minoan dynasty. To ascribe to an enemy invasion a disaster so violent and so extensive would be altogether absurd. Moreover, such an invasion could have come only from Mycenae, which at that time had close and friendly relations with Crete. Besides, no indications of any such activity have been found anywhere. At Zakros, in particular, the palace and the houses were found inviolate and undisturbed. Therefore, this destruction also appears to have had a geological origin. In fact, there were strong indications that Crete had again suffered a series of catastrophic earthquakes. This conclusion could be supported by certain observations of seismic activity. At the Palace of Zakros careful study was given to such evidence: the clay partitions thrown down, the displacement of masses, the inclination of walls from the perpendicular, and the curving or hollowing of the partitions. All the heaps of fallen stone were cleaned carefully, and it was thus confirmed that huge stones, some dressed, some not, had been hurled to a distance or had fallen and shattered, blocking passages and filling open spaces. Whole sections of the upper story had been thrown down, at many points preserving their relative continuity. Sections of the walls of the façade, carefully constructed of dressed stone, fell in a block from their bases in such a manner that the stones were spread out in a series on the floor. Walls of mud brick in the area of the kitchen were detached and fell inside the rooms in one piece. Huge sections of walls had collapsed into the deep storerooms; some of these walls were sharply bent. The southern approaches to the central court were impassable because of the large heaps of massive stones strewn there. The parapet of the circular cistern was completely crumbled, the stones having fallen within the cistern. The walls of ashlar masonry surrounding the fountain were partly dislocated and partially inclined from the vertical. The steps of the stairways had subsided, and in many cases were displaced from their original position. All these effects and many other similar ones were photographed and recorded with care, as proofs that the damage had been caused by earthquakes; such phenomena could not possibly be ascribed to any deliberate human activity of ravaging and destruction. Long and laborious excavation work was required to clear the courts and passages of the masses of fallen material.

The only question is whether simple earthquakes having their center along a geological fault line would have sufficient force to cause such widespread and violent destruction. The course of the investigation revealed many other analogous effects. Many of the pithoi in the deep storerooms of the West Wing, mainly those arrayed along the west wall, had been compressed and squeezed as if pressure from a great force had been applied from east to west. A similar enormous pressure was evidenced by whole walls of dressed poros stones that had fallen from their foundations in one piece. Could seismic vibrations alone cause this? And if so, why had other walls of unworked stone not fallen? SEE PAGES 288 289

The effects of fire also required study. Everywhere, though most noticeable in the West Wing, there was a very thick layer of a russet-brown color, which doubtless resulted from the dissolution of the burned mud bricks of the partitions of the upper floor. Where mud-brick partitions existed on the ground floor this layer was still thicker and many burned bricks, most of them of large size, were found within it. Under this layer

*Fallen poros blocks, at some places in tiers,
from the façades of the Banquet Hall in the Central Court,
attesting to the force of the catastrophe*

there was another thinner layer, 0.2–0.3 meter in thickness lying almost immediately above the floor. This layer was black from the charred materials and from the ash. In certain places, however, as in the half-underground storerooms for pithoi, the layer of ash was very thick. In one of the storerooms it even rose above the rims of the pithoi and was dark gray in color. The fire was certainly of large extent and of great intensity; it reduced everything to ashes. Fed by inflammable materials such as the oil in the storerooms, it turned many stones into lime, charred completely all the wooden parts of the palace and the internal timber of the walls, burned

288

*Fragments of large jars pressed against the west wall
of a storeroom in the West Wing*

the columns, and in some areas transformed by conflagration even the
clay pots, some of which were crumbled and distorted or changed into a
shapeless mass. Some wall surfaces were blackened, and dressed stones
were split or fell into fragments. Lead objects and raw lead stored in the
palace dissolved into molten material which covered parts of the floors.
The few inscribed tablets that survived owed their preservation to having
been baked by the fire, which had changed most of them to a russet or
chestnut color. Nowhere, however, did the fire reach the temperature required to melt bronze objects or those made of precious metals, and these

for the most part were found in good condition. The fire had consumed almost the whole palace complex but the same effects of the fire were observed also in the houses of the town.

Extensive fires have often accompanied great earthquakes both in ancient and in modern times. Notable examples are the disasters of San Francisco, of Messina in Sicily, and recently of the cities on the Ionian islands of Cephalonia and Zakynthos. Sometimes the fires are more destructive than the earthquake tremors themselves. Fires could easily originate accidentally from lighted lamps, from hearths, or furnaces in workshops. However, the fact that most of the effects of fire were observed at a series of settlements abruptly destroyed cannot be considered the result of mere accident. One might say that the catastrophe occurred when many lamps were alight. The intensity of the conflagration, however, does not explain the thickness of the layer of ash in the storerooms, where only a door, a window, and ceiling beams were made of wood.

Another circumstance which should be considered in any attempt to explain the cause of the destruction is the presence of pumice. So much of this material occurred in the fill covering the remains of the buildings that the significance of its appearance in the palace was easily overlooked. The pumice nowhere constituted an actual stratum, but abundant pieces were found mixed in the soil. Since the workmen removing the fill did not always distinguish the pumice from the earth, the actual quantity must have been many times the amount collected. However, at Zakros, as on Amnisos, a quantity of stored pumice was found, chiefly in the room immediately north of the two-columned portico of the central court, near the cage of the stairway. Of even greater significance was the fact that pieces of pumice had been placed in conical cups to be offered to the divinity along with other offerings deposited both in the built well where a cup containing olives was found and in the Well of the Fountain. The offering strongly suggests that the sudden arrival of pumice on the shores was recognized as being related to the danger threatening the site, against which attempts were being made to propitiate the divinities by offerings. Pumice in such great quantities could have reached the shores of Crete only by means of a volcanic wave. Such a wave, some 50 years earlier, had spread pumice over the northern shores; now the phenomenon was being repeated. That the appearance of this material heralded approaching disaster at both times was proved by the fact that at Zakros pumice was also found in a layer which covered the remains of the earlier palace.

We do not know whether the storage of pumice served a practical purpose or a ritual one. If the storing was done at a time when the threat of the rapidly approaching catastrophe had begun to be sensed, a practical use seems improbable. In favor of the second theory is the fact that pieces of painted stucco from portable altars were found with the pumice, and a pair of stone horns of consecration and the stepped pyramidal base of a double axe were not far away. Another example, exactly contemporary and similar, of offerings of lumps of pumice inside conical cups was noted some years before the Zakros excavations at the Minoan villa of Nirou Chani, 13 kilometers east of Heraklion, when I was working among the ruins there. The offerings were discovered in a deposit under the threshold of a blocked door of the shrine of the villa. The remains of ash from sacrifices were found in an enclosure next to the deposit, and four huge bronze double axes were standing nearby. This deposit, which apparently belonged to the shrine, included a large quantity of conical cups. Presumably the same ceremony of propitiating the divinity was being carried out.

The inhabitants of the island would have promptly recognized the significance of the arrival of pumice. It was brought by small volcanic waves produced by minor eruptions preceding the great eruption, and this had happened before. The catastrophe of 1500 B.C. would certainly have been well remembered. During that catastrophe other ceremonies were also conducted, including the sacrifice of bulls, as the investigations of the destroyed houses near the Palace of Knossos showed.

In addition to the pumice, another indication pointed even more clearly to the kind of destruction that was to occur. At many points about the palace, mostly in the layer immediately covering the walls and floors, were found cores of a strange substance which at first could not be identified. Some of these cores were as large as a boy's head, but most were much smaller. They were either spherical or irregular in shape and consisted of a molten metallic substance, spongy in parts, mixed with a yellowish material which suggested sulfur. Such a material could not have been produced by fusion of metals in the fire, since none of the bronze objects of the palace had melted. Besides, these cores were not found on the floor but only in the covering fill. Their texture and their wide dispersion precluded the possibility of their being cinders from a furnace; moreover no remains of such a furnace were found. As evidence gradually emerged to indicate that the destruction had been caused by an eruption of the Thera volcano, the suggestion was made that the material could be magma hurled from the crater. At first view, the distance of about 130 to 140 kilometers between Thera and eastern Crete made this explanation seem improbable. But in the Krakatoa eruption cores of solidified volcanic magma about the size of a human head had been hurled 60 kilometers, and certainly the Thera eruption had at least four times the force of that at Krakatoa. For the full verification of the origin of the molten mass it is necessary to have certain analyses and crystallographic researches, which so far for many reasons have not been effectuated. James W. Mavor, who carried out submarine investigations around Thera with the research ship *Chain,* examined a piece of the Zakros material and expressed a provisional opinion that it might be volcanic magma hurled directly from the erupting crater. Other scientists, however, showed some skepticism about such a possibility.

There is thus a considerable body of evidence that the destruction of Zakros resulted from the eruption of the volcano of Thera, estimated to have occurred about 1450 B.C., in which the greater part of the island of Thera was submerged. The phenomena accompanying the eruption must have been of great extent and intensity and would account for the destruction of the Minoan centers of central and eastern Crete, although the effect would have been greatest on the northern shores. By a comparison with the phenomena that accompanied the eruption of Krakatoa and also those of other volcanoes, it is possible to re-create the dramatic events of which Professor Marinatos has tried to give a general picture. As at Krakatoa, the awakening of the volcano was anticipated for months previously by small successive eruptions which poured forth lava and ashes. The pumice overflowed into the surrounding sea and was carried by small volcanic waves as far as the shores of Crete. The island of Thera was henceforth inaccessible. Earthquakes at intervals bore witness that the rock strata along the length of a volcanic crack going through Thera had become unstable.

The inhabitants of Crete were already suffering the results of the unchaining of the infernal powers. They must have believed that the chthonic divinities had been angered by their sins and that a way to appease them must be found. Ceremonies were conducted in the shrines, and offerings were made at the points where the presence of these divinities was most felt—at the sources of water, in the depths of sacred caves, in the underground repositories, in the lustral basins where steps led down toward the underworld. From time to time roaring, like that of an enraged bull, was heard, and the earth shook. Fear mounted. The soothsayers and augurs were constantly consulted.

Suddenly came the monstrous eruption, on a scale unique in human history. Because of its enormous force, already described as equaling that of several hundred hydogen bombs, the phenomena must have been more frightful than the most vivid fancy could conceive. Even at Crete the noises which accompanied it would have been deafening. The violence of the wind would have had force enough to damage buildings. The ash must have risen to a stratospheric height and immediately afterward spread into a very thick dark cloud, driven by the wind. The impenetrable darkness created by the cloud of ash must have lasted for several days. Day became night, and lamps had to be lighted everywhere. Fires started by the overturning lamps would have been spread very quickly by the wind. Then ash would have begun to fall, rendering the already overheated air almost unfit for breathing. Heavy glowing shells of solidified magma, hurled from the volcano, must have rained like bullets, reaching to incredible distances. The ground was shaken continuously by tremors. Poisonous exhalations began to reach the island. A condensation of vapors mingled with ash and particles of andesite would have caused showers of mud to fall, and the resulting whirls of wind by picking up dust from the red soil would have produced the phenomenon of sanguinary rain.

The inhabitants, in the utmost distress, must have fled toward the coast or taken shelter in caves until the disaster ended. Since they would not have had time or presence of mind to save many belongings, they would have taken with them only the things most precious to them. Imme-

diately afterward, however, an even worse calamity occurred. With unimaginable force and violence, with roaring and crashing, the tidal wave
caused by the collapse of the center of Thera reached the shores of Crete
an estimated 20 to 30 minutes later. At the bay of Zakros the impetuosity
of the wave would have been somewhat checked because the site is shel-
tered by projecting promontories. Nevertheless, the vehemence of the
wave would have been great and possibly would account for the tumbling
of whole solid walls from their foundations and for the compression and
squeezing of the pithoi toward the west walls of the magazines. The phenomenon certainly took the form of tides which continued for a long time
to rise and fall, gradually losing force. Such waves have also been observed
in cases of earthquakes having a sea center; one which occurred in the
south Aegean in 1956 caused a tidal rising and ebbing which continued
for many hours and altered the shape of the north shores of Crete. I have
watched the course of these phenomena with amazement, but they were as
nothing compared with the vehemence of the volcanic wave at the time
of the Thera eruption, which caused the subsidence of part of the Cretan
coasts and completely destroyed harbor installations such as those of
Zakros. The ships moored in the harbor would have been capsized by the
waves; many of them could have been hurled far inland. In one instance
reported of the tidal wave from the eruption of Krakatoa, a gunboat, lifted
up above the city of Telok Betong in Sumatra, was found 3.5 kilometers
from the shore at a height of 9 meters above sea level.

The hypotheses proposed concerning the consequences of the volcanic wave on the shores of Crete must not be considered exaggerated.
Observations carried out concerning the radius of activity of simple earthquake waves in relation to their height and power show that the estimates
were rather moderate. Thus the seismic wave of an earthquake of moderate
intensity occurring in 1956 on Amorgos, an island of the Cyclades, reached
the shores of Crete and Palestine with considerable force. The waves from
the earthquake in Chile in May 1960 had repercussions as far as Japan.
The seismic waves of Alaska in 1958 reached a height of 225 meters. Ancient chroniclers reported in connection with earthquakes in the Aegean
that waves were created which swept the shores and reached the mountains, hurling ships upon them. Historical accounts of the smaller volcanic

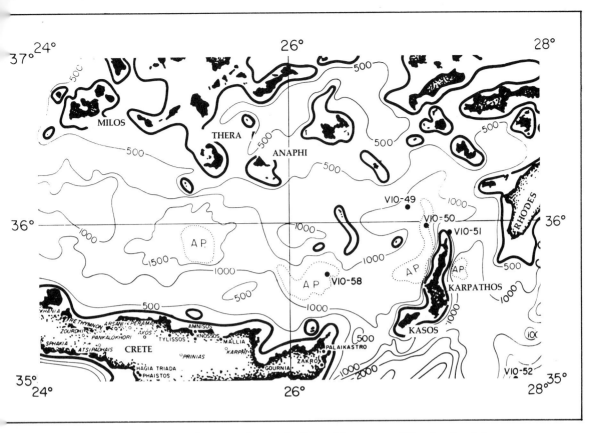

The eastern Aegean, with ocean depths indicated in meters. The depth of the sea in this area contributed to the height and velocity of the volcanic tidal wave

eruptions of Thera relate that the accompanying phenomena, although confined to the narrower circumference of the eastern Aegean, were very significant. The ash was swept by the winds to a distance of 100 kilometers, and on the neighboring islands were observed marked disturbances of the health of the inhabitants, a partial poisoning of the water, discoloring of the houses from the vapors, and other effects. Analysis of the waters of Thera showed significant quantities of iron and sulfur; this pollution was the cause of the signs of poisoning observed during the eruption of 1866. Vegetation was also destroyed at this time.

These accounts help to explain the devastation which followed the catastrophe at Zakros and the other Minoan palaces. The immediate effects of the eruption were destructive enough to cause panic and to create persistent phobias in the population. Such symptoms of panic and their consequences have been observed in other catastrophes of geological origin. In an earthquake in 1954, the most recent to occur in the Ionian Islands, for example, especially in Cephalonia and Zakynthos, a military force was required to prevent the population from abandoning those islands. But in Crete at the time of the great eruption subsequent conditions also were such as to render life in the central and eastern parts of the island almost impossible. The thick layer of ash destroyed all vegetation for a considerable time and made cultivation unproductive if not impossible. The water in the springs, where it had not dried up entirely, would have been polluted or at best rendered hardly drinkable. The scarcity of water added to the suffering. Various diseases, endemic and epidemic, increased the mortality, especially among children. The only possible course was to abandon the cursed land at least for a time, and to seek homes in the less damaged area of western Crete or even to leave the island entirely. Minoan elements found in settlements of the western Peloponnesus, especially in the regions of Messenia and Triphylia, and dated to this period, may have resulted from such emigration. The practice of deserting hitherto rich lands as a consequence of a volcanic eruption is very well known. In Iceland, after the eruption of 1362 A.D., when ash covered the cultivated lands to a thickness of 0.1 meter or more, the region around Oraefajökull was abandoned for ten years. Following the eruption of Hekla in 1104 A.D. the population of the region of Thjorsardalur left the area and never returned.

Obviously, full elucidation of the consequences of the eruption of the volcano of Thera at the middle of the fifteenth century B.C. will require detailed study of all evidence produced by investigation of the Minoan centers. Unfortunately, much of the excavation took place before any theory of seismic or volcanic causes for the destruction had been considered, and consequently a great deal of evidence was overlooked. Only a few sites provide a basis for definite conclusions.

The fact remains, however, that all the Minoan centers were destroyed and devastated at one time. At Knossos, Mycenaean elements took advantage of the situation to establish their own dynasty, very probably with the tolerance and possibly with the aid of such Minoans as had remained, and the palace was rebuilt. The rest of the Minoan centers survived only as simple village settlements, with greatly diminished populations. The subsequent domination of nearly all of Crete by the Mycenaean power at Knossos is easy to understand. That this occurred is proved by the tablets in the Knossian archives, which also reveal the foundation of many new Mycenaean centers. Gradually the results of the eruption disappeared; the layers of ash slowly dissolved and new soil built up; the waters cleared; climatic conditions returned to almost their original state. Only the extensive forests of great cypresses and cedars had permanently disappeared. Evans noted that in the last phase at Knossos wooden frames for doors and windows were unusual, as were wooden beams; his explanation was that the island had been stripped of its woods for earlier building operations. The political consequences of the destruction were also serious. The newly created conditions shifted the center of gravity to the Mycenaean world, which on the one hand was strengthened by the presence of Cretan refugees on the Greek mainland and on the other hand found its opportunity to dominate the entire eastern Mediterranean basin. The Mycenaean centers also suffered from the consequences of the volcanic eruption, but studies indicate that in that area the destruction was on a minor scale. The smaller Aegean islands, however, suffered in the same way as did Crete. The Minoan settlements of Phylakopi on Melos, of Kea, of Peparethos, of Trianda on Rhodes, of Cythera, were completely destroyed.

The Kefti disappeared from Egypt, and the Mycenaeans succeeded them in trade relations, as is evident from the strong Mycenaean influence and the abundance of Mycenaean objects in Egypt during the reigns of Amenhotep II, Thutmose IV, Amenhotep III, and Akhenaton (Amenhotep IV).

34   Once catastrophe has occurred, the survivors may bury the event in their memories, mentioning it so rarely that at last its history is forgotten—except in the recounting of myth or as an embellishment of fanciful story. Yet such accounts have grains of truth at their core. Finding those grains is also part of archaeology.

Reminiscences of the Catastrophe in Greek and Other Traditions

It is curious that the historical recollections of a disaster on such a scale and of such catalytic consequences are so slight. The explanation can undoubtedly be found in the dark and turbulent conditions of the period which followed the epoch of the Minoan-Mycenaean civilization. Dim memories of this brilliant civilization and the historical events of Mycenaean times were all that survived, and these are shrouded in the mists of myth.

According to myth, Thera was created by a lump of earth which Euphemus let fall into the water. The name of the latter is reminiscent of the Cyclops Polyphemus, who is described in the *Odyssey* as hurling huge rocks from his island into the sea. Many mythologists and other scientists have interpreted the myth of Polyphemus as relating to the action of the volcanoes of the Mediterranean, including that of Thera. Volcanic activity is reflected also in the myths of the gigantomachy, the war between the gods and the giants. That Enceladus, one of the giants, personified the terrible underground roaring is proved by his name, which means "infernal uproar." When the Greeks colonized Sicily, the activity of Enceladus was localized in the volcanoes of that island.

The only myth in which a volcanic destruction is definitely related to the disappearance of a land of highly developed civilization is the story of Atlantis, which is discussed in detail in the following chapter. Similarities between Minoan civilization and that described for Atlantis have long been recognized, and since the recent discoveries in connection with the partial collapse of Thera, other parallels have been noted.

Much more numerous are accounts of floods, sometimes attributed to long-continued rains, as in Genesis and the Babylonian epic of Gilgamesh, and sometimes to huge waves. The former category includes the Greek myth of Deucalion and Pyrrha, dated according to ancient chronology in the year 1529 B.C., but by Sir John Myres, according to his theories of genealogy, about 1430 B.C. Their boat grounded after nine days on the peak of Lykoreia of Parnassus, as did that of Noah on Ararat. In the Greek story, however, the waters drained away through the chasm of the river Ilissos in Attica. The Greek historian Herodotus, writing in the fifth century B.C., reported a tidal flood of the Thriasian Plain of Eleusis during the reign of Cecrops, traditionally the first king of Athens. According to legend, the sea god Poseidon contested with the goddess Athena for the possession of the city; when Cecrops decided in favor of the goddess, the vengeful Poseidon sent the flood. Herodotus's contemporary Euripides in his tragedy *Hippolytus* introduced an episode, probably based on tradition, of a gigantic wave which arrived with a terrible roar, as of underground thunder, and behind which the shore of Attica on the Saronic Gulf disappeared completely. Other traditions concerning a flood from the sea existed locally in different regions of Greece, as in Argos, and on some of the islands of the Aegean. In Lycia, where a Cretan settlement was believed to have been established under Sarpedon, the inhabitants preserved the memory of a huge wave that flooded the level shore to a great extent.

In the Orient and in Egypt, where historical tradition was almost continuous and many inscribed monuments have been preserved, it is natural to seek echoes that may relate to a catastrophe. A Phoenician poem from the ancient city of Ugarit (modern Ras Shamra, Syria), recently recognized as having been a Minoan settlement, attributed the total destruction of the city to the arrival of a sudden hurricane and a flood of water. The French archaeologist, Dr. Claude F. C. Schaeffer, who excavated the Phoenician city of Ugarit in 1929–1936, attributed the final destruction of the harbor, occurring between the years 1450 and 1400 B.C., to a seismic wave. Egyptian sources record that during a military expedition in Syria astonishing events of a supernatural character occurred which put to flight the Egyptian army. From the description it is not impossible that these were phenomena accompanying a volcanic eruption, the repercussions of which were felt to that remote area.

After the end of the Eighteenth Dynasty (1350 B.C.) prophetic texts referring to events of a much earlier period began to be circulated in Egypt. The conditions described in these texts, which have been cited by various scholars, could have been those that occurred as a result of the huge volcanic eruption on Thera: "For nine days there was no exit from the palace and no one could see the face of his fellow." "It is inconceivable what has happened in the land—to its whole extent confusion and terrible noise of tumult. Oh that the earth would cease from noise. . . . The towns are destroyed. . . . Upper Egypt suffered devastation . . . blood everywhere . . . pestilence throughout the whole country. . . ." "Men no longer sail to Byblos. What shall we do for cedar for our mummies . . . and for the oils with which chiefs are embalmed as far as the country of the Kefti? They come no more. . . ." "The sun is covered and does not shine to the sight of men. Life is no longer possible when the sun is concealed behind the clouds. Ra has turned his face from mankind. If only it would shine, even for one hour! No one knows when it is midday. One's shadow is not discernible. The sun in the heavens resembles the moon."

Since it was after the eruption that the Kefti ceased to come to Egypt bringing the cedars of Lebanon, the resin, and the aromatic oils so much used in burials and so indispensable for the after life, the meaning of the accounts in the prophecies now become clear.

The American scientist J. G. Bennett, and the Greek seismologist Angelos Galanopoulos have both suggested that these events may be related to the biblical account of the Exodus and of the plagues endured in Egypt. The chronology of the Exodus has always been disputed among the specialists, some placing it toward the end of the reign of

Thutmose III or about 1450 B.C., others during the reign of Ramses II (1301–1234 B.C.). Many scholars have suggested that Mosaic monotheism would probably have begun in the reign of the reformer pharaoh Akhenaton (c. 1372–1354 B.C.); Psalm 104 of the Bible has a very close resemblance to the hymn to the sun (Aton) composed by that king. The Hebraic Messianic prophecies are very similar to the Egyptian prophecies, though they are considered unrelated; possibly, then, they referred to the same events.

In the Bible Crete is called Kaphtor (a name related to the Egyptian term Kefti and the Anatolian term Kaptaru). The Cretans are called Philistines, because the latter people were believed to have come from Crete to establish themselves on the south shore of Palestine, after their expulsion from Egypt. According to the biblical prophets, the Israelites and the Cretans settled in Palestine at the same time—the period of the terrible events, often represented prophetically in the future. Thus the prophet Amos says: "Have not I brought up Israel out of the land of Egypt, and the Philistines from Caphtor [Kaphtor] and the Syrians from Kir?" (Amos 9:7). Zephaniah: "That day is a day of wrath, a day of wasteness and desolation, a day of darkness and gloominess, a day of clouds and thick darkness. . . . And I will bring distress upon men, that they shall walk as blind men. . . . Woe unto the inhabitants of the sea coast . . . the land of the Philistines. . . . I will even destroy you that there shall be no inhabitant" (Zephaniah 1:15; 2:5). Jeremiah: "Behold, the waters rise up out of the North and shall be an overflowing flood and shall inundate the land . . . because of the day that cometh to spoil all the Philistines . . . for the Lord wishes the extermination of the Philistines, the remnant of the country of Kaphtor" (Jeremiah 47:2, 4).

As Bennett first (1963) observed, the plagues of Egypt at the time of Exodus could probably be explained as results of the eruption of the volcano of Thera. But Galanopoulos also associated the resulting events with the tidal wave. The plagues, as described in the Bible, included the red color of the waters, the poisoning of the fish, the whirlwinds, the formation of swamps, the falling of red rain, the three-day darkness, the strong and violent winds, the swarms of locusts, the sudden epidemics of illness, and the death of the first-born. The Israelites, taking advantage

301

of the ensuing confusion, fled, following the beach as far as the lagoon of Sirbon, between the Nile Delta and Palestine. There the pursuing Egyptians almost overtook them. According to the explanation given by Galanopoulos, the Israelites did not pass through the Red Sea itself but through the narrow strip separating the shallows of Yam Suf (the Red Shoal or Shoal of Reeds) from the sea at the peninsula Bardawil, east of Port Said. The rising and falling of waters caused by the volcanic tidal wave could have produced a dry passage for the Israelites and then immediately afterward drowned the Egyptians by covering the narrow strip and the shallows.

Naturally this is only a hypothesis, and it is weakened by the disputed chronology. However, the dating of the Exodus at about 1450 B.C. is further supported by the tradition that this event happened 480 years before the beginning of King Solomon's reign in 970 B.C., which again places it at about 1450 B.C.

35

In the end it was the legend of Atlantis that remained in men's minds, while the ancient Minoan civilization fell out of memory. Now that modern excavation has revealed that civilization, is it true that Crete is Atlantis and Atlantis Crete?

Atlantis

Plato's story of Atlantis, the great island with a highly developed culture, which reportedly vanished into the sea during historic time, has had a stronger hold on the fancy of Western man than any other subject. The bibliography relating to it includes several thousand books, articles, and studies. The location of the island has been sought all over the world. The most generally accepted theory has been that it was a land in the Atlantic Ocean which was submerged in geological time, but so long ago that the widespread transmission of the details of so advanced a civilization cannot be satisfactorily explained. However, Plato's account, contained in the dialogues *Kritias* and *Timaios*, cites a definite source—the narrative of the priests of Saïs in Egypt—and relates specifically to a conflict between two great powers—one being the Atlanteans and the other the inhabitants of Attica and their allies. If Attica was indeed one of the powers, both the place and the time can be fixed: the area can only be the eastern Mediterranean and the time that of the height of Attic strength in the Mycenaean age.

Such an assumption, however, involves the necessity of explaining how the actual historical events could have been transformed into the shape which Plato gives them. In the dialogue *Kritias* Plato represents the younger Kritias as telling a story which he had heard from his grandfather, also named Kritias, whose father, Dropidas, had been told it by his friend Solon, the Athenian statesman and poet (c. 640–560 B.C.).

Solon traveled extensively over the then known civilized world and in the course of his journeying visited Egypt. There he had heard from the priests of Saïs an account of ancient historical events which had added glory to his country but about which no memory had been preserved in Greece. The subject was the conflict of Attica and her allies with the extensive island continent of Atlantis, which had developed a civilization of a preeminently high standard. The acme of the power of Attica, determined by the names of the hero kings mentioned, may be placed at the early Mycenaean period. The two powers that were contending for the control of the seas and the monopoly of trade in the eastern basin of the Mediterranean are now identified as the rulers of the Mycenaean mainland centers and those of Minoan Crete. According to the priests' account, after preparations on both sides, the conflict had just begun when it was suddenly interrupted by a geological catastrophe. Marked by violent earthquakes and floods for a day and a night, the disaster exterminated the entire Attic fighting force, stripped the Attic lands of their soil, and caused the whole land of Atlantis to vanish under the sea. The civilization of the sunken island disappeared, and in Attica the few survivors were reduced to a bare level of subsistence and all traces of their culture were also lost.

In the search for the lost continent of Atlantis, undue importance has been given to the fact that Plato's account places it outside the Pillars of Hercules—that is, the Straits of Gibraltar. Modern studies have shown that as the colonial expansion of Hellenism acquainted the Greeks with the Mediterranean world, many sites of semi-mythical events originally placed within the closed sea were relocated in the outer ocean. According to the earlier cosmographic conceptions, it was in the center of the Mediterranean that Atlas held the columns supporting the vault of heaven. Only later was the giant correlated with Mount Atlas on the northwest extremity of Africa, not far from the Pillars of Hercules. From this mountain the outer sea was given the name Atlantic Ocean.

Again, Plato's figure of 9,000 years for the time since the submersion should not be considered as precisely defining. That would place the events at the end of the Paleolithic Era, well beyond the beginning of recorded history. Some scientists have suggested that, instead of nine millennia, the figure could be interpreted as meaning nine centuries. Since Solon's journey to Egypt, which is a historical fact, is dated about 590 B.C., events 900 years earlier would have occurred about 1490 B.C. Egyptian chronicles, which cover only events later than 3000 B.C., could easily have preserved memories of that period, whereas the earlier date is far outside their scope. Moreover, the rise of the power of Attica, represented as contemporaneous with the catastrophe, has now been dated as not earlier than 1500 B.C.

The description of Atlantis contributes to a more accurate knowledge of Attica's rival than is provided by Hellenic tradition. The island is described as a large continent, and indeed the Egyptians had known Crete as an island continent, dominating the eastern Mediterranean. Its area of 3,200 square miles made it, for them, the largest island in the Mediterranean—even larger than Cyprus, which actually exceeds it in extent. And Crete, like Atlantis, was connected by a bridge of islands to the shores of the continents surrounding its sea.

Moreover, Plato's account contains other analogies with Crete and its civilization. In the country of the Atlanteans, runs the narrative, the kings had developed unique power; not only did they rule their own island but their influence extended to the surrounding islands and reached as far as Egypt and Libya and Etruria as well. The Atlanteans prepared a large expedition for the conquest of Attica and the other surrounding lands and began the struggle. However, they had not expected a valiant opponent with strong military preparation, which they found in the united power of the Greeks with Attica heading the coalition. In the matter of Attic leadership, Athenian chauvinism perhaps somewhat altered the facts, but the antagonism of the two powers, the Minoan and the Mycenaean, in the eastern Mediterranean is an undisputed historical fact. This antagonism brought about the coalition of the Mycenaeans and their allies and the final counterattack against Minoan Crete; their success was certainly due at least in part to the destruction of the palaces by the natural forces unleashed by the eruption.

These historical facts have been clarified by recent discoveries, and the decipherment of the Knossian archives of Linear B script has provided definite proof of the establishment of an Achaean dynasty at Knossos in the last phase of that palace. Also confirmed was the presence in Crete of large numbers of Achaeans, bearers of the late Mycenaean civilization. In Plato's account, however, the Hellenic element is represented as having already prevailed at the time the catastrophe occurred, whereas the historical fact is that those who established the Achaean dynasty at Knossos took advantage of that event.

According to the concise account in the dialogue *Timaios*, the island-continent was entirely submerged, and the sea at the spot for a long time was impassable because of the mud which remained after the submergence. In *Kritias*, the narrative digresses into a detailed description of an imaginary ideal form of government. This dialogue, however, was left unfinished, and the account ends abruptly exactly at the point when the struggle was about to begin and the gods had already decided upon the penalty for the arrogant power. Possibly this was the point at which the epic poem that Solon was said to have written on the subject was cut off.

The royal line of the rival power is represented as unique and wonderful, deriving its descent from a divine origin. The description begins with a mythological account of the marriage of Poseidon to Cleito, a mortal, and their founding of the first settlement on a mound in an immense plain. The security of the divine establishment was assured by means of three circular zones of water enclosing two zones of land and a central spot. The connection of these zones was achieved by bridges and canals, a larger and longer canal joining the outer zone to the sea, where the outside harbor was constructed parallel to other harbors in each of the zones. On the hill there was a palace, which each succeeding king did his utmost to adorn.

Poseidon and Cleito had ten sons. The eldest, named Atlas, was given the overlordship of the island, and it and the ocean were named after him. He retained the plain and the original establishment, and the remainder of the island was divided among the other nine brothers who were also the heads of royal families. There was thus created a hierarchy of kings, first among whom was the one descended of Atlas.

The kings of this family accomplished great works. They built three circuits of walls and coated these respectively with copper, tin, and orichalc. With an innate inclination for color they combined stones of a variety of hues to cover the façades of the buildings. In the process of quarrying stone for their building operations they hollowed out shipyards along the shore. Inside the palace there was a shrine to Poseidon and Cleito, at which offerings of their finest products were made. The shrine was adorned with rich metals and ivories; the walls, columns, and floors were covered with orichalc, in which the light was reflected. Many and rich were the offerings of the kings and numerous the worshipers. They constructed buildings around the springs and planted trees to shade them. Cisterns, some with hot water, some with cold, supplied comforts for all classes, and drinking troughs refreshed the domestic animals. Water was diverted for irrigating the sacred grove of Poseidon and conveyed by aqueducts to the outer zone.

Special buildings in the outer zones housed most of the royal guard; of these, however, some were housed in the inner zone, and the most trusted of all had dwellings around the palace, near the apartments of the king.

The harbors were full of movement and noise from the continuous coming and going of ships and people and the loading and unloading of merchandise.

The city was on an extensive plain, surrounded by mountains, of which the south slopes fell abruptly toward the sea. On the slopes and the foothills of these mountains were many settlements. The landscape surrounding this plain was varied, as was the vegetation and animal life. An elaborate system of irrigation canals so increased the productivity of the plain that two crops could be harvested every year. Navigable canals connecting the zones of water aided the transport of the harvests and of timber from the mountains. The water collected from the mountains was distributed through a peripheral canal.

The organization of political, social, economic, and religious life was equally admirable. The military organization depended on a feudal system. The areas ruled by each of the ten kings were divided into allotments, with a leader in each responsible for providing men and equipment for military and naval service.

Each king ruled his particular area, but the relations among the kings and the general exercise of authority were regulated by the commands of

Poseidon transmuted through the law and the records of the first rulers inscribed on a stele of orichalc in the central sanctuary. There the ten kings assembled at regular intervals to make decisions on important common affairs and to judge themselves and others.

Before passing judgment, the kings took part in a very old ceremony. It began with the capture of a bull within the sacred grove, which was accomplished with only a staff of wood and a noose. The bull's throat was cut so that its blood was shed on the inscribed stele. Various rites followed, including libations of wine and of blood of the sacrificed bull in golden vessels. When night fell, the fires were extinguished, and the kings, wearing blue robes, seated themselves on the ground among the ashes of the sacrifice and made judgments and decisions. When morning came, the decisions were written on golden tablets and deposited in the sanctuary along with the robes.

Many laws defined the royal authority, among the most important being that the kings should never make war upon one another, that they should make common cause against every attempt to overthrow the royal power, and that decisions upon significant subjects should be made in common under the leadership of the king descended from Atlas.

Through many generations the kings were distinguished for their prudence, piety, and love of peace; they never aspired to excess of power and regarded virtue and amity as more important than wealth. But when at last the divine part of their nature became degraded through marriages with ordinary mortals, their noble qualities degenerated into greediness and arrogance. In their new lust for power, they planned, according to the Egyptian priests, to enslave the whole Mediterranean world. This attempt was completely frustrated by the Greeks, a preeminently war-like people who, organized into a powerful coalition, had accomplished great deeds under the effective protection of Athena, herself a warlike divinity.

Among the Greeks the warrior class was distinguished among the other classes—priests, artisans, shepherds, hunters, and farmers. They were guardians of the laws and they held property in common. The land of Attica before the catastrophe was naturally rich and productive and rendered more so by the exceptional diligence of its inhabitants. But after the floods and the terrible earthquakes its soil was stripped and became unproductive. The Acropolis of Athens had previously been extensive and provided ample support for the warriors and the priests who lived on it. The strength and merit of Attica were proved in the great conflict with the colossal power of Atlantis. Although the account in *Kritias* breaks off before the war began, the outcome and the catastrophe are described in *Timaios*.

After Plato's time most Greeks seem to have been indifferent or skeptical in regard to this astonishing narrative. Aristotle reportedly said of Atlantis that its creator, meaning Plato, had done away with it. However, the philosopher Krantor (c. 335–275 B.C.), whose commentary on *Timaios* was the first of numerous commentaries on Plato, was assured of the authenticity of the narrative by Egyptians, who showed him related hieroglyphic inscriptions which he was unable to check. The Stoic philosopher Posidonius (first century B.C.) was among the few who believed that the legend embodied facts of ancient history and actual geological events.

Many changes were later made in the legend. The most important variant was that transmitted by the Graeco-Roman historian Diodorus Siculus (first century B.C.), who located Atlantis in western Libya. Upon this basis, the French writer Pierre Benoît wrote his novel *L'Atlantide*.

The first modern scholar to point out the astonishing analogies with Minoan Crete in Plato's account of Atlantis was an English archaeologist, K. T. Frost, who first published his theory anonymously in *The Times* (London) in 1909 only a few years after the first Minoan discoveries, and later expanded it in an article entitled "Critias and Minoan Crete" (*Journal of Hellenic Studies*, 33 [1913]). Frost rejected the idea that Atlantis was an invention by Plato. The transmission of the tradition through Solon, Dropidas, Kritias the elder, and the younger Kritias, all historical figures, seemed plausible to him, and the source of the details from the priests of Saïs, on the basis of hieroglyphic records, not improbable. Solon's intercourse with the priests through interpreters would not have been different from that held by the historian Herodotus when he visited Egypt in the following century. That Solon, well known as a poet, should use such material in an epic was natural. Solon's epic would have had a didactic purpose, to show how a well-governed and peaceful people of brilliant achievements through lawless arrogance embarked on an iniquitous war against the admirably organized Hellenic coalition. The historical basis of the account is not invalidated by the alterations inserted to aggrandize Attica.

Frost attributed to the epic imaginative exaggeration based on details drawn from Egypt and the Orient. He theorizes, however, that behind all this Minoan Crete is clearly evident, with its marvelous harbors and luxurious palaces, its training of athletes, its bull games, its mysterious ceremonies. The disappearance of Atlantis for the Egyptians, he suggests, was not a physical disappearance but the failure of the Kefti to return and the cutting off of communications with them. The correspondence to known facts makes clear, in Frost's view, the improbability that the account was merely a fictional narrative. Recollections of the historical facts also lingered in myths and epics. The Egyptians preserved memories of their own close connection with a rich island continent of exceptional political development, with a centralized and basically theocratic administration, of its rivalry with the Mycenaean centers, of the penetration of the Cretans into Attica, of the catastrophes that devastated the island, and of the final successful aggression of Greek invaders in Crete. The myth of Theseus bears witness to the struggle of Crete with Attica. Notwithstanding the exaggerations, the achievements of the latter reflect the military organization of the Mycenaean power, which was destroyed by the surging migrations of the Peoples of the Sea and by the Dorian invasion of Greece.

Frost also recognized the correspondence in the geographical description of Atlantis as the chief of the series of islands connected with the neighboring continent. Its dominion extended to the eastern as well as to the western Mediterranean, through settlements and the establishment of trade stations, and the position of the palace on the plain surrounded by mountains also corresponded to Minoan Crete. Frost explained the translocation to the Atlantic Ocean by a misinterpretation of the name of Mount Atlas. For the Egyptians Crete was the faraway land, the contemporary Far West. The Mediterranean was considered an ocean, and around it were situated the four columns supporting the vault of the heavens. The Greeks of the fifth century B.C. would never have connected Atlantis with Crete, which to them was merely a Dorian island, the past history of which was completely forgotten. Nor did they relate Crete to the civilization of Homer's Phaeacians, which today is believed to reflect the Minoan culture.

Since Frost, many scholars have supported the identification of Atlantis with Minoan Crete, in articles, lectures, studies, and books. In 1945 I delivered two lectures on the subject at Heraklion. Later Spyridon Marinatos, who first connected the destruction of the Minoan centers with the eruption of the volcano of Thera, wrote about it in his book *Crete and Mycenae* (New York, Abrams, 1960). The geological evidence of the eruption has made the identification more convincing, and in 1960 it was presented in a new form by Angelos Galanopoulos, professor of seismology in the University of Athens. The British archaeologist J. V. Luce, in *Lost Atlantis* (New York, McGraw-Hill, 1969), places himself in accord with the view that Plato's account is based on historical facts relating to the events in the eastern Mediterranean basin at the time of the great eruption of the volcano of Thera. The transformation of these events before their transmission to Solon by the priests of Saïs and their further revision in Solon's epic can be attributed to the influence of surviving legends; Plato's dialogues interpreted these for didactic purposes.

In this connection it must be emphasized that the elements of Plato's narrative which correspond to historical reality are much more numerous than present-day studies have yet made clear. The dominion of the Atlanteans over a large part of the Mediterranean world, extending as far as Libya and Etruria, and their intention of expanding it to mainland Greece reflects the wide program of Minoan commercial penetration through trade stations and colonies, which research confirmed. The antagonism of the Minoan and Mycenaean worlds in the sphere of economic enterprise has been proved, as well as the domination of the Mycenaeans in Crete after the destruction of the Minoan palaces. Attica's primary role in this movement, as described in Plato's account and attested by many traditions, is not yet confirmed, but it does not seem at all improbable if we take into account the legends of Minoan penetration into the Saronic Gulf of Attica.

That penetration by Crete as far as Libya took the form of the establishment of a permanent colony is not impossible. A Cretan from Itanos later led a colony from Thera to found Cyrene. Evans attributed to Minoan initiative the construction of the Pharos harbor in the Delta of the Nile. For Cretan penetration of Lycia and Caria not only many ancient traditions bear witness, but also many data from recent investigations. Schaeffer recognized a Minoan installation at Ugarit and others along the shore of Phoenicia. Some scholars, including myself, today believe that the older form of the Phoenician civilization was largely due to these establishments. Cadmus, the founder of Thebes, probably led from Phoenicia a colony in which Minoan elements participated, a fact which explains the Minoan-Phoenician character of the settlement in Thebes. Cretan penetration as far as Etruria has also been ascertained, and current research seems to indicate that the Tyrrhenian-Etruscans emigrated from the eastern Aegean and had connections with Minoan Crete.

Concerning the military organization of the Mycenaean world, many details are known from the numerous weapons found, as well as from the representations of fighters and from the archives. The coalition of Mycenaean leaders for common purposes is attested by tradition; the Seven against Thebes, the Epigonoi (sons of the Seven), the Argonauts, the expeditionary force against Troy, and what we know about the enterprises of Achijava into the eastern Aegean and the opposite coast. These enterprises are later than the events of the great destruction, but a wide ethnic movement is evidenced even for the time immediately preceding. Otherwise the establishment of an Achaean dynasty at Knossos would have been inconceivable.

The description of events relating to the eruptions of the Thera volcano and its terrible consequences is sufficient to associate these with the destruction of Atlantis in Plato's account. There is no doubt that the inhabitants of Crete attributed the catastrophe, as Plato's narrative did, to the wrath of the gods. About 1500 B.C. many offerings to the deities were deposited in the caves of Crete. Most of these offerings seem to belong to a definite time. Immediately thereafter, the sacred cave of Arkalochori collapsed as a consequence of the first eruption, covering the offerings. At the same time the palaces and the surroundings houses were ruined, and huge stones from them were hurled about. In some of the houses, ceremonies accompanied by the sacrifice of bulls were performed. There were offerings on the sacred sites, in which pumice was included. This catastrophe, however, was in no way comparable to the final one, which a steadily increasing amount of evidence relates to the last cataclysmic eruption of the Thera volcano. (At Krakatoa also, an eruption two hundred years before the final one had indicated that the volcano was becoming more active.)

There is one significant difference between the disaster of Atlantis and that of Crete. The first was submerged and disappeared; the shores of the latter were flooded by the volcanic tidal wave and its centers were destroyed but the island was not actually submerged. Its shores, however, were altered, and parts of them subsided into the sea. Today one can distinguish some ruins of the Minoan harbors, shipyards hewn in the rocks, lying partly or entirely under the surface of the sea—for instance, at Katsambas, near Heraklion, in the little harbor of Haghii Theodoroi near Nirou Chani, at Mochlos, and near Sitia. Whether these were submerged at the time of the eruption or later, whether the sinking occurred abruptly or was a gradual process, are questions not yet answered. Current opinion among geologists tends to the theory of sudden submergence after the eruption.

The submergence of two-thirds of the island of Thera inevitably had colossal repercussions throughout the Mediterranean area; certainly it could have been recorded in accounts of the disasters striking the country of the Kefti, which was known to the Egyptians.

Professor Galanopoulos, seeking a closer correspondence with Plato's story, has suggested that Thera, which was partially submerged, should be identified at Atlantis. He based his theory principally upon the description of the zones of water and land around the main center of Atlantis, which he related to the shape of Thera before the submergence. His views are presented in *Atlantis: The Truth Behind the Legend* (Indianapolis: Bobbs-Merrill, 1969). To check this theory, soundings were made by the research ship *Chain*, and Mavor conducted further research near the shore, described in his *Voyage to Atlantis* (New York: Putnam, 1969). The results, however, were not definitive. In any case, most of the evidence to date suggests that though Thera, like other islands in the Cyclades, had Minoan settlements, it could hardly have been the center of the exceptional civilization which is described for Atlantis and which corresponds in so many respects to the archaeological findings in Crete.

Whether the destruction on Crete was caused chiefly by the direct force of the eruption or by its aftereffects of tides, falling ash, and earthquakes with resulting fires cannot yet be determined. However, since no human remains from either the final disaster or the preceding one have been discovered, it seems obvious that people had time to escape. Further evidence of this is provided by the numerous treasures of bronze objects which were found buried under palace floors, especially at Knossos, apparently hidden by the inhabitants in the great haste of their departure, with the hope of recovering them later. Almost without exception, these treasures belong to the final phase of the palaces, although Evans dated most of them to the end of the preceding period.

The earthquakes that preceded, accompanied, and followed the eruption were sufficiently powerful to destroy the Cretan cities. Several times since, Crete has suffered terrible earthquakes, some of which produced tidal waves analogous with those of the volcanic eruptions. Reports which have been preserved tell of the sea's inundating many miles of the coast and in one instance of ships being hurled more than a kilometer from the beach onto the surrounding hills. A Sibylline oracle was said to have prophesied that Crete would ultimately disappear under the water.

The layer of mud which prevented access to the area of Atlantis after the island was submerged, as recorded by Plato, was probably the very dense layer of pumice which filled the seas after the eruption. No other material could have floated on the deep swell of the Aegean. After the eruption of Krakatoa the Sebesi channel was totally blocked for ships by floating volcanic material. The Greek geographer Strabo, writing in the first century B.C., characterized as floating mud the layer of pumice from the eruption of the Stromboli volcano in Sicily. This material is described as subsequently congealing and hardening. This phenomenon was later connected with accounts of nautical adventure, as on the mythical island of Kerne, which was later, like Atlantis, transposed to the Atlantic Ocean. This island was related to Atlantis in a later variation of the narrative preserved by Diodorus.

The high evaluation of Cretan power by the Egyptians is known from their records. The land of the Kefti was included among the great powers. The participation of women in the bull games and other activities represented in Plato's narrative is also well known in the Creto-Mycenaean world; women participated in hunts and bull fights, appearing in armor, and engaged in other occupations more often regarded as manly. The armed female divinity is the same one who appears in the Mycenaean world, the forerunner of Athena. In Crete also arms were dedicated to the great goddess and to the young god later identified with Zeus.

The stripping and despoiling of the soil as a consequence of the disaster has been confirmed for Crete as well as for the Mycenaean area. It seems rather probable that these consequences of the catastrophe were very serious. Upon this subject special studies have been written, including Rhys Carpenter's *Discontinuity in Greek Civilization* (New York: Norton, 1968). However, these attribute to different causes the alteration in the conditions of life. Regions with luxuriant vegetation, such as the hill of Colonus north of Athens, were stripped, and the rock appeared on the surface. Rivers changed to simple streams or to torrents, as was the case with Kairatos, the river of Knossos, a contributary of which was formerly bridged by a huge viaduct. The extensive cypress and cedar groves ceased to exist.

The special worship of a male god identified with Poseidon, god of water and earthquakes, among whose titles were "earthshaker" and "dominator of the earth," and to whom bulls were sacred, has been proved for the Minoan as well as for the Mycenaean area. The myth of the beautiful bull sent by Poseidon and his union with Minos's queen Pasiphaë is related to the marriage of Poseidon and Cleito in the Atlantis story. Hellenic myth includes also the union of Zeus, king of the gods, with the maiden Europa. In the form of a bull, Zeus carried Europa to Crete, where she bore him children, one of whom was Minos, and she afterward married the king of Crete, who adopted her sons.

Poseidon was also the principal divinity of the Minyai, possibly a branch of the Minoans, who settled in the district of Orchomenos in continental Greece. The same god was worshiped in Pylos, which was colonized by the Minyai, as well as in Scheria, the country of the nautical

Phaeacians. He is said to have punished the Phaeacians by covering their land with a mountain, a destruction not unlike that which overtook Atlantis. In the civilization of this nautical people most scholars recognize basic similarities to the Minoan culture.

The principal center of Atlantis, that of the family of Atlas, as Frost and other scholars agree, bears less resemblance to Knossos than to Phaistos, which is on an extensive plain, surrounded by mountains, analogous to Plato's description, with slopes falling abruptly to the sea—the Asterousia range—and having on the slopes and foothills many settlements, of which a number have been traced. To these belong the numerous excavated tholos tombs of Pre-palatial and Proto-palatial date and the many cemeteries of rock-cut chamber tombs of the Neo-palatial and Post-palatial periods. The Egyptians were best acquainted with this region, disembarking at the southern harbors of Matala and Lebena (ancient Leben). In this vital area, according to Evans, the first Minoans settled. Its location would explain the influx of people from ancient Libya. The principal Minoan settlement there was built on a hill, as was that of Atlantis.

However, whether in this and in other important regions the Minoans had carried out technical works corresponding to those described for Atlantis is still not clear. Systematic improvement of the plain of Mesara around Phaistos, mainly by irrigation, appears very probable; otherwise so many settlements could not have subsisted around it. Irrigation systems consisting of a network of crossed canals connected with a peripheral one assembling the waters and with other ones draining them are not unlikely to have been established by the Minoans in the plain of Mesara, as similar works have been proved to be on the plateau of Lasithi, where some of the irrigation canals crossing one another in a checkerboard pattern, known as *linies*, have been cleaned out and are again in use. Similar too, but on a larger scale, was the system of irrigation canals carried out by the Minyai at Orchomenos for the draining and irrigation of the Kopais swamps. These works were partly rediscovered in 1886 by the English company which drained the swamps and reclaimed much land for agricultural use.

Other huge works, such as viaducts, shipyards cut into the rock, harbors, and the type of enceinte walls which were later developed in the Mycenaean region into gigantic defensive works, with towers, monumental gates, arched galleries and storerooms in the thickness of the walls, and systems of guarding and control, have become known through exploration in Crete and in the whole Creto-Mycenaean area, showing the source of some of the elements utilized in the account of Atlantis. Although the descriptions of these are poetically aggrandized in the narrative, they do not seem to depart essentially from historical fact. It is thought today that small ships could have come up the Kairatos River as far as the Palace of Knossos, and in the bed of the river at a villa in the Sitia area a wharf for landing and narrow stairways leading directly from the river to the terraced sections of the villa have been found.

While not much is known about the Minoan harbors, we do know something about certain harbor works, such as shipyards, beacons, storerooms, and wharfs. So great a work as the harbor at Pharos in the Nile Delta, which the researches of the French archaeologist Gaston Jondet in 1915 proved to have been constructed by Cretans, shows that the Minoans possessed technical abilities equal to those described in the account of Atlantis. Concave double shipyards hollowed out of rock are visible even today on the beach near Heraklion. While inner harbors accessible through a channel have not yet been found in Minoan Crete, the technique of building the so-called *kothones* was probably first developed by the Minoans, who seem to have taught it to the Phoenicians. In the region of Phalasarna of western Crete there are traces of a "closed harbor," away from the shore and accessible through a channel, which date from early Hellenic times. The correspondence to Atlantis is too close to be ascribed to pure chance. The walls described as surrounding the zones encircling the central seat of the Atlanteans suggest enceinte walls such as have been found at Knossos and Phaistos, rather than strong fortifications.

The shrine of Poseidon at the center of the central hill, evidently inside the palace, seems similar to the central shrines of the Minoan palaces. The richness and decoration of the latter have become so well known through extended investigations that detailed comparisons are not necessary. Although no wall linings of precious metals have been found, lining with crystallic gypsum is well known, especially at Knossos and Phaistos, and this with its reflections produced an effect analogous with the lining of orichalc Plato described. The pursuit of polychrome effects by a combination of different materials is one of the principal characteristics of Minoan architecture. The interior of the Treasury of Atreus at Mycenae, adorned, as was its gate, after Minoan prototypes, provides an illustration of the combination of carved stones and metal elements, such as were described for the palace of Atlantis.

That the principal richness of the Minoan palaces came from the offerings to the gods and from the ceremonial equipment of the shrine has been proved by the various excavations. The storerooms were full of offerings of the finest products, and the utensils in the depositories amount to many hundreds; both offerings and deposits are similar to those described for Atlantis.

Equally significant analogies are contained in the section on the amenities of life, especially those related to water. In no other early civilization have so many installations for water been found as existed among the Minoans, from whom the Mycenaeans learned the technique. It is sufficient to mention only the various bath chambers, the lustral basins, the system of hot water in the Caravanserai at Knossos, the built-in spring chambers of Knossos and Zakros, the cisterns and spring wells in the Palace of Zakros and at Arkhanes. Royal gardens and groves with various exotic animals are pictured in wall paintings, and sites of such gardens have been discovered. The paintings also show athletic exercises, dances, games, somersaults, almost always closely connected with ceremonies in honor of the goddess. Corresponding details were described in the *Odyssey* in relation to the land of the Phaeacians. Wall paintings at Knossos showed the use of chariots in earlier periods than those in the Mycenaean area, where similar chariots are represented in the wall paintings. However, chariots are more often represented on seal stones and rings. Chariots races like those on Atlantis are by no means unlikely.

Moreover, the political and social organization of Atlantis offers many analogies to that of Minoan Crete. The four palace centers so far discovered seem to confirm the co-existence of several kings, among whom the one at Knossos appears to have ranked first among equals (*primus inter pares*). A theocratic political organization like that described for Atlantis would have provided the basis for the so-called *pax Minoica* which was the source of the Cretan *eunomia,* that exemplary condition of civil order under excellent laws. The capture of the sacrificial bull so closely corresponds to the Minoan custom represented in various works of art that the source for the Atlantis narrative can only be regarded as genuinely historical. The engraved stele in the shrine corresponds to the quadrangular pillars with incised sacred signs in the center of the Minoan crypts. Basins for the collection of the libation liquids have been discovered, there, and the existence of layers of sacrificial ashes has also been ascertained. The golden cups used in the Atlantis ceremonial have parallels in the famous Vaphio chalices with their representations of the capture of bulls and in the tall golden chalice of Nestor found at Mycenae, as well as in the stone chalices for sacred communion, found mainly at Zakros, but also in other palaces. Even the blue of the kings' robes seems to have verisimilitude; that color predominated in the Minoan crypts and in the equipment for rituals in shrines and in tombs. The sacrifice of a bull is very frequently portrayed in Minoan and Mycenaean art in the same way that is described as occurring in Atlantis.

There are still other analogies, but enough have already been cited to show how faithfully the narrative about the civilization of the Atlanteans reflects the Minoan world which so suddenly and strangely vanished.

Even the reference to the mingling of the sacred breed with inferior families can be explained by the intrusion in Crete of people from continental Greece, since recent discoveries have shown that the introduction of Achaean customs and practices had begun before the destruction. Conservatives would have considered such changes as a defiance of the divinely inspired laws, provoking an unleashing of the infernal powers to punish the people. Priests and elders would have inveighed against the younger people for arrogance and lawlessness. The soothsayers would have seen the premonitory portents of the coming disaster. By the time the people began trying to propitiate the deity by supplications and sacrifices, the terrible punishment was already arriving, implacable and unavertible. The civilization once so favored was destroyed, its brilliant creations were swept away, and the land was devastated for many years. The people who survived became wanderers, seeking new homes in less damaged areas or in other countries and surviving only by continuous struggle. The abrupt total devastation of the flourishing harbor of Zakros is one of the most characteristic instances of the ruin. Whatever remained vanished from the historical consciousness of the neighboring Mediterranean peoples, who for so long a time had accepted the cultural leadership of the Minoan civilization. Only a memory, itself darkened by the shadow of myth, survived until the time of Solon, to be transmitted to that wise representative of the new Greek world in the form of a narrative—the story of lost Atlantis.

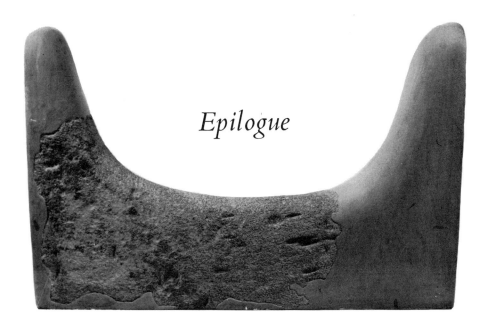

Epilogue

The excavations at Zakros will be continued until the palace is revealed in its entirety, showing the full extent of the East and South wings, as well as the exterior courts. The annexes on the North Slope will be further explored and their interpretation clarified; further study of the stratigraphy will be necessary to understand the evolution of the whole complex. Much more remains to be learned also about the town and its harbor installations.

The results already attained have not only added much corroborative detail to the picture of Minoan culture revealed by the earlier excavations but have also provided solutions to many controversial problems and data that should lead to the solution of others. Since the Palace of Zakros had not been plundered or even seriously disturbed, scientific methods developed since the period of the first excavations could be applied there to an extent that would not have been possible with the other palaces.

Perhaps the most significant result was the dating of the final destruction of all the Minoan palaces. This has been proved to have occurred during the gigantic eruption of the Thera volcano around 1450 B.C. To obtain this date it was necessary to survey afresh the whole chronology of all the palaces and the problems of Minoan chronology in general. By a fortunate coincidence, new explorations of the Minoan settlement on Thera, destroyed at the same time, have paralleled the Zakros work.

Naturally new questions have been raised, and further investigation and study will be required to find their answers. When the explorations at Zakros are completed, the results will be published in full archaeological detail. The publication will provide scholars with abundant material from which to draw conclusions on many of the most controversial aspects of Minoan civilization. Meanwhile, with increasing evidence of the extent to which archaeology, and prehistoric archaeology in particular, has captured the imagination of the general reader, the excitement of the discovery of the palace and the significance of the finds already made seem to provide sufficient justification for the present book.

CHRONOLOGICAL TABLE

MINOAN CRETE

EGYPT		Evans's Chronology (Revised)		Chronological System Used in This Book		DATES (B.C.)
OLD KINGDOM	Third Dynasty	NEOLITHIC ERA		NEOLITHIC PERIOD		AFTER 2700
	Fourth Dynasty					2600
	Fifth Dynasty	EARLY MINOAN PERIOD	Phase I	PRE-PALATIAL PERIOD	I	2500
	Sixth Dynasty					2400
FIRST INTERMEDIATE PERIOD	Seventh to Tenth Dynasties		Phase II		II	2300
						2200
MIDDLE KINGDOM	Eleventh Dynasty		Phase III		III	2100 2000
	Twelfth Dynasty	MIDDLE MINOAN PERIOD	I A	PROTO-PALATIAL PERIOD		1900
			I B		I	
			II A		II	1800
			II B		III	1700
SECOND INTERMEDIATE PERIOD	Thirteenth to Seventeenth Dynasties		III A	NEO-PALATIAL PERIOD	I	1600
			III B		II	
NEW KINGDOM	Eighteenth Dynasty	LATE MINOAN PERIOD	I A		III	1500
			I B		IV KNOSSOS	1400
			II A, B			
	Nineteenth Dynasty		III A	POST PALATIAL PERIOD	I	1300
			III B		II	1200
	Twentieth Dynasty		III C		III	
		SUB-MINOAN PERIOD		SUB-MINOAN PERIOD		1100

GREEK PERIOD { PROTO-GEOMETRIC GEOMETRIC ORIENTALIZING

METRIC TABLE

Equivalents of Units Used in the Text

Metric Unit	Abbre-viation	Metric Equivalent	Approximate U.S. Equivalent
LENGTH			
kilometer	km	1,000 meters	0.62 mile
meter	m	1	39.37 inches
centimeter	cm	0.01 meter	0.39 inch
MASS AND WEIGHT			
metric ton	MT or t	1,000,000 grams	1.1 tons
kilogram	kg	1,000 grams	2.2046 pounds
gram	g or gm	1	0.035 ounce

GLOSSARY

ACROPOLIS. Term used to describe any fortifications built on high ground for the purpose of defending a city in ancient times. From the Greek words meaning "high" and "city." Most famous acropolis is that of Athens, built fifth century B.C.

AMPHORA. A large, two-handled pottery jar, with a slender neck and pointed base, usually used to store oil or wine.

ARCHITRAVE. Beam, the lowest element of an ENTABLATURE, sometimes referred to as the epistyle.

ASHLAR. Squared, dressed stone used for building or facing a wall, as opposed to rough, unfinished stone.

ASHLAR MASONRY, DRESSED. Masonry made of cut, squared, and finished building stone.

BALUSTRADE. Rail supported by closely spaced symmetrical posts, as on a staircase, a parapet, balcony, etc.

BETYL. From bet-el, a stone as domicile of the god. A conical sacred stone which was worshipped as symbolic of a deity.

BEZEL. The top part of a ring; may be a flat surface, hold a gem, or bear an intaglio or other decoration.

CALCINE. The ashy substance which remains after stone or metal has been heated to a high temperature.

CALDERA. The large, basinlike depression which occurs as the result of an explosion of a volcano and the collapse of its center.

CALYX. Wine bowl shaped like the calyx of a flower.

CARTOUCHE. A rounded scroll-shaped space which is surrounded with carvings and ornamental scrollwork designs.

CHALICE. Drinking vessel with a stem and base; usually, such a vessel employed for sacred communion in religious ceremonies.

CHTHONIC. Pertaining to underworld deities or spirits.

CIST. Box, usually of stone slabs, used for storage or ritual deposits of objects after a burial is placed in a cist.

CLERESTORY. Upper portion of a room, which is located above surrounding rooftop level and has windows to let in the light.

COLONNADE. A row of columns spaced at regular intervals.

CORBEL. Architectural element projecting from a wall; corbels in graduated steps form a vault.

CORNICE. An ornamental, horizontally projecting band which forms the highest portion of an ENTABLATURE.

CRATER. A former volcano opening, which is usually defined by a circular, basinlike depression.

CREPIS. A compact foundation platform which supports walls, colonnades, or other structures.

CULT, adj. Related to religious rites and worship—cult room, cult object.

CYCLADIC CULTURE. Culture which arose during the Bronze Age on the islands of the Aegean, specifically on the Cyclades Islands.

CYCLOPEAN MASONRY. Masonry built of large, irregular blocks of undressed stone.

DOUBLE AXE. A two-bladed axe used as a sacred symbol in Minoan and Mycenaean culture and found as a writing sign and as a mason's mark.

DOWEL. Cylindrical or quadrangular peg which is fitted into a hole in order to fasten or align adjacent pieces.

DROMOS (pl. DROMOI). Hall or passageway, leading into a subterranean tomb.

ENCEINTE. An enclosing wall, or the enclosed area, sometimes fortified.

ENTABLATURE. In classical architecture, the three elements of a wall between the columns and the gables (pediment): the lowest of these elements is the architrave, or epistyle; the next, the frieze; and the highest, the cornice.

EPISTYLE. See ARCHITRAVE, ENTABLATURE.

ETEO-CRETAN. "True" Cretan, term applied to people of Cretan blood who survived after the Dorian invasion of Crete c. 1100 B.C.

EWER. A tall, slender, pitcherlike vessel having a wide spout, a handle, and a base.

FAÇADE. In architecture, a face of a building, especially one that is given special decorative treatment.

FAÏENCE. A fine, colorfully decorated variety of glazed clay.

FLORAL STYLE. Style of Minoan pottery in which flower and plant motifs are used in informal over-all patterns (1550-1500 B.C.).

FRIEZE. Plain or decorated horizontal band forming the central part of an ENTABLA-TURE; any decorative horizontal band.

GLASS PASTE. Strass; glass used for making artificial jewels.

Glossary

GLYPTIC. Process of carving or engraving, especially on gems.

GRIFFIN. Mythical monster having the head and wings of a bird and the body of a lion.

HORNS OF CONSECRATION. Horns, sometimes of oxen and bulls, which symbolically refer to religious rites or beliefs; sometimes imitated in stone.

HYPAETHRAL, adj. Unroofed; open to the sky.

HYPOSTYLE, adj. Having a roof or ceiling supported by rows of columns.

IDEOGRAM. A written symbol representing an idea or object, rather than a specific word or sound.

INTERSTICE. A small or narrow opening or interval between parts of a structure or body.

ISODOMIC. Pertaining to masonry consisting of blocks of equal size laid in courses with the vertical divisions of each row coming directly above the middle of the blocks in the row below.

KAMARES STYLE. Style of Minoan pottery of great delicacy, with light-colored decorations in abstract or naturalistic patterns on a dark background, named for the cave sanctuary where it was first found (2000-1700 B.C.).

KERNOS (pl. KERNOI). A ceramic ring or clasp to which were attached cups or small vases, joined together to form a vessel.

KRATER. Large bowl for mixing wine and water.

KYLIX. Drinking cup with a wide shallow bowl, two horizontal handles, and a stemmed foot.

LIGHTWELL. A shaft providing light to interior rooms of a building.

LINEAR A SCRIPT. An ancient Minoan system of writing found on clay tablets and ritual vessels.

LINEAR B SCRIPT. A later script, resembling Linear A in some respects, found on clay tablets in Crete and elsewhere in the Aegean and the Peloponnese; deciphered by Michael Ventris, it proved to represent a form of the Greek language in use from c. 1450 B.C.

LINTEL. A horizontal structure which supports the weight above a door or window.

LOOM WEIGHT. Disk of lead, stone, or pottery, used to weight the threads in weaving.

LUSTRAL BASIN. A large receptacle, or special area, containing holy water used by worshippers to purify themselves before participating in a religious ceremony.

MACE HEAD. A round or oval stone having a hole in its center for the insertion of a handle.

MAGMA. Molten material within the earth's crust.

MARINE STYLE. Style of Minoan pottery using motifs of sea life—octopuses, shells, etc.—in over-all patterns (1500-1450 B.C.).

MEGARON. A building, or complex of rooms off the main building, which is generally used as a royal apartment or living quarters.

MORTICE. A notch, slot, or hole in a piece of wood into which a tenon of corresponding shape is fitted.

ORICHALC. A zinc-rich brass prepared and used for decoration in ancient times; yellow metallic substance considered precious by the ancient Greeks.

PANTHEON. A temple dedicated collectively to all the gods of a particular mythology; the body of gods officially recognized.

PEAK SANCTUARY. An ancient Minoan sanctuary constructed on a mountain peak.

PEPLOS. A loose-fitting, draped, and folded outer garment worn by women in ancient Greece.

PERISTYLE. A courtyard or open space surrounded by a system of columns.

PIER. A square pillar or post, from which a door is hung, or which serves as a support to some structure such as an arch, gate, or lintel.

PIER-AND-DOOR PARTITION. A structure which, by opening or closing the door, made it possible to divide a room into two private chambers or open it into a single unit; see POLYTHYRON.

PITHAMPHORA. A wide-mouthed amphora.

PITHOS (pl. PITHOI). Large wide-mouthed earthenware jar or vase used to store wine, oil, or grain, or for the burial of the dead.

POLYCHROME, adj. Made or decorated in many or various colors.

POLYCHROMY. The art of using many colors in decoration.

POLYTHYRON. Pier-and-door system arranged in a connecting series to control the subdivision of large sections of a palace or building.

POROS STONE. A type of fine-grained sandy limestone widely used in the construction of Minoan and Greek buildings.

POSTERN ENTRANCE. A private back door or side entrance apart from the main one.

POTSHERDS. Fragments of pottery.

PROPYLAEUM (pl. PROPYLAEA). Impressively constructed entrance or connecting chamber to a temple, palace, or other important building.

PROPYLON. An imposing archway or gateway, one of a series in front of the entrance gateway to a temple or other building of importance.

Glossary

PSEUDO-ISODOMIC. See ISODOMIC.

PYLON. A monumental tower, consisting of a masonry mass with sloping sides and a door at the center, which forms the entrance to important buildings.

PYXIS. A cylindrical box with a lid and a handle, used to hold cosmetics.

RHYTON. A libation vessel of stone, metal, or pottery, conical, ovoid, or spherical in shape, sometimes molded in the shape of an animal's head.

SAPROPEL. Sediment formed in water, consisting largely of organic matter.

SARDONYX. Quartz mineral in layers of more than one color, used for cameos, seals, and other ornaments.

SEAL. A small object of metal, stone, wood, or clay upon which letters or pictures were engraved, used for making an impression upon wax or clay by stamping or rolling.

SEALING. A small piece of clay upon which the impression of an engraved seal has been fixed; used to close a jar or vessel.

SHAFT GRAVE. A deep rectangular or square burial pit.

SHARD. Fragment of broken pottery; see POTSHERD.

STEATITE. Soapstone or massive talc, a soft stone used to make utensils or seals.

STELE. Upright stone or slab with an inscribed or sculptured surface, used as a commemorative tablet or monument.

STEPPED, adj. Having a series of steps or risers.

STIRRUP JAR. Vessel with a spherical body, an arched stirruplike handle, and a spout in the shoulder.

STOA. Portico with a wall at one side and a colonnade at the other side facing an open space.

STUCCO. A fine plaster consisting of a mixture of sand, lime, mortar, and water used for decorative work, molding, facings, or finishings.

STYLOBATE. A course of masonry that is the foundation for a colonnade.

TEMENOS. Room or enclosure containing a shrine or dedicated to a god.

TENON. Projection or peg at the end of a piece of material which is inserted into a mortice to make a joint.

TEPHRA. Volcanic debris, such as cinders, dust, and bits of volcanic glass, ejected during an eruption.

TERRACOTTA. Baked clay, often red or orange-brown in color, used for the manufacture of figurines, vessels, and other objects.

THALASSOCRACY. Maritime supremacy.

333

THOLOS (pl. THOLOI). A circular vaulted subterranean burial chamber, often reached by a horizontal passageway.

TOPARCH. Prince or ruler of a small district or city-state.

TRITON. Mollusk having a pointed, spirally twisted shell.

VASILIKI STYLE. Style of Minoan pottery, with a mottled surface, fired by oxidizing flame; found most abundantly at Vasiliki in eastern Crete (2400-2200 B.C.). Later (2200-2000 B.C.) designs were in white on a background of black paint.

BIBLIOGRAPHY

Asterisks indicate books used as source material by the author.

Alsop, Joseph. *From the Silent Earth,* New York: Harper & Row, 1962.

Bossert, H. T. *Alt Kreta.* 3rd ed. Berlin: Wasmuth, 1937.

Childe, V. Gordon. *The Dawn of European Civilization,* 6th ed. New York: Knopf, 1958.

Demargne, P. *Aegean Art.* London-New York: Thames and Hudson, 1964.

*Evans, Sir Arthur J. *The Palace of Minos,* 4 vols. London: Macmillan, 1921-1936.

——. "The Prehistoric Tombs of Knossos," *Archaeologia,* LIX, London, 1906.

——. "The Tomb of the Double Axes," *Archaeologia,* LXV, London, 1914.

*——. "Mycenaean Tree and Pillar Cult. *Journal of Hellenic Studies,* XXI, 1901.

*Fimmen, D. *Die Kretisch-Mykenische Kultur,* 2nd ed. Leipzig-Berlin: Teubner, 1924.

Forsdyke, E. J. "Minoan Art," *Proceedings of the British Academy,* 15, London, 1929.

*Glotz, G. *La civilisation égéenne.* 2nd ed. Paris: Albin Michel, 1952.

*Graham, James W. *The Palaces of Crete.* Princeton, N.J.: Princeton University Press, 1962.

Hawkes, Jacquetta. *The Dawn of the Gods.* New York: Random House, 1968.

Higgins, Reynold. *Minoan and Mycenaean Art,* New York: Praeger, 1967.

Hood, Sinclair, *The Home of the Heroes. The Aegean before the Greeks.* New York: McGraw-Hill, 1967.

*Hutchinson, R. M. *Prehistoric Crete.* Baltimore: Penguin Books, 1962.

Lacey, A. D. *Greek Pottery in the Bronze Age,* London: Methuen, 1967.

*Marinatos, Spyridon, and Hirmer, Max. *Crete and Mycenae.* New York: Abrams, 1960.

Matt, Leonard von, *et al. Ancient Crete.* New York: Praeger, 1968.

Bibliography

*Matz, Friedrich. *Kreta, Mykenae, Troya,* Stuttgart, Kilpper, 1958.

*——. *Kreta und Frühes Griechenland,* Baden-Baden, 1962.

*——. *Minoan Civilisation—Maturity and Zenith* (Cambridge Ancient History. Facsimile 12). New York: Cambridge University Press, 1962.

Nilsson, Martin Persson. *The Minoan-Mycenaean Religion and Its Survival in Greek Religion,* Lund: Aleerup, 1950.

Palmer, Leonard. *Mycenaeans and Minoans.* rev. ed. New York: Knopf, 1964.

*Pendlebury, J. D. S. *The Archaeology of Crete.* London: Methuen, 1935. New York: Norton, 1965, paper.

——. A Handbook to the Palace of Minos, rev. ed. New York: Dufour, 1954.

*Platon, Nicholas. *Crete.* Archaeologia Mundi series. New York: World Publishing Co., 1966.

*——. Preliminary Reports (in Greek) since 1961 in the Proceedings of the Archaeological Society in Athens (*Praktika Archaeologikis Etaireias*).

*——. "Kunst des Anmutigen," *Merian* 16 (1963), Heft 12, 34 ff.

*——. "A New Minoan Palace," *Archaeology* 16 (1963), 269 ff.

——. "A New Major Minoan Palace Discovered in Crete," *Illustrated London News,* February 29, 1964, 312 ff., March 7, 1964, 350 ff.

——. "Sir Arthur Evans and the Creto-Mycenaean Bullfights," *Greek Heritage,* I, 4 (1964), 91.

——. "A Rediscovered Palace," *Horizon,* 7, Section 3 (1965), 76 ff.

——. "Der minoische Palast von Kato Zakros," *DU,* 27, January 1967, 49 ff (Reprinted in Aleyiou *et al., Ancient Crete,* 163 ff.

*——. "Bathrooms and Lustral Basins in Minoan Dwellings," *Europa,* Festschrift E. Grumach, 236 ff.

*Shachermeyr, Friedrich. *Die minoische Kultur des alten Kreta,* Stuttgart: Kohlhammer, 1964.

*Snijder, G. *Kretische Kunst,* Berlin: Mann, 1936.

Thomson, George. *Studies in Ancient Greek Society: The Prehistoric Aegean.* New York: Citadel Press, 1936.

*Willetts, R. F. *Everyday Life in Ancient Crete.* New York: Putnam, 1969.

*Zervos, Christian. *L'Art de la Crète néolithique et minoenne.* Paris: Cahiers d'Art, 1956.

PICTURE CREDITS

Photographs

National Aeronautics and Space Administration (NASA): pages 15, 16

Anastasia Platonos: pages 7, 38, 54, 61, 65 (bottom), 67, 84 (top and bottom), 118 (bottom), 119 (top and bottom), 128, 130, 134 (top and bottom), 197, 206, 207

Emil Sarafis: pages 2, 6, 10, 14, 65 (top, left and right), 118 (top, left and right), 138 (top and bottom), 139 (all), 142, 144, 165, 168

R. V. Shroder: page 3

George Xylouris: pages 9, 11, 17, 30, 32, 58, 60, 68, 69, 73, 75, 78, 87, 90, 93, 97, 100, 105, 106, 107, 108, 109, 110, 111, 112, 113, 114, 117 (top and bottom), 121, 122, 123, 124, 125, 126, 131, 137, 140, 141, 146 (top and bottom), 147, 148, 149 (top and bottom), 150, 153, 157, 159, 160, 167, 173, 198, 212, 214, 215, 218, 219 (top and bottom), 220, 221, 223, 229, 237, 261, 288, 289

Maps, plans, and drawings

J. Demetriades: page 91

M. Filippa: pages 176, 177

D. G. Hogarth, *British School Annual*, VII (1900-1901): pages 25, 26 (top and bottom), 27, 28

J. V. Luce, *Lost Atlantis*: pages 1, 271, 274

M. Lydidaki and N. Platon: page 62

D. Ninkovich and B. Hegen, "Santorini Tephra," *Colston Papers*, XVII: pages 268, 275, 278, 279, 295

Thomas Phanourakis: pages 167, 217

Nicholas Platon: page 63

John and Effi Sakellaraki: page 71

K. Sarris: pages 180, 186, 193, 211

Charles Scribner's Sons: page 241

Joseph W. Shaw: pages 80-81, 102, 132, 150, 171, 205

Maria Shaw: page 96

INDEX

Index

ABOUT THE AUTHOR

Nicholas Platon was born in Cephalonia, Greece, and educated at the Gymnasium in Heraklion, the University of Athens, and the Sorbonne in Paris, receiving his M.A. from the University of Athens. He served the Greek Government as Assistant Curator of Antiquities for Crete from 1930 to 1935. As Curator of Antiquities he was in Thebes from 1936-38, and in Heraklion from 1939-1961. During this period he was also Director of the Museum in Thebes until 1936 and Director of the Heraklion Museum until 1961. From 1961 to 1965 he was Director of the Acropolis Museum in Athens. Since then he has been a professor at the University of Thessaloniki. Professor Platon is a member of numerous archaeological institutes and societies and is the author of *Crete*. He lives in Athens and Thessaloniki and divides his time between the excavation at Kato Zakros and the University of Thessaloniki.